THE TOLEDO WAR

THE TOLEDO WAR THE FIRST MICHIGAN-OHIO RIVALRY

DON FABER

THE UNIVERSITY OF MICHIGAN PRESS

ANN ARBOR

Copyright © by the University of Michigan 2008
All rights reserved
Published in the United States of America by
The University of Michigan Press
Printed and bound by CPI Group (UK) Ltd, Croydon, CR0 4YY

A CIP catalog record for this book is available from the British Library.

Library of Congress Cataloging-in-Publication Data

Faber, Don, 1939–
    The Toledo War : the first Michigan-Ohio rivalry / Don Faber.
       p.   cm.
    Includes bibliographical references and index.
    ISBN-13: 978-0-472-07054-1 (cloth : alk. paper)
    ISBN-13: 978-0-472-05054-3 (paper : alk. paper)

    1. Toledo War, 1835.   2. Ohio—Boundaries—Michigan.
3. Michigan—Boundaries—Ohio.   4. Toledo (Ohio)—History—19th
century.   5. Ohio—History—1787–1865.   6. Michigan—History—To
1837.   7. Lucas, Robert, 1781–1853.   8. Mason, Stevens Thomson,
1811–1843.   9. Ohio—Politics and government—1787–1865.
10. Michigan—Politics and government—To 1837.   I. Title.

F497.B7F33   2008
977.1'03—dc22   2008032082

For my wife, Jeannette Luton Faber,
without whose loving support this book
would not have been possible

PREFACE

Thirty years before the War between the States, as the Civil War was referred to in the South, there occurred another war between states. Not a war in the military sense, this conflict between two states had no fatalities, grand battle plans, or five-star generals plotting their places in history. But make no mistake about it, Michigan and Ohio, eyeball to eyeball, were at serious swords' points in 1835. Statehood and a disputed boundary were the two intertwined issues.

The Harris survey of 1817 agreed with the Ohio Constitution in placing the mouth of the Maumee River in that state. The Fulton survey of 1818 agreed with the language of the Northwest Ordinance, placing that geographic area in Michigan. The land between the two surveys was the Toledo Strip—a wedge-shaped slice five miles wide at the Indiana border and eight miles wide at Lake Erie.

Before it was over, the Toledo War would involve, marginally or directly, six U.S. presidents. James Monroe threw his presidential authority behind the boundary re-marking carried out by Captain Andrew Talcott. James K. Polk was the Speaker of the House when the Michigan statehood bill was signed into law. Martin Van Buren was vice president under Andrew Jackson and was the latter's hoped-for successor during the political jockeying in 1835; it was Old Kinderhook, as Van Buren was known, who signed enabling legislation for Michigan's statehood application. James Buchanan of Pennsylvania took the Senate floor to argue against Michigan's claim to the Toledo Strip. Andrew Jackson, Old Hickory, was president when the Toledo War occurred, and it was he who fired Stevens T. Mason as Michigan's territorial governor. No less a personage than former president John Quincy Adams delivered more than one passionate defense of Michigan's position from his seat in the U.S. House of Representatives. Robert E. Lee got into the act, too. The future Civil War general and commander of the Army of Northern Virginia served on the 1834 Talcott survey team that fixed Michigan's southern boundary along the line of that state's original claim.

Newspaper accounts of the day tell of colorful characters and political one-upmanship that involved not just the frontline players in the two states but also men in the nation's capital. The stage was set for a showdown when President Jackson referred the boundary dispute to his attorney general, who ruled that Michigan was clearly in the right. The attorney general's opinion does not have the force of law, of course, but it made a compelling argument that Michigan used to promote its case. Michigan likely would have won its claim to the Toledo Strip in a court intent on the letter, rather than the spirit, of the law. As it turned out, Ohio took its case to Congress and won.

Even the date of statehood is open to debate. The official date given is January 26, 1837, but the Great Seal of the State of Michigan gives 1835 as the date of statehood. On November 1 of that year, Michigan began functioning as a state, with a full slate of officers and a constitution ratified by the people. Could Michigan help it if Congress dragged its heels on admission?

Michigan's birth was not an easy one. Its earliest petitions for statehood were rejected by Congress as inexpedient. Then, as a condition for statehood, Michigan was forced to cede its claim to the Toledo Strip. Additionally, in the federal capital, slavery was a ticking time bomb, and Michigan, as a free state, could not come into the Union unless it was paired with a slave state—in this case, Arkansas.

There was much rejoicing in Michigan when statehood became a fact, but strong feelings over losing the Toledo Strip lingered for a long time. Bad blood between the two states did not go away. Disputes over the boundary occurred as late as the 1970s. And one of the fiercest rivalries on the American gridiron is the interstate clash between the University of Michigan and Ohio State University, two titans who annually contend for regional and national supremacy. The game, whether in Ann Arbor or Columbus, is simply referred to as "the Big One." Whatever feelings of animosity the two states still share may be said to date to Michigan's bid for statehood and Ohio's determination to block that application until wresting control of the Toledo Strip from the territory of Michigan.

The canals that prompted such interest in the Toledo Strip on Ohio's part were soon surpassed by the railroads. Toledo's importance on Lake Erie was overshadowed by Cleveland. The Upper Peninsula, which was the consolation prize given to Michigan, has become a tourist mecca for much of the region and a source of great pride for all Michiganians, despite the fact that many in 1836 regarded it as a mostly valueless chunk of real estate, thrown into the deal to atone for the loss of all that valuable farmland and swamp in the Toledo Strip.

Throughout this narrative, reference will be made to the Northwest Ordinance of 1787. Along with the Declaration of Independence, the Constitution, the Bill of Rights, and Lincoln's Gettysburg Address, it is one of the most important documents in American history. It called for the orderly development of land and established government on the frontier while providing for the creation of future states.

The language of the Northwest Ordinance still resonates today. It proclaims, "Religion, morality and knowledge being necessary to good government and the happiness of mankind, schools and the means of education shall forever be encouraged." The need for education to illuminate the darkness is as compelling now as it was in frontier days. It is a timeless message that is still the best hope for humanity in a changing world.

ACKNOWLEDGMENTS

I wish to thank the fine staff of the William L. Clements Library in Ann Arbor, especially former director John Dann, who advised in the publication of this book; Clayton Lewis, curator of graphic materials, for his time and patience; the late John Harriman, who so ably located the appropriate materials for research; and Brian Dunnigan, the "maps man," who provided invaluable assistance. In Lansing, Eve R. Weipert, curator of collections and exhibits at the Michigan Historical Museum, was most helpful. Michael W. Lora, assistant manager and curator of rare books in the local history department of the Toledo-Lucas County Public Library, is thanked for his cheerful and speedy cooperation in the areas of photography and research.

The Detroit Public Library was a valuable place for scholarship, and I am especially indebted to David L. Poremba, manager, for his assistance with the Burton Collections. Mark E. Harvey, reference archivist at the Michigan Historical Center in Lansing, and Dave Johnson, Michigan archivist at the Michigan Historical Center, were most helpful, as was Roger Rosentreter, editor of *Michigan History* magazine. Connie Ostrove, reference librarian at the State Library of Ohio in Columbus, provided material on Robert Lucas. I thank James R. Ryland, curator of the Monroe County Historical Museum, for allowing me to photograph artifacts there. Lynn Reaume, archives assistant, and Chris Kull, archivist, at the Monroe County Historical Museum, gave me plenty of their time. Thanks also go to the highly trained staff at the Bentley Library in Ann Arbor, especially Malgosia Myc, assistant reference archivist, and to the Lenawee County Historical Museum in Adrian, Michigan.

A special acknowledgment goes to Eleanor Rubingh, my fifth-grade teacher. Just the way she said "Constantinople" fired me with a love of history and of parts unknown waiting to be visited. Robert Vanderlaan was my high school government and history teacher; he served in the Michigan legislature and aspired to Congress. He made history as fresh as today's newspaper. Dr. Sidney Fine was a University of Michigan teaching treasure for decades. No one could infuse an hour-long lecture with more energy than he. Dr. Fine is among the finest professors of history who ever drew breath.

There are many people who encouraged me in this project, including Keith Molin of Ann Arbor; David Pollack of Ann Arbor; the late Robert Warner, former archivist of the United States; Donald R. Adams of Temperance, Michigan; and Philip P. Mason, distinguished professor of history, emeritus, at Wayne State University. Allison Faber helped in the formatting of the manuscript. Photographer Jen Luton added her considerable skills to any possible success this book may have. Finally, my wife, Jeannette Luton Faber, is thanked from the bottom of my heart for her critical appraising eye as an editor and for her writing expertise, which enormously improved the manuscript and speeded its way to production.

CONTENTS

THE TOLEDO WAR

CHAPTER ONE

THE BATTLE OF PHILLIPS CORNERS

I need not remark to you that this Act of Michigan will be wholly disregarded by Ohio.

—GOVERNOR ROBERT LUCAS OF OHIO TO A CORRESPONDENT

Like lions stalking prey, a posse of thirty armed Michigan men crept forward, shushing each other all the while. They had gathered in Adrian the previous night, before marching fourteen miles south to where they expected an encounter with the enemy. The men were carried part of the way in wagons before the roads gave out, in this part of southern Michigan near the Ohio border. A veteran of the march, Benjamin Baxter of Tecumseh, Michigan, remembered being furnished with U.S. arms and ammunition. His recollection of who supplied the arms was to be the subject of a heated dispute between the governor of Ohio and the secretary of war. In an official report, Baxter's commanding officer said muskets for his men were supplied by the territory of Michigan, an important distinction.

In any event, it was noon on Sunday, April 26, 1835, at a field belonging to a certain Phillips, later known as Phillips Corners, when the men under the command of Lenawee County undersheriff William McNair surprised a party of Ohioans who were lounging about. The Ohioans' duty had been to re-mark the William Harris survey line in a steadily worsening border dispute between the state of Ohio and the territory of Michigan. A strip of land, five miles wide at the Indiana line and eight miles wide at Toledo on Lake Erie, totaling 468 square miles, was the bone of contention. The Ohio contingent consisted of three

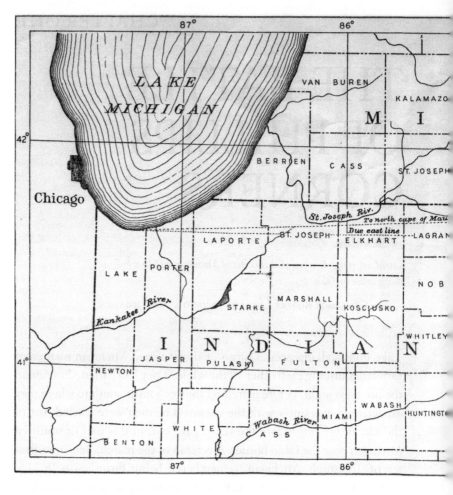

survey commissioners appointed by Governor Robert Lucas and some sharpshooters for their protection. The survey party had been followed—harassed, by some accounts—ever since they had begun running the line eastward from Indiana toward the mouth of the Maumee River.

Both sides were on military high alert. A month earlier, on March 27, Governor Lucas ordered part of the Seventeenth Division of the Ohio militia mustered. Across the border, Governor Stevens T. Mason had also placed his Michigan militia in a state of readiness, under the command of Major General Joseph W. Brown. Brown was an apt choice to lead the militia. One of the original founders of the Michigan town of Tecumseh, he now found himself in a position to put his medals on parade, so to speak, right in his own backyard.

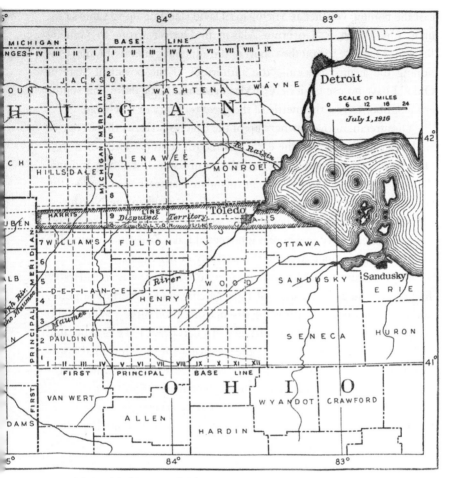

A joint Michigan and Ohio survey in 1916 produced this map showing the disputed territory known as the Toledo Strip. (Courtesy of the Ohio Historical Society.)

The press in both states whipped up war fever. The March 28 issue of the *Cleveland Herald* reported, "Michigan is marching her troops to the scene of action, to repel any attempt on the part of this state to extend her jurisdiction over the territory in question." On April 22, a rival paper, the *Cleveland Whig*, trumpeted, "In the boundary dispute between Michigan and this state, the citizens of Michigan have taken men prisoners just as if it were war. Ohio women have been treated with violence. We can destroy this band of ruffians, but the governor wishes us to forbear, and it is probably for the best." Newspapers in Michigan tended to cast the coming conflict as Michigan's David standing up to Ohio's Goliath. On March 6, Governor Mason in Detroit wrote to General Brown, "I enclose to you the report of the adjutant general of Ohio, cautioning me against resisting 'the authorities of the powerful State of Ohio.' I have no use for it here."[1] Mason seemed to be daring his southern neighbor to test the mettle of the great territory of Michigan.

Disagreement over ownership of the Toledo Strip, as this wedge of land was called, dated to the early nineteenth century. The Northwest Ordinance of 1787, which created the future states of Ohio, Indiana, Illinois, Michigan, and Wisconsin, mandated an east-west line as the boundary between the northern and southern states in the Northwest Territory. That line would begin at the southernmost tip of Lake Michigan and run eastward to where it intersected Lake Erie, thus placing the mouth of the Maumee River in the territory of Michigan.

But maps in those days were not precise, and there was considerable doubt as to the exact location of Lake Michigan's southernmost point. Adding to the uncertainty was the absence of a good survey. When Ohio became a state in 1803, the importance of a harbor on Lake Erie became evident. To provide for this need, the state's constitution included a provision that claimed the mouth of the Maumee River for Ohio, disregarding the boundary line placed by the Northwest Ordinance.

Congress accepted Ohio's constitution, a necessary step to statehood, but did not expressly give consent to the changed boundary. After the War of 1812, a survey run by an Ohio-paid engineer named Harris, angling from the Indiana line to Maumee Bay, put a strip of land ostensibly owned by Michigan in Ohio. Not to be outdone, Michigan employed a survey engineer named Fulton, whose line closely followed the original Northwest Ordinance line. A federal survey by U.S. Army engineers in 1834 also put the disputed territory in Michigan. Although both states claimed the 468-square-mile chunk of territory, matters were quiet until Ohio began underwriting a series of canals that were intended to link up with the Maumee River near where it empties into Lake Erie. In 1827, with no opposition from Ohio, Michigan actually organized the Toledo Strip into tax-collecting, law-enforcing, local government agencies.

In the early 1830s, Michigan began to push for statehood. By now, many people in Ohio, including its political leadership, believed the planned canals would make Toledo, not yet organized as a city, a great maritime center. Until it was assured possession of the Toledo Strip and the mouth of the Maumee, Ohio planned to use its strength in Congress to block Michigan's bid for admission to the Union. George Fuller, in his *Michigan Centennial History*, writes, "The immediate cause of the war was the announced intention on the part of Ohio to survey and mark the line described in its constitution as the state's northern boundary, that is, a line running on a diagonal from the southern end of Lake Michigan to the northernmost cape of Maumee Bay. The surveyors in marking this line from the Indiana border had to cross Lenawee and Monroe counties in the Territory of Michigan."[2]

At the request of President Andrew Jackson, U.S. attorney general Benjamin F. Butler addressed the jurisdictional dispute and opined that Michigan was in the right. Furthermore, he said, Michigan's Pains and Penalties Act, making it a criminal offense, punishable by a heavy fine or imprisonment, for anyone to attempt to exercise any official functions within the jurisdiction of Michigan under any authority not derived from the territory or from the United States, was a valid law. As early as February 23, 1835, just eleven days after the act was passed, Governor Lucas wrote to a friend, "I need not remark to you that this Act of Michigan will be wholly disregarded by Ohio."[3]

When Butler's ruling came in March, Lucas brushed it aside as inconsequential and ordered a survey crew to run the line when the weather warmed up. Mason bided his time, ordering General Brown to keep an eye on the movements of the interlopers. Scouting reports indicated that the Ohioans were armed, and enforcement of the warrants for their arrest would require a posse of armed men. When the Ohioans arrived within the county of Lenawee, Undersheriff McNair and his posse of thirty men were poised to pounce. The next six months of hostilities, such as they were, would be known as the Toledo War.

But the men on both sides of the line at Phillips Corners that Sunday morning were not thinking about history or the Pains and Penalties Act. A few were nursing hangovers. After a "night of jollification" in Adrian, Benjamin Baxter wrote, "we started out on a Sabbath morning for the invaded territory."[4] Baxter was not even of legal age to join the troops, but like many a young lad ambitious of military glory, he ran away from home and joined McNair's forces. He must have wondered why they had time to party in Adrian, given the seriousness of the situation.

Undersheriff McNair was prepared to serve warrants for alleged violations of the Pains and Penalties Act. His marching orders were to arrest the Ohio survey party or to run them out of the territory, and it was with a sense of heightened anticipation that his men, peering through the trees, spied their quarry taking their ease. McNair stopped to consider what to do next. Ordering his men to stay a distance off, he warily approached the camp of the enemy with an aide.

It was a tense situation for both sides, this first meeting of "statesmen" and "territorialists." McNair inquired as to the whereabouts of the survey commissioners. Told they had left and would return shortly, he decided to wait. But when his men, impatient for activity, arrived on the scene to ask for instructions, the Ohioans suddenly grabbed their rifles. One of the Ohio party, Colonel Hawkins, was immediately arrested, and a few more surrendered on the spot. Nine other riflemen fled and took refuge in a nearby cabin, where they barricaded themselves inside. Surrounded by the Michigan posse, who were spoiling for a fight, the Ohioans were ordered by McNair to give up; they refused. Eventually they came out with their rifles cocked. The Michigan and Ohio men faced each other, about eight rods apart, according to McNair's report, when the Ohioans suddenly bolted for the woods "in double quick time."[5]

Reports of what happened next vary. According to McNair, his men fired a volley over the heads of the fleeing Buckeyes and gave chase. The discharge of thirty or so Springfield muskets echoed and reechoed in the woods. A number of the pursued escaped and, meeting up again with the survey commissioners, made their way through the Black Swamp to Perrysburg, with the added humiliation of tattered clothing and numerous mosquito bites.

Back at Phillips Corners, a handful of Ohio men were taken into custody and jailed at Tecumseh, then the Lenawee County seat. Two of the prisoners were released for lack of evidence; six others posted bail; and one, Colonel J. E. Fletcher, refused bail and opted to remain a prisoner—under orders, he said, from Governor Lucas. Benjamin Baxter later reported, "Our prisoner, Col. Fletcher, remained with us for many months, a genial gentleman not suffering apparently from his incarceration, but sometimes subjecting us to the inconvenience of hunting him up when we had occasion to use the jail for some counterfeiter or horse thief, as he was likely to be found riding with one of the sheriff's lovely daughters, having taken the jail keys with him."[6] In the Battle of Phillips Corners, the first real skirmish of the Toledo War, no one was injured. A claim by the Ohioans that a Michigan musket ball had "passed through the clothing" of a member of their party was dismissed as a joke. McNair humorously reported to Governor Mason that "the commissioners made good time through the swamp" and arrived at Perrysburg that next morning "with nothing more serious than the loss of their coats."[7]

The events of Phillips Corners were not so amusing to Ohio. The re-marking of the state's northern boundary was stopped dead in its tracks. The upstart territory had given the established state a comeuppance. Governor Lucas had lost face with his people. The three Ohio survey commissioners who eluded capture at Phillips Corners wrote to Lucas that they deemed it "prudent" to suspend their activities until such time as they could adequately be protected. Unbeknownst to them, on April 15, Lucas had ordered Major General John Bell to muster 500 men as a protection squad for the surveyors, but Bell was only able to raise 292 men.

The commissioners appointed by Governor Lucas and charged with re-marking the Harris line were Jonathan Taylor of Licking County, Uri Seely of Geauga County and John Patterson of Adams County. In a letter to Lucas from Perrysburg, Ohio, dated May 1, the trio gave a report of what happened at Phillips Corners. They clearly tried to put the best face on an embarrassing situation. Thus they wrote, "During our progress [of marking the line], we had been constantly threatened by the authorities of Michigan; and spies from the Territory . . . were almost daily among us."[8] On Saturday, April 25, the commissioners and their party "retired to the distance of about one mile south of the line, in Henry County, within the state of Ohio, where we thought to have rested quietly, and peaceably enjoy the blessings of the Sabbath."[9]

In their report, Taylor, Patterson, and Seely doubled the size of McNair's invading force: "An armed force of about fifty or sixty men hove in sight within musket shot of us, all mounted upon horses, well armed with muskets, and under the command of General Brown of Michigan. Your commissioners . . . thought it prudent to retire and so advised our men."[10] They were, in fact, outnumbered. The commissioners said they had only five armed men as lookouts among them; other reports had nine or ten armed men. The Ohio version has the retreating Buckeyes being "fired upon" by the enemy. In any event, no one was wounded. On that, both sides agree.

Interestingly, the commissioners, who were not even at the camp when McNair's men arrived, nonetheless counted "thirty to fifty shots" fired at them and noted, "Our party did not fire a gun in turn." They reported to Lucas, "Your commissioners, with several of their party, made good their retreat to this place. But sir, we are under the painful necessity of relating that nine of our men, who did not leave the ground in time, were taken prisoners, and carried away into the interior of the country." The nine named are "Cols. Hawkins, Scott and Gould, Major Rice, Capt. Biggerstaf and Messrs. Ellsworth, Fletcher, Moale and Rickets."[11] If there was any question about Michigan retaining jurisdiction of the disputed land, all doubts now were removed. In fact, after the Battle of Phillips Corners and throughout the summer of 1835, Michigan continued to vigorously enforce the Pains and Penalties Act by serving process on alleged violators.

For now, it was enough that the routed Ohio forces arrived at Perrysburg in disarray and with their clothing torn, there to relate to Governor Lucas how they bravely escaped the attack of General Brown and how their missing comrades were taken prisoners. Lucas reported to President Andrew Jackson in Washington, who sent a copy to Governor Mason, requesting a statement of facts from the officers engaged in the melee. McNair's report said the proceedings were civil in character and not a military expedition.

While the politicians deliberated on what to do next, the people of Michigan rejoiced at the news from Phillips Corners. In a headline story of May 9, 1835, the *Detroit Free Press* blared, "The First Blow Struck!" The story gleefully related how Charles Hewitt, a magistrate of Michigan, had issued warrants for the apprehension of the survey party "and other persons engaged in violating the laws of the territory." Continuing its fanfare, the *Free Press* reported, "The warrants were given to the sheriff of Lenawee, who summoned a posse of 30 or 40 respectable persons of that county. On arriving near the house of Phillips, seven miles within the Michigan line, they found nine or ten armed men, ascertained to be a portion of the Ohio party and demanded their surrender, which the latter refused to do." The newspaper account has McNair's men, undaunted, "pressing hard upon their Ohio neighbors and, in obedience to orders, firing over their heads—a maneuver which instantly caused them to take to their heels." The account reports, "They were, however, chased by the Michiganians, and captured."

Not surprisingly, the *Columbus Hemisphere* saw things in a different light. As reprinted in the *National Intelligencer* of May 12, 1835, the

Hemisphere's story told of how General Brown "made an attack upon the commissioners and their party who were stopped during the Sabbath with some private families." The report continued, "Brown and some 80 armed men made captive nine of our Ohio corps. Governor Lucas postpones further active measures for 2–3 days. General Andy Jackson [President Jackson] will veto the proceedings of the Hotspur of Michigan." The Hotspur mentioned in the report is Stevens T. Mason, who, in his supposed youthful impetuousness, recalled Shakespeare's character known by that name.

As for the foot soldier veteran Benjamin Baxter, the whole experience at Phillips Corners was a bit of a lark. Some of the men, he says, had not yet arrived at the enemy camp but were "rapidly approaching the forest." Confused by the sound of musket fire reverberating through the tall trees, Baxter stopped for a minute "to consider," he said, "how I could best find out which side I was on." He then "started for the battlefield very excited and nearly on the run." Baxter recalled that about twelve of the invaders were taken and as many got away, "running some 15 or 20 miles to Maumee, where they arrived in the night, very peculiarly and lightly clad, it is said, by reason of the prickly ash and blackberry bushes through which lay their line of retreat." Many years later, Baxter would describe "thrilling events and hairsbreadth escapes" of the Toledo War.[12]

Today, Phillips Corners is a peaceful place. A battered barn sits on the site where the men of Michigan surprised the Ohioans resting on the Lord's day. The woods that echoed with musketry are long gone. Flat farm country dotted with grain elevators and silos marks the scene. A historical marker fourteen miles south of Adrian, Michigan, one mile south of the Michigan-Ohio line, awaits the curious traveler through these less-traveled byways. One side of the marker, titled "The Ohio Michigan Boundary War," reads:

> The Northwest Ordinance of 1787 defined the boundary of the northern and southern tier of states to be carved out of the Northwest Territory, as a line drawn east from the southernmost tip of Lake Michigan until it intersects Lake Erie. Controversy over the exact location of that line led to the 1834–1837 boundary dispute between the State of Ohio and Michigan Territory. Passions ran high as everyone on both sides of the boundary knew that a great port city would emerge in the disputed territory. President Andrew Jackson settled the dispute in 1836 when he signed an act that

Historical marker at the site of the Battle of Phillips Corners, near present-day Seward, Ohio. (Photograph by Jen Luton.)

recognized the current border between Ohio and Michigan, giving Michigan 9,000 square miles of Upper Peninsula land and awarding the disputed strip of approximately 470 square miles to Ohio. Michigan then joined the nation as a state the following year.

The side of the marker facing southward, toward Ohio, reads:

The Battle of Phillips Corners took place on April 26, 1835, and is sometimes referred to as the Toledo War. The altercation began when Ohio Governor Robert Lucas sent a survey party to re-mark the 1817 William Harris survey line, located on land claimed by Michigan Territory. When the survey party stopped to rest on land owned by Colonel Eli Phillips of the Michigan Militia, Under-Sheriff William McNair formed a posse of local deputies. Acting under authority of Michigan Territory Governor Stevens Mason, McNair and his force attempted to arrest the survey party for illegal trespass on Michigan Territory. The three Ohio Boundary Commissioners escaped accompanied by Colonel Sebried Dodge of the Ohio Corps. of Engineers and Pennsylvania & Ohio Canal surveyor and engineer. Shots were fired in the direction of the surveyors, but no one was killed or wounded; however, nine members of the armed party were arrested.

The Phillips Corners site marker, at the intersection of Ohio Route 109 and Route 120, was erected in 2002 by the Ohio Historical Society, working with the Ohio Bicentennial Commission and the Fulton County Historical Society. There is no mention of Ohio's vigorous insistence that Michigan be blocked from statehood until it had yielded the Toledo Strip, despite having strong legal claim to the territory. Ohioans may credit President Jackson with "settling the dispute," but Old Hickory tried to take a hands-off approach. Also, the altercation did not really begin when Governor Lucas sent his survey party to re-mark the line but when his state slipped a proviso into its constitution that claimed ownership of the mouth of Maumee Bay for Ohio. History records that the Battle of Phillips Corners was the first battle in the Toledo War. The next six months would provide for, if not rattling good history, at least entertaining reading.

ROOTS OF THE DISPUTE I THE NORTHWEST ORDINANCE

Bad maps sometimes produce a lot of history.

—CARL WITTKE, FORMER PROFESSOR OF HISTORY,
OHIO STATE UNIVERSITY

The Toledo War is best understood in the context of the Northwest Ordinance of 1787 and the events that preceded that historic document. John Dann, former director of the William L. Clements Library in Ann Arbor, writes, "It is sometimes said that the basic documents for the founding of the United States are the Declaration of Independence in 1776, the Northwest Ordinance of 1787 and the Constitution of 1787–88. The books, manuscripts, maps and prints selected to illustrate the life of the Ordinance begin with a growing consciousness of our first West, the rejection of colonialism and the guarantee of individual rights."[1] The Northwest Ordinance is the lesser known of the three great documents Dann mentions, but it is by no means any less important. Among other things, it called for the orderly development of land and established government of future states.

The North America that the explorers found and later claimed under their respective national flags was unowned. For the indigenous people, instruments of landownership, such as deeds, surveys, titles, and boundaries, were alien concepts. When the Old World met the New World, the clash of cultures produced a profound change in regard to the land.

Early in their history, the original states of the Atlantic Seaboard used their royal charters to claim vast tracts of lands far to the west. For example, the charter granted by the royal government in London to Virginia in 1609 granted to the company "all that space and circuit of lands from the Atlantic on the east to the sea on the west, west and northwest."[2] After the American Revolution, Virginia used this vague and uncertain boundary to make a claim to all the territory north and northwest of the Ohio River. That claim was disputed by other states.

Then there was Connecticut, whose charter in April 1662 granted to the governor or company "all that portion of territory formed from Narragansett Bay on the east to the south sea or the west part." We cannot now conjecture where this south sea was, but Connecticut used this undefined boundary to the west to make claim to a portion of the country northwest of the Ohio River. In all, five of the original thirteen states—Virginia, Pennsylvania, New York, Massachusetts, and Connecticut—claimed portions of the Old Northwest by either charter grants or treaties with the Indians. Michigan, or what would be Michigan, was claimed by Virginia.

The Northwest Territory, which included present-day Michigan, Ohio, Indiana, Illinois, and Wisconsin, came into being when the five previously mentioned states gave up their land claims across the mountains. In 1787, Congress adopted the Northwest Ordinance, which outlined how this territory would be divided. In this ordinance, officially titled "An Ordinance for the Government of the Territory of the United States, North-West of the River Ohio," Congress used the description of an east-west line as the southern boundary of the northern tier of states. That line used the southernmost tip of Lake Michigan as its starting point. As we shall see, the territory of Michigan later claimed that line as its rightful southern boundary with Ohio, and Ohio said that the line was negated by both inaccurate data and the Ohio Constitution.

What bearing does all this have on the Toledo War? To answer that, we have to go back to 1755, when John Mitchell, a Virginia physician and botanist, produced for the Lords of Trade in London a map of British North America. The Mitchell map was regarded for many decades as the definitive cartographic delineation of the continent. But as Carl Wittke, former professor of history at Ohio State University, once wrote, "Bad maps sometimes produce a lot of history."[3] It was not Mitchell's fault he drew a map that placed the southern end of Lake Michigan too far north. Cartography was an inexact science, and

Mitchell was only using the knowledge at hand. When the framers of the Northwest Ordinance of 1787 deliberated over how the territory should be divided into future states, they used the Mitchell map as their guide.

Between 1780 and 1786, with certain reservations, all five states ceded to the general government their claims to western lands. They were induced to do so for several reasons, not least of which was the belief that the western country was a heritage of the Revolution, purchased by the common blood and treasure of all the states. Overlapping claims to these western lands would have proved difficult to settle. And there was the realization that protecting this area from foreign aggression and hostile Indians was a shared responsibility.

The process of ceding claims began in 1780, when Pennsylvania agreed to a definite western boundary. A year later, New York surrendered its claims, followed successively by Virginia in 1784, Massachusetts in 1785, and Connecticut in 1786. The cession of those states gave the jurisdiction of the Northwest Territory to the United States. In this way, after the Revolution, the U.S. Congress took ownership of the lands lying "northwest of the River Ohio." The Northwest Ordinance of 1787 is the model to be followed by all the territorial governments. The first steps toward settling the Northwest Territory were the congressional resolutions of 1776 and 1780 presenting land bounties to the officers and soldiers of the Revolution, or the Continental Army.

Before 1763, both France and England claimed title to the Great Lakes region. But when the British defeated their mainland rivals on the Plains of Abraham in Quebec in what was known as the French and Indian War, the French were driven out of North America. By right of conquest, the British claimed those lands northwest of the Ohio River, as well as taking indisputable title to the public lands as far west as the Mississippi River.

When the Treaty of Paris was signed in 1763, Great Britain had reached an apex of glory. All of Canada and the American West from the Appalachians to the Mississippi had been added to Britain's empire. But only twenty years after the first, a second Treaty of Paris would considerably diminish the Crown's North American holdings. When the British were defeated by the United States, the victorious Yankees fell heir to a large chunk of inland America. One of the provisions of the 1783 Treaty of Paris, ending the Revolutionary War, was the establishment of boundaries that would allow for American expansion westward.

But this treaty did not terminate the difficulties between Great Britain
and the United States. The British would not abandon their forts in the
Northwest Territory, as they were reluctant to give up the lucrative fur
trade in the Great Lakes region. Hostile Indians also remained. In 1794,
at the Battle of Fallen Timbers near Maumee, Ohio, General "Mad An-
thony" Wayne defeated the Indians and forced the British to abandon
forts they were holding in the northwest in violation of the treaty ending the Revolution. The War of 1812 was still in the future, however,
and it would be left to Oliver Hazard Perry to sweep the British out of
Lake Erie.

In the 1780s, the issue facing the victorious former colonists was
one of nation building, more particularly that of union. What interests
would bind easterners and westerners together? Was it possible to rec-
oncile individual liberty and republican forms of government with a national government capable of maintaining law and order at home while
providing a strong defense against foreign enemies? The Articles of
Confederation, which established a "perpetual Union" of the states in
1781, had failed to unite them in common cause. Congress was financially broke, and the confederation was hamstrung by the provision requiring the unanimous consent of the states to amend the articles.
Without the power to tax or to regulate commerce or to enforce the
terms of the Treaty of Paris, the new nation floundered.

As to what sort of union Congress was considering, that question
was addressed in the two central statements of western expansion policy:
the Land Ordinance of May 20, 1785, and the Northwest Ordinance.
These two statements of western policy were preceded by the act of October 10, 1780, that called on the large, "landed" states to relinquish
their extensive western claims to make possible the creation of a national domain. Congress then promised—and the promise was repeated
in state land cessions—that land sales revenue would be used for the
"common benefit" of the United States and that western settlements
eventually would be formed into new, equal states and be admitted into
the Union. Unlike the original thirteen states, which had to break from
the empire to assert their equality, the new American states in the West
would go through an orderly preparation before being received as equal
members of the Union.

The territorial government ordinance of April 23, 1784, the direct
predecessor of the Northwest Ordinance, reaffirmed Congress's commitment to new state equality. So, in 1784, when Virginia became the

third state to cede its trans-Ohio claims, Congress had to do something quickly. The lands to the northwest were rich in natural endowments sure to attract new settlers, land speculators, and other opportunists. In 1785, an ordinance was passed that provided for a survey and sale of lands. Speculators were buying land and then selling to farmers at higher prices. Congress desperately needed the revenue from land sales, and it needed to pacify the Indians. It also needed to build a navy and provide for the common defense. But what was it to do with those western lands? How were the Indians to be dealt with, and what was to be the policy for settlement?

The Revolutionary War left the new nation burdened with debt and with veteran soldiers who were entitled to land bounties. The people of the country began to regard the western lands as a potential fund to aid in the liquidation of this national debt. It was maintained that since the war was prosecuted for the general defense and benefit of the country, the states claiming the lands far to the west ought to relinquish them as a common fund for the benefit of the United States. The states also concluded that the conquest of the Indians, the building of roads, and the protection of the northwest from aggressors (i.e., the British) were beyond the resources of any one of them and must necessarily become a common responsibility.

Maryland, which had no claims to the west, was the first to suggest that the western country be made public domain, the common property of all the states. Those states having claims to any portion of the territory would cede their claims to the general government, with the understanding that sovereign states would in time be erected from these lands. To induce the states to make cessions of land to the general government, Congress declared, on October 10, 1780, that the territory ceded should be disposed of for the common benefit of the Union and should be formed into republican states, possessing the same rights and privileges of the other states.

Michigan territory, as I have said, was claimed by Virginia. In 1784, Virginia ceded its western holdings, and the greatest of her native sons, Thomas Jefferson, proposed a plan for the division of the western territory into ten future states. Jefferson even gave some of these states-to-be classical names, such as *Polypotamia* and *Cherronesus*; others were adaptations of Indian words. Interestingly enough, on Jefferson's map, Michigania included part of the present state of Wisconsin but none of Michigan. Not that it mattered. Congress did not buy into Jefferson's fanciful names, and it similarly rejected his arbitrary division of states by lines of longitude and latitude. The essentials of Jefferson's plan were adopted in 1784, only to be superseded three years later by the Northwest Ordinance of 1787.

The name *Michigan*, incidentally, derives from an Algonquin word for "great lake." A tribe of the Illinois Confederacy was called Michigamea. Thomas Jefferson Latinized their name to come up with *Michigania*, which he applied to one of the ten states he created out of the Northwest Territory. That name, thankfully, did not stick, but *Michigan* did, and when the territorial act was passed in 1805, the name *Michigan* became official.

The Ordinance of 1784 provided that the western lands would not remain in subjection to the east, stating that when a sufficiently large population was gained, it would be divided into states and accepted into the nation on an equal footing with the older states. That was controversial stuff at the time. There were other major concerns as well. Would a large number of new states in this distant region soon outvote the original thirteen? Those thirteen did not want the Northwest Territory broken up into so many future states that they would rival the powers of the original states in the general government. Would a dynamic frontier culture outstrip the settled, landed interests of the east?

James Monroe had taken the trouble to tour the western settlements. He concluded that the interests of the people living there "were little connected with ours." Monroe thought Jefferson's plan of dividing the region into ten districts that would eventually become states would not "sell" with the older colonies. He favored reducing Jefferson's plan by at least half, so that when the proposed states should enter the Union, their influence would be weakened. The future fifth president of the United States was not alone in his reasoning that the western states "will outnumber us in Congress unless we confine their number as much as possible."[4] In the debates leading up to passage of the Northwest Ordinance, men from the established states articulated the fear of being ganged up on by these upstart westerners. During the early discussion of how this vast territory was to be administered, Monroe proposed that the territory northwest of the Ohio River be divided into not less than three nor more than five states.

A practical method of transition from territorial status to statehood was needed. Future states would grow into their new role in the same way a child gains experience and attains maturity. In 1785, the Continental Congress made its intentions clear when it asked Virginia and Massachusetts, in regard to their western lands ceded to the United States, to remove all restrictions that might hinder division of the territory into "not less than two, nor more than five states." This was the first official declaration of the number of states that might be formed in the Old Northwest. The number was changed in 1787 to "not less than three nor more than five states."

The commitment to continental development embodied in the Northwest Ordinance was as crucial to the new nation's future as the nearly simultaneous decision to institute a more "energetic" national government (to replace the Articles of Confederation). The value of the ordinance to our country's historical development cannot be overstated. John Dann writes, "The Ordinance is the story of a stable but flexible charter that allowed thirty-one of our fifty states to be carved out of the public domain under the Ordinance of 1787 as amended from time to time. With the admission of Minnesota as a state, the application of the Ordinance to the old Northwest came to an end but the pattern remained in force."[5] In other words, the Old Northwest embodied the republican values of unfettered freedom, limitless opportunity, and independence. It served as freedom's laboratory as it promoted orderly progress to self-rule.

Michigan's early political history begins, then, with the Northwest Ordinance and, to a lesser extent, with the Constitutional Convention of 1787, meeting in Philadelphia. For the purposes of this book, foremost consideration will be given to the Continental Congress, which drafted the Northwest Ordinance. The Constitutional Convention was charged by the Continental Congress in February, as Pauline Maier puts it, "the sole and express purpose of revising the Articles of Confederation . . . which had failed to unite the states in common purpose."[6] It sounds so commonplace, this call to revise the country's basic charter, but concern over the fate of the young republic and of the ideals of the American Revolution helped to attract a truly remarkable gathering of minds to Philadelphia.

The Constitutional Convention worked simultaneously with the Continental Congress, meeting in New York. While one body formulated a constitution that would establish a uniquely American federal system, the other group of men drafted an ordinance that envisioned a dynamic, expanding union of equal states. What a happy conjunction of events! Long before e-mail, without benefit of instant consultation, the

framers of the Northwest Ordinance and the federal Constitution crafted documents that depended on each other. Without the Constitution, the ordinance would have lacked a sense of validity. By the same light, the success of republican government depended on the ordinance's commitment to an expanding union of equal states. Soon enough, in 1803, Jefferson's bold purchase of the Louisiana Territory would bear out what the ordinance envisioned all along.

The Continental Congress had a lot on its table. Scarred by its experience with the failed Articles of Confederation, Congress had to balance states' rights with the federal concept that the framers in Philadelphia were considering. Eastern prejudices were brought to bear on the settlers then flooding into the northwest. How could these "white savages"—presumed to be fleeing the restraints of taxation, the rule of law, and civilized society by moving west—be brought into the Union? Congress had debated this matter for years, many members doubting the capacity of frontiersmen to govern themselves. The lack of political character and virtue of frontier people were the butt of jokes by conservative easterners. Thus Congress set about fashioning its expansion policy. It was clear to most contemporaries that the central government would have to be much stronger to implement a vigorous western policy. "A most fortunate antecedent to the making of Michigan," wrote George Willard, "and one which served to essentially shape its structure, is seen in the fundamental law which the founders of the American republic provided for molding the institutions of the old northwest territory. The Continental Congress gave to that territory in the ordinance of 1787 a political bible."[7]

The record shows that the Reverend Manasseh Cutler of Massachusetts, while negotiating a deal with an official of Congress who handled land sales, demanded that Congress take action to provide government for the region in which his (Cutler's) tract was located, which happened to be in southeastern Ohio. The outgrowth of Cutler's demand eventually came to be the Northwest Ordinance. In the case of the Northwest Ordinance, haste did not make waste. A committee, made up of Edward Carrington and Richard Henry Lee of Virginia, Nathan Dane of Massachusetts, John Kean of South Carolina, and Melancton Smith of New York, was formed on July 9, 1787. The *Journal of Congress* shows that the ordinance took the same course in its passage as any other law. It was given a first reading, tabled, amended and changed, given a second and third reading, and finally passed. Dane modestly allowed that he might be considered "the principal author" of the document: "We met several times and at last agreed on some principles, at least Lee, Smith and myself . . . when I drew the ordinance which passed . . . as I originally formed it."[8] It took only two days for Dane's committee to make its recommendations. On July 13, 1787, Congress passed the ordinance that created the Northwest Territory, 260,000 square miles of land. (Two months later, the founding fathers in Philadelphia birthed the Constitution.)

This far-reaching, visionary document was drafted, debated, and approved in an economy of time, yet its creators seemed to give little thought to their place in history. Other than Lee of Virginia, the members who helped to formulate western policy are not well known, in contrast to the framers at Philadelphia. Jefferson, who did not help to write the Constitution (because he was serving his country overseas at the time), termed the Philadelphia gathering of delegates "an assembly of demigods."

The Northwest Ordinance prohibited slavery throughout the territory, a remarkable statement in itself, while declaring freedom of religion and the sanctity of contracts. Its most famous article is the third, which states, "Religion, morality and knowledge being necessary to good government and the happiness of mankind, schools and the means of education shall forever be encouraged." From now on, one section in each township would be sold for school purposes.

The ordinance stipulated the stages of development through which its divisions would pass as they moved toward statehood. A temporary government with a governor, secretary, and three judges would be appointed by Congress. These would adopt suitable laws necessary to administer the territory. When a territory had five thousand free adult males, it would have the right to elect a legislative assembly with power to make laws, and it would have the right to send a territorial delegate to Congress. Finally, at a population of sixty thousand, a territory would be at liberty to form a constitution and state government.

As Thomas Smith has explained, the people living in what became Ohio, the first state established under this policy, "tested the notion that democratic government could evolve during a tutorial period under centralized supervision." "Despite eastern state rivalry, political factionalism, foreign intrigues and Indian warfare," wrote Smith, "the young American government was able to combine private entrepreneurship and federal responsibility to control settlement and to provide a governmental structure that insured the westward growth of the country, based on equal rights for states and white citizens."[9] That put to rest the colonial concept to which the British were wedded.

Geography provided a bigger hurdle than anticipated. If more than three states were formed, the northern boundary of the southern three states, corresponding to Ohio, Indiana, and Illinois, was to be a line drawn straight east and west from the southern end of Lake Michigan, with Congress exercising its discretion as to whether one or two states would be created north of the line. This provision was to have a profound effect on Michigan's evolution to statehood and was often cited to support Michigan's claims in the Toledo War. When Michigan claimed for its southern boundary a line from the most southerly extreme of Lake Michigan to Lake Erie, it did so as a vested right, a right accruing to the state by compact. The compact was the Northwest Ordinance of 1787, the parties to which were the original thirteen states and the territory northwest of the Ohio River. The ordinance, providing for government of those lands, declared that the acts therein contained "articles of compact between the original states and the people and states in the said territory" and were "forever to remain unalterable unless by common consent." Because the Northwest Ordinance protected every potential state against the encroachment of another and even of Congress itself, it made the alteration of any boundary subject to mutual consent of the states involved. Michigan leaned heavily on that argument in justifying its occupancy of the Toledo Strip.

However, such terms as *unalterable, forever,* and *common consent* take on a different quality over time, particularly when subjected to the vagaries of politics. Given that Congress was working with imprecise geographical knowledge in demarcating Michigan's southern boundary, "unalterable" becomes somewhat less of an absolute. Likewise, "forever" is a long time, and for the most part, laws simply do not hold up that long. We also cannot be sure what Congress meant by "common consent." Did Congress propose in the Northwest Ordinance to make "common consent" mean unanimous consent? Majority consent? Should the language of the ordinance be given a strict interpretation or a liberal construction? By the time Michigan based its claim to the Toledo Strip on the immutable and sacred quality of the Northwest Ordinance, it was unlikely to gather support for its position. As time passed and the Constitution became preeminent, the authority of the ordinance waned. The language and terms it employed, at once so ringing and definitive, could also admit to different interpretation.

In its bid for statehood and its claim to the ribbon of land over which the Toledo War was fought, Michigan would, time and again, cite the Northwest Ordinance as its legal bible. But as we shall see, in 1835, when Michigan battled Ohio over the former's southern boundary, the Northwest Ordinance was for all intents and purposes a dead letter. Today, we would say that much of the ordinance had built-in obsolescence. For example, the first section, establishing a system of temporary territorial administration, became null with the attainment of statehood. Later Congresses came to regard the work of this Continental Congress as the fruits of the old regime, that is, the Articles of Confederation. The Constitution assumed iconic status, many of the framers going on to serve the new republic in heroic manner. By contrast, the mostly anonymous drafters of the Northwest Ordinance came to be seen as lesser revolutionary statesmen who served the old Congress in its dying days.

In 1789, Congress reenacted the Northwest Ordinance in slightly altered form, to make the territorial system compatible with the new federal system. The Constitutional Convention in Philadelphia had empowered Congress to administer national territory and admit new states, in Article IV, Section 3, of the new Constitution. The Constitution, with its Bill of Rights and procedures for amendment and judicial interpretation, grew in stature. The ordinance's diminished standing made it a historical, rather than a dynamic, document. Its critics said that actions of the Continental Congress were not binding on its successors and that it had no authority to preempt the will of the people as expressed through their delegates in Philadelphia.

Not until 1850, fifteen years after the Toledo War, were last rites pronounced over the Northwest Ordinance. In *Strader v. Graham*, U.S. Supreme Court chief justice Roger Taney asserted that the ordinance was a constitutional nullity. The compact articles were said to be perpetual, but they had not been incorporated in the federal Constitution. They were not superior and paramount to the Constitution, said Taney. In his estimation, the text of the ordinance no longer had any authority at all but, in fact, had virtually disappeared. Taney's opinion accurately reflected the prevalent understanding of the relationship between the ordinance and the Constitution. The former had served its purpose, and it deserved a decent burial.

Mitchell map of 1755 (here rendered by David Burr), used by the framers of the Northwest Ordinance of 1787 to establish a due east line from the southern bend of Lake Michigan to demarcate the southern boundary of the Michigan Territory. (Courtesy of William L. Clements Library, University of Michigan.)

The beauty of the Northwest Ordinance is that it allowed new territories to become states and to be admitted to the Union on an equal footing with the original thirteen states. There would be no colonies as existed before the Revolutionary War. That was a radical departure from the British concept. Division of the Northwest Territory into states of reasonable size and the maximum use of natural boundary lines were settled upon. To further prepare these territories for the political responsibility of statehood, the ordinance proclaimed the value of education. A grid pattern of land surveys would eliminate the quarrelsome title conflicts that undercut communal harmony in some frontier areas. Finally, the document contained a bill of rights guaranteed to the people who settled in this region. Peter Onuf writes, "The Northwest Ordinance not only affirmed Congress's faith in the Union, but also included specific measures for assuring its survival and expansion. The Northwest Ordinance was an integral part of America's new constitutional order."[10] Thomas Smith would say, "The Northwest Territory created in 1787 served as an experiment in systematic and controlled expansionism, unequaled in the western world."[11]

In 1803, Ohio became the first of five states to be carved out of the old Northwest Territory. It may be said that with Ohio's becoming a state, the Northwest Ordinance, having prepared territories for statehood, began to pass from existence. On January 11, 1805, President Thomas Jefferson signed a bill that created Michigan from the Indiana Territory. The population may have been about four thousand, and the capital of Detroit, founded in 1701, was then a backwater of eighteen hundred persons. In late June, Michigan became a functioning territory, its boundaries recognizably those of the present state.

The roots of the dispute over the Toledo Strip date to the Northwest Ordinance's reliance on the Mitchell map. The defects in Mitchell's geography were to become self-evident, as survey after survey was ordered to establish certainty about Michigan's southern and Ohio's northern border. Other maps than Mitchell's were more accurate, but his had the clout of royal approval. And with royal approval, this map with numerous geographic errors was the official record in fixing the boundaries of the United States and Canada in the treaty ending the Revolutionary War. The weight of the map's authority was so great that it was used by Congress for the Ordinance of 1784 as well as the Northwest Ordinance of 1787. But if the Northwest Ordinance, as the instrument that precipitated a state of war, was based on a faulty map, the more immediate cause of the border dispute was another document— Ohio's constitution of 1803.

CHAPTER THREE

ROOTS OF THE DISPUTE II OHIO STATEHOOD

A disputed jurisdiction is one of the greatest evils which can happen to a country.

—LEWIS CASS, MICHIGAN TERRITORIAL GOVERNOR

As settlers poured into the lands west of the Appalachians, Ohio became the first land tract to qualify for statehood under the terms of the Northwest Ordinance. Meeting in Chillicothe, then the state capital, delegates gathered in 1802 for a constitutional convention. The enabling act for Ohio, passed by Congress in 1802, fixed the northern boundary of that state by the line named in the Northwest Ordinance, that being an east-west line drawn from the southerly extreme of Lake Michigan until it intersected Lake Erie and thence through Lake Erie to the Pennsylvania line. However, Ohio had other ideas concerning that boundary.

The Ohio delegates wanted to be sure the mouth of the Maumee River, then known as Miami of the Lake, was in Ohio. The area in which Toledo eventually would be sited had no great value at the time, but frontage on Lake Erie was deemed desirable for the state's development. Because maps were so imprecise, the delegates at Chillicothe worried that an east-west line drawn from Lake Michigan's southern end might compromise Ohio's geographical objectives. As delegates were pondering this dilemma, a hunter who was familiar with the region around Lake Michigan showed up among them and related the chilling intelligence that the southern end of Lake Michigan was farther south than was shown on the maps of the time. By logical extension, the western end of Lake Erie and the mouth of the Maumee River would be out-

25

side their new state if they accepted the line specified by the Northwest Ordinance.

Accordingly, to that section of its proposed constitution describing boundaries, the convention attached a proviso stating that if the line from the tip of Lake Michigan "should be found not to intersect Lake Erie, or to intersect it east of the mouth of the Maumee River, then with the assent of Congress, the boundary should be a straight line running from the southerly extreme of the lake to the most northerly cape of Maumee Bay."[1] The proviso was so phrased that the description of the boundary would be accepted unless Congress pointedly refused its consent. As it turned out, Congress never officially approved the change but did accept the constitution as drafted. Ohio would later claim that this was implied consent for its altered line.

The Chillicothe convention tried to have it both ways. Delegates who feared that the Northwest Ordinance line might strike Lake Erie farther south than they wished argued for a northern boundary either as ordained by the ordinance or, if that should strike Lake Erie below Maumee Bay, so located as to run along a line (the Ohio angle) sufficient to place all of Maumee Bay in Ohio. Ohio was accepted into the Union in 1803 with this uncertain boundary. It was so uncertain, in fact, that settlers along the Maumee River were concerned as to whether they were in Ohio or Michigan. The real confusion lay with Ohioans themselves. Despite claiming that they had Congress's implied consent and that they were in the right all along, the Ohio legislature passed resolutions, in 1807 and again in 1809, asking the federal government to survey the boundary line. By insisting that Congress take some action in its disposition, Ohio appeared to consider the question unsettled.

In the meantime, in 1805, Congress established the Michigan Territory, with the Northwest Ordinance line as its southern boundary. This left Ohio's claims null and void, and it placed within the boundaries of Michigan the strip of land Ohio wanted. Ohio continued to press for acceptance of its altered northern boundary. As the years passed, Michigan would assert that its southern boundary was inviolable because it was provided in the Northwest Ordinance and could be changed only by mutual consent. In Michigan's opinion, the ordinance protected every potential state against the encroachment of another, which is why it made the alteration of any boundary subject to mutual consent of the states involved.

Ohio's claim rested on Congress's failure to address the question of boundary at the time of accepting the Ohio Constitution. Ohio would say that when the Northwest Ordinance was adopted in 1787, the true location of the southern extreme of Lake Michigan was unknown. But when Congress declined either to accept or to reject the boundary proviso, it was precisely because the proviso pivoted on a point of geographic uncertainty. The congressional committee that dealt with the matter objected to the boundary proviso on the grounds that it depended on a fact not yet determined. When, in 1800, the Indiana Territory was created out of the Northwest Territory by running a line north from the Ohio River through the Straits of Mackinac to the international boundary, Ohio's western boundary was settled. And when another Congress, in 1805, carved the Michigan Territory from the former Indiana Territory, Congress, in defining Michigan's southern boundary, opted to accept the Northwest Ordinance line.

This occurred two years after Ohio joined the Union. In other words, Congress chose to ignore the proviso that Ohio inserted into its constitution. The consent of Congress had not been given to the line conditionally proposed in the Ohio Constitution; in fact, the dissent of Congress is expressly shown by the act of January 11, 1805, creating the Michigan Territory. Ohio made no protest against the definition of its northern boundary in the act creating the Michigan Territory.

By altering the northern boundary to include the mouth of the Maumee River, the Ohio Constitution laid the basis for the Toledo War. As Lewis Cass, Michigan territorial governor, would say, "a disputed jurisdiction is one of the greatest evils which can happen to a country."[2] Subsequent surveys, one ordered by Ohio (Harris) and another by Michigan (Fulton), created a strip of land claimed by both states. It would be years, however, before Ohio actively pushed its claim to the Toledo Strip, and it did so only after a flurry of canal projects made it evident that a commercial center would arise wherever these canals (joining the Wabash and Ohio Rivers to Lake Erie) terminated by entrance to a river or lake. It was also clear that any canal linking to Lake Erie ought to enter the northeast-flowing Maumee for its lake connection.

John Doyle explained, "Ohio wanted the Toledo Strip for development purposes, ignoring the presence of the Great Black Swamp in the northwest portion of the state, which was believed by many to be the natural barrier between Ohio and Michigan. Michigan wanted to prevent development in the Strip because any commercial center there would rival Detroit and Monroe."[3] In the meantime, the Michigan Territory administered the disputed tract of land right up until hostilities. The effect of all this on the inhabitants of the Maumee Valley was to raise their anxiety level. Did they belong to Ohio or to the Michigan Territory? If they identified with any political unit, it was Detroit, founded way back in 1701 and itself hoping to be the capital when Michigan became a state.

CHAPTER FOUR

PRELUDE TO WAR 1815–30

There isn't one tillable acre in the whole Territory.

—EDWARD TIFFIN, U.S. SURVEYOR GENERAL,
ON THE MICHIGAN TERRITORY

*Here is the place to live at ease / To work or play just as you please. /
With little prudence any man / Can soon get rich in Michigan.*

—POPULAR SONG

On January 11, 1805, President Thomas Jefferson, still flush from his triumph in expanding the nation through the Louisiana Purchase, signed legislation that significantly altered the Northwest Territory. What was known as the Indiana Territory was divided into two separate governments. By this act, the territory of Michigan was established and its boundaries defined. The western boundary was to be a north-south line running through the middle of Lake Michigan and then from the Straits of Mackinac to the international boundary in Lake Superior, thus placing a large section of the eastern Upper Peninsula in Michigan. There were a few settlers in the Upper Peninsula—chiefly on Mackinac Island, profiting from the fur trade—and in such mission settlements as Sault Ste. Marie and St. Ignace, both of them old cities. This is the first time that a political division of land by the name of Michigan appears on the maps of the day. The Michigan Territory included the eastern end of the Upper Peninsula, all of the Lower Peninsula, and a strip of land now contained in Indiana and Ohio.

One would think that any question of boundary between Michigan and Indiana or between Michigan and Ohio would be settled by an act that had congressional approval and a presidential signature. Michigan's southern boundary would be that established in the Northwest Ordinance. Even if this ordinance was not binding in its delineation of boundaries, the act of 1805 was conclusive. Ohio's delegation in Congress continued to lobby for the Maumee Bay tangent that would put the mouth of the Maumee River in Ohio. As late as 1812, Congress was still ignoring Ohio's claim; that year, Congress passed a resolution providing for a survey of the ordinance line drawn straight east from the southernmost extreme of Lake Michigan.

If the War of 1812 had not intervened to short-circuit that survey, Michigan might have had an even stronger legal case, as a survey under federal imprimatur would have carried considerable weight. But when, in 1815, a federal survey was ordered by the surveyor general of the United States, the timing for Michigan could not have been worse. The surveyor general was Edward Tiffin, the first governor of Ohio, who had helped to draft the Ohio Constitution when the boundary defined by the Northwest Ordinance was challenged. In 1817, he instructed his deputy, William Harris, to survey the boundary, but with special instructions: to run the line to conform with the if-then provision in the Ohio Constitution.

Tiffin ordered his man to "repair to the northwest corner of the state of Ohio," where, "having found the post at the N.W. corner of Ohio," he was to "survey and mark a line, due East, as nearly as it can be done with the compass, to the border of Lake Erie." Tiffin added a final note of caution: "Great accuracy and care must be observed in running this line, as the jurisdictional limits between the State of Ohio and the Territory of Michigan are to be determined by it."[1] Using all the tools of the trade, including surveyor chains, Harris's crew ran the line on an angle from the Indiana border to the most northerly cape of Maumee Bay. In that way, the Harris line turned out to be the boundary desired by Ohio. The Harris survey struck Lake Erie seven miles and forty-nine chains north of a line due east from the southern end of Lake Michigan. Michigan territorial governor Lewis Cass cried foul, saying that Tiffin had failed to honor the requirements set down by Congress.

Cass, a towering figure in Michigan's early history, succeeded in persuading President James Monroe to order a second survey. This was made in 1818 by John A. Fulton, who ran his line in accordance with a greater awareness of where the most southerly end of Lake Michigan was. The Fulton line intersected Lake Erie to the east of the mouth of the Maumee River, leaving the opening to the lake in Michigan Territory. The two widely varying surveys produced the Toledo Strip—the area of roughly 470 square miles between the Harris line on the north

and the Fulton line to the south. The strip was a tapering piece of land
seventy miles long, five miles wide on the west at the Indiana line and
eight miles wide on the east. Today, the strip contains mostly flat farmland of no great intrinsic value to either state, but in 1818, the Maumee
Valley was deemed to have great economic potential.

There was another major reason why Edward Tiffin did not endear
himself to Michigan. Just as an earlier Congress had earmarked the
Northwest Territory as bounty lands for Revolutionary War veterans,
another Congress had come along to offer two million acres in the territories as a bounty for service in the War of 1812. Under a survey ordered by Tiffin as surveyor general, commissioners from the Federal
Land Office in Washington "scoped out" the Michigan Territory. In
their 1817 report, commissioners said they could not find one tillable
acre in the whole territory. Tiffin's version of the report portrayed
Michigan as a land of bogs and lakes, mosquitoes and ague, swamp critters and noxious fevers. Just a poor, barren sandy land, Tiffin called it;
and as a result of his report, President James Madison recommended
that other lands should be designated to take the place of Michigan's
proportion of the military bounty lands.

Governor Cass took the Tiffin report to task, saying the lands of
Michigan had been "grossly misrepresented."[2] He was in a position to
know, as he was as familiar with the territory as anybody. In 1818, he
persuaded the federal government to locate a land office in Detroit, and
he later obtained funds from Congress to build a road from Detroit to
Fort Dearborn. He had finished surveying two roads across the peninsula and knew very well there was fine farmland in the interior.

But Cass was also a visionary. He did not want the Michigan Territory populated with war veterans and land speculators. Hoping to attract a better class of settlers, he rose to Michigan's defense in criticizing
the Tiffin report, but he pulled his punches to some extent. He would
take his time promoting Michigan in eastern circles. For his patience, he
was ultimately rewarded.

But the short term took its toll. As a result of Tiffin's unflattering
report, Michigan's settlement was slowed, and the government's disap-
proval of Michigan's agricultural potential found its way into the nation's newspapers. School geographies contained maps with "inter-
minable swamp" scrawled across peninsular Michigan. A traveler's guide
of that day depicted Michigan with sand hills "extending into the inte-

rior as far as the dividing ridge, . . . sometimes crowned with a few stunted trees, and a scanty vegetation, but generally bare, and thrown by the wind into a thousand fantastic shapes."[3]

In 1816, Indiana entered the Union, having placed its northern border ten miles north of the Northwest Ordinance line. The new state wanted frontage on Lake Michigan and boldly staked its claim. At the time, southwestern Michigan was undersettled, and Cass was busy elsewhere, so Indiana's northern border, which was in contravention of the ordinance line, went uncontested. Indiana's northward expansion met with no opposition in Congress.

The apparent indifference of Michigan to its western lands must have emboldened Indiana. In 1827, the latter state secured a law providing for a survey of its northern boundary as defined in the act of 1816. Then in 1833, the Committee on Territories in the national House of Representatives was instructed to report on the advisability of extending Indiana to the St. Joseph River, which empties into Lake Michigan at the present cities of St. Joseph and Benton Harbor, Michigan. This bid for another lake port also seems to have gone unnoticed in Michigan, although in the following year, Michigan governor Stevens T. Mason appointed commissioners to treat with Indiana, as well as Ohio, on this matter of boundaries. So confident was Indiana of its right to all the land Congress had given it, writes Annah May Soule in her treatise on the Michigan-Indiana boundary, "that one of her senators at this time supported the claims of Michigan against Ohio,"[4] saying in the debate on the Michigan-Ohio boundary that Ohio had no claim to the strip of land in question. (Later, Indiana would change its tune and side with Ohio, when it became clear that if Michigan won its dispute with Ohio, Michigan might also best Indiana in any strict interpretation of the Northwest Ordinance line.)

In 1818, the ordinance line was debased again, when Illinois placed its border with Wisconsin sixty miles north of the most southerly end of Lake Michigan, to include Fort Dearborn, now Chicago. In accepting Indiana's and Illinois's borders in their statehood applications, Congress thus chose to ignore the language of the Northwest Ordinance. A year earlier, Cass had protested the Harris line by arguing, "Why add to an already strong state at the expense of an undeveloped territory?" On November 1, 1817, writing from Detroit to Tiffin, Cass gets right to the point: "Report says that the line which has been recently run between the State of Ohio and this Territory was not run a due east course from the southern extremity of Lake Michigan to Lake Erie, but a course somewhat to the north of this. The Act of Congress organizing the Territory marks its southern boundary a due east line, . . . and this act is in strict conformity with the fifth article of the Articles of Compact in the Ordinance for the government of the Northwestern Territory. These are declared to be unalterable, except by mutual consent, and although the boundary of Indiana was extended, contrary to these provisions ten miles north, yet I believe it was done inadvisedly and will, when this Territory is heard in the Legislature of the Nation, be a subject for revision and examination."[5]

As Michigan would discover repeatedly in the near future, both in its bid for statehood and in affirming its rights to the Toledo Strip, influence in the halls of Congress is what it sorely lacked. Ohio and, later, Indiana and Illinois, as states, had voting delegations in "the Legislature of the Nation," which Michigan, as a territory, could only dream about. In the letter already cited, Cass goes on to remind Tiffin that Congress never agreed to the line run by Ohio "to the most northerly cape of Miami Bay," and he argues that the altered boundary "only adds strength to the strong, and makes the weak still weaker." He adds, "By reducing it, its period of admission into the general confederation is indefinitely postponed. The country upon the Miami has no natural connection with the interior of Ohio."[6]

Responding from Chillicothe, then Ohio's capital, Tiffin replied, "I was directed by the President of the United States . . . to have the boundary surveyed and marked, and that Mr. William Harris, a surveyor, was designated to do this work. By the enclosed sketch you therefore see the two lines, and let the proper authorities say which shall govern and divide the State of Ohio from the Territory of Michigan. It is my opinion that the black line is the true line." The black line referenced by Tiffin is, of course, the Harris line. He recounts the act of Congress enabling Ohio to be admitted to the Union and mentions the Ohio Constitution's express call for a line to be drawn "to the most northerly cape of the Miami." "By attending to the words 'with the assent of the Congress of the United States' and calling to mind that Congress did assent by receiving the State into the Union upon the terms and conditions above expressed," Tiffin concludes, "I should suppose no doubt can arise relative to the true boundary."[7]

Although Tiffin had clout in Congress, he was up against a formidable foe in Lewis Cass. Born in 1872, Cass is Michigan's dominant political figure. Today, he is its star personage in the National Statuary Hall, under the dome of the U.S. Capitol. There, his inscription reads: "General Lewis Cass, 1782–1866, dedicated to the memory of the foremost of Michigan's pioneers. More than any other man he shaped the development of Michigan and the whole Northwest Territory. He negotiated twenty-two Indian treaties, supervised the movement of numerous tribes to the hinterlands west of the Mississippi, conducted important exploration tours into the wilderness to discover and measure its resources, enforced the edicts of a young nation on one of its most difficult frontiers. As territorial governor, he set up geographic boundaries throughout the state, created judicial districts, organized many of the counties of the state. He served his country in the War of 1812, attaining high rank. After 18 years as Michigan territorial governor he served in two presidential cabinets, 12 years in the U.S. Senate. Appointed minister to France he published in Paris his celebrated 'Inquiry into the Right of Search' which made maritime history. He was nominated for President in 1848. Often ranked first in the second generation of American statesmen—which included Clay, Webster, Calhoun—he is Michigan's permanent representative in the Nation's Hall of Fame."

Cass's long public career spanned the period from the War of 1812 to the Civil War. A Yankee who was born in Exeter, New Hampshire, he emigrated to the Northwest Territory in 1801, settling near Zanesville, Ohio. He studied law, was admitted to the bar, and, at the young age of twenty-four, was elected to the Ohio House of Representatives. His strong support for Thomas Jefferson led to his appointment as U.S. marshal for the district of Ohio. At the outbreak of the War of 1812, he enlisted in the army. As a colonel of the Third Ohio Infantry under General William Hull, he was present when Detroit was surrendered, later writing a report critical of Hull's performance and testifying at Hull's court-martial proceedings. He was brevetted brigadier general on March 20, 1813, and contributed substantially to the American victory in the Battle of the Thames the following year.

Cass rode his military reputation to political fame, serving as the military and civil governor of the Michigan Territory between 1813 and 1831. During this time and later, as Andrew Jackson's secretary of war, Cass became deeply involved in formulating a government policy toward Native Americans and was a central figure in promoting removal as a general policy. He was appointed U.S. envoy to France in 1836, but

Lewis Cass, Michigan's territorial governor. Cass labored to portray Michigan as a favorable place to settle and farm. He served in many capacities and is Michigan's most highly regarded statesman. (Courtesy of William L. Clements Library, University of Michigan.)

his outspoken Anglophobia led to disagreement with Secretary of State Daniel Webster and prompted his resignation in 1842.

Cass was elected as the U.S. senator from Michigan in 1845 and again in 1851 and was an unsuccessful candidate for president on the Democratic ticket in 1848. As a senator, Cass had approved of the Compromise of 1850, but after joining the Buchanan cabinet as secretary of state, as disunion threatened, he became convinced that strong measures were necessary. He resigned from the cabinet when President Buchanan refused to fortify federal garrisons.

After the Harris and Fulton surveys, the dispute over the boundary quieted down. Ohio seemingly forfeited its rights to this wedge of land by leaving its administration in the hands of the Michigan Territory. Michigan continued to extend its authority over the Toledo Strip. In 1820, the Michigan delegate to Congress, William Woodbridge, urged that a report concerning the boundary be brought before the House of

Representatives. It was referred to the Committee on Public Lands, which heard arguments from Woodbridge and the Ohio representatives before the committee chair, Richard Anderson of Kentucky, reported to the House in favor of Michigan's interpretation.

Again in 1828, the subject of boundary received the attention of Congress, or at least a small element of that body. The Committee on Territories in the House reported it was obviously just and fair that the states to be formed out of the Northwest Territory should enjoy, as nearly as possible, equal advantages in their access to and communication with Lakes Erie and Michigan. Members of the committee seemed to think that maybe the framers of the Northwest Ordinance intended that all the states should benefit from frontage on the lakes.

Michigan solidified its claim to the disputed area when Monroe County was created in 1822 with the Fulton line as its southern boundary. The pioneer villages of Port Lawrence, Vistula, Manhattan, and Tremainsville, all part of present-day Toledo, functioned under Michigan jurisdiction. Postmasters in those communities marked the mail with "M.T." or "Mic Ty" for "Michigan Territory." In 1827, the Michigan Legislative Council organized the area into Port Lawrence Township, with taxes being paid to the Monroe County treasurer. Judicial proceedings beyond the realm of the justice of the peace were handled at Monroe, the county seat. Public land was purchased at the government land office in Monroe, and the deeds were recorded in that town. The case can be made that when Michigan organized the Toledo Strip, enforcing laws and collecting taxes there, Ohio waived its last legal claim to the disputed tract.

More fundamentally, it was an error on the part of Congress to allow Ohio to assume the functions and duties of a state merely from the state's enabling act, without addressing the issue of boundary in its constitution. The if-then provision should have been summarily rejected, and Ohio should have been told that if it had a problem with its northern boundary, there were legal channels to employ. As long as Michigan pressed its rights and its legal claim stood a chance of being upheld, an air of uncertainty hung over the matter, which annoyed Ohio.

In the meantime, public attitudes back east were changing. Governor Cass was doing his best to promote Michigan. Some of the early guidebooks for travelers and settlers were very favorable to the area. In his *Pedestrious Tour*, published in 1818, Estwick Evans wrote, "In travelling more than four thousand miles, in the western parts of the United States, I met no tract of country which, upon the whole, impressed my mind so favorably as the Michigan Territory. . . . The soil of the territory is generally fertile, and a considerable proportion of it is very rich."[8]

More newspaper articles about Michigan were appearing in the eastern press, while water transportation and the Erie Canal made Michigan look attractive. New editions of Morse's *Geography* painted a better picture of the peninsula. The construction of roads and the opening of land offices in Detroit and Monroe lured settlers and developers. By about 1825, the Tiffin report had lost its sting in the East. There was a popular song whose first verse runs thus:

> Come all ye Yankee farmers who wish to change your lot
> Who've spunk enough to travel beyond your native spot
> And leave behind the village where Pa and Ma do stay
> Come follow me and settle in Mich-i-gan-i-a-
> Yea, yea, yea, in Michigania.[9]

Another song hymned the praises of Michigan girls:

> Here is the place to live at ease
> To work or play just as you please
> With little prudence any man
> Can soon get rich in Michigan
> Ye who have led a single life
> And now would wish to get a wife
> I tell you this, now understand
> We have first-rate girls in Michigan.[10]

By the time statehood was being talked up, a mass influx of New Englanders to Michigan was in progress. "Michigan fever" was claiming more victims all the time. Because of the Tiffin report and Cass's clever downplaying of Michigan's potential during the early development of the Northwest Territory, it was Michigan's good fortune to avoid being settled by land speculators and veterans of the earlier wars with England. One writer said, "Soldiers' bounty lands, granted without survey, led to a rush of land-hungry veterans everywhere. Wild speculation ensued, quite at variance with the situation in Michigan where settlers arrived with money to pay for their land and tools to build their homes."[11]

The Michigan area received a more sophisticated class of settlers. They came mostly from New England and upper New York State. Despite the cholera epidemics, hundreds of immigrants began pouring into southern Michigan every week via the Erie Canal and Lake Erie steamboats. How fast was this growth? Michigan's population was believed to number thirty-one thousand in 1830, with Detroit holding about three thousand. By late 1834, a census put the population at eighty-five thousand. The push for statehood was in full cry.

The success of the Erie Canal got people's minds to dreaming of profits and prosperity for the two new states of Indiana and Ohio. Canals were seen as the transportation solution in getting goods to market and in promoting trade. Steamships on the Great Lakes were not long in coming, so the wedding of canals and steamers to facilitate commerce was inevitable.

In 1830, Toledo was still a collection of villages. But because of its geographical positioning at the mouth of the Maumee River on Lake Erie, it was envisioned as a great port, certain to surpass Detroit. There were about a thousand inhabitants in Port Lawrence and Vistula at this time, far more than in Chicago, but fewer than in Detroit. It was thought that Toledo, not yet officially a city, would link the commercial activity of the two eastern lakes of the Great Lakes with the potential wealth of the three western lakes. The city would be the eastern terminus for a vast network of canals.

In February 1825, the Ohio legislature adopted a canal act that plunged the state heavily into canal construction. A state system of waterways would connect Lake Erie with the Ohio River. At the same time, Indiana leaders hit on the idea of building a canal to connect the Wabash River (which reached the Ohio River at Evansville, Indiana) with the Maumee River, whose outlet is in Lake Erie at Toledo. One of Ohio's proposed canals, running northward from Cincinnati, would juncture with the Wabash and Erie Canal in the Maumee Valley.

By 1830, the boundary issue flared up again, with a great convergence of explosive issues. Michigan was experiencing rapid growth and appeared ready for statehood. Ohio was becoming greatly concerned about the eastern terminus of its canal system. In Congress, the Ohio representatives were hoping to get that body to ratify the provision in the Ohio Constitution that the northern boundary should include Maumee Bay within the limits of that state. Until it was assured control over the Toledo Strip, or until Congress ratified Ohio's version of its northern boundary, Ohio planned to block Michigan's bid for admission into the Union.

This was what poisoned the waters before and after the Toledo

War. Michigan would find its way to full admission as a state blocked, time and again, by a collusion of political forces. Michigan asked Congress for permission to proceed with statehood in the early 1830s, but Ohio, a supporter of President Jackson and the Democratic Party, adopted the policy of blocking Michigan's entry until it agreed to accept Ohio's boundary claim. Ohio persuaded Illinois and Indiana to join in pressing for deferment of Michigan statehood until the boundary question was settled—an easy piece of persuasion on Ohio's part, because the other two states had already breached the Northwest Ordinance line and might be forced to give up territory if Michigan's claim was upheld.

If the political deck was stacked against Michigan, the economic forces at work against that state were also formidable. The federal government wanted to promote internal development and did so with grants of land and money for canal building. Years before the Wabash and Erie Canal was completed, eastern speculators had invested heavily in real estate in the Port Lawrence (Toledo) area, in the expectation that the area would become a commercial capital. Investors wanted to keep their holdings within a healthy and established state (Ohio), rather than trust their financial fortunes to a new and uncertain government in Michigan. The prospect of the lower Maumee being connected by canal with the Wabash River and the Ohio River at Cincinnati appealed to promoters and investors, nearly all of whom were Ohio people. The future of their enterprises depended on the generosity of the legislature in its public works appropriations, so they naturally appealed for a hasty settlement of the boundary dispute.

In the early 1830s, residents of the Toledo Strip, who were placidly pro-Michigan if they had any allegiance at all, suddenly found themselves rabidly pro-Ohio. It was clear that the residents of the strip stood to gain financially if the canal was allowed to have its terminus at Toledo, safely in Ohio's jurisdiction. At a public meeting held in Toledo in November 1834, the sentiment voiced was in favor of Ohio asserting and maintaining jurisdiction over the disputed region.

For their part, Michigan capitalists wanted to keep the Toledo Strip within their state because two sizable railroad projects had been initiated in Michigan, one of which was to terminate in the Toledo area. The Erie and Kalamazoo Railroad had been chartered in 1833; it operated its first horse-drawn coach over thirty-three miles of oak rails from Port Lawrence to Adrian on November 2, 1836. The next year, it got a steam engine. So in the early 1830s, both investors in canals in Ohio and investors in railroads in Michigan supplied colorful patriotic rhetoric arguing that the Toledo Strip rightfully belonged, respectively, to the sovereign state of Ohio or the new state of Michigan.

As it happened, the canal craze died out in the 1840s, as railroads became more and more popular. Ohio's Wabash and Erie Canal was not completed until 1845, ten years after the Toledo War. A waterway to connect the Great Lakes with the Mississippi River by way of the Illinois River was not finished until 1848. Canal building was dealt a serious blow when the federal government, under President Andrew Jackson, sharply curtailed appropriations for internal improvements. The financial panic of 1837 did the rest.

In 1830 and the years immediately following, the stage was set for conflict between Michigan and Ohio. The economic and political forces at work would bring matters to a head in the land between the Harris and Fulton lines. Michigan, under a youthful—some would say impetuous—territorial governor, was knocking on the door of Congress, asking for statehood. Ohio, holding the trump card of political influence in that body, was determined to keep Michigan a territory until the northern boundary was decided in Ohio's favor. Because statehood for Michigan and the Toledo War are inextricably intertwined, Michigan's difficult path to statehood is worthy of more study if the ensuing war is to be properly understood. For that, we must introduce Stevens T. Mason, a young man who was destined to write his name in capital letters on Michigan's early history.

CHAPTER FIVE

PATH TO STATEHOOD

Shall it be expedient for the people of the territory to form a state government?

— QUESTION POSED TO VOTERS OF THE MICHIGAN
TERRITORY, OCTOBER 1832

It is not expedient to admit Michigan at the present time.

— COMMITTEE ON TERRITORIES, HOUSE OF REPRESENTATIVES,
WASHINGTON, D.C., MARCH 11, 1834

By any standard, Michigan had a most difficult birth. Carved out of the Northwest Ordinance as the Michigan Territory in 1805, the land between the lakes experienced slow growth at first, thanks in part to the off-putting Tiffin report. But when Lewis Cass became territorial governor in 1813, Michigan found itself in the capable hands of a frontiersman with a first-class mind. Part of Cass's giant reputation came from his skill with Indians in negotiating treaties. Large quantities of land were given up by these original settlers in terms considered fair at the time. And when Ohio, through Tiffin, made its first tentative claims to the Toledo Strip, Cass was there to uphold Michigan's right.

Andrew Jackson won the presidency in 1829 and tapped Cass to be his secretary of war. Washington's gain was Michigan's loss. Cass left his duties as territorial governor in 1831, just about the time Michigan had reached the population requirement (sixty thousand) for statehood as set forth in the Northwest Ordinance. The process for statehood began in earnest in October 1832, when Michigan citizens voted to petition Congress for admission as a state. Neither House nor Senate acted on this petition. Not until January 26, 1837, did Michigan finally win its star on the national flag.

The "boy wonder" who transformed Michigan from bumptious

territory to vigorous state in a single decade was Stevens T. Mason, whose pedigree was the peerless Virginia family of that name. Born to wealth in Virginia on October 11, 1811, Mason's great-grandfather, George Mason, was a friend of George Washington and Patrick Henry. Stevens T. Mason moved to Kentucky at a young age, when his restless father, John T. Mason, followed his urge to explore and settle the frontier for the new nation. Fortunately for John T., who wanted to head west and needed a job, he had a friend in President Jackson, the great champion of patronage politics. As luck would have it, there just happened to be a vacant position in the Michigan Territory.

With Michigan bereft of the services of Cass, it was thought that William Woodbridge or Austin E. Wing were the best-qualified citizens for the governorship of the territory. Woodbridge had served as a delegate to Congress and as secretary of the territory. Wing had also served in Congress. But Jackson, happily doling out appointments under the spoils system, ignored local sentiment and summoned Mason to the White House. John T. Mason's business ventures were not always successful, and he needed something that both paid reasonably well and satisfied his questing spirit. So when Jackson met with Mason in May 1830 and offered him the post of secretary of the Michigan Territory, with the responsibility to act as governor, with full executive responsibilities, until that job was filled, Mason said yes.

Thus it was that young Stevens T. Mason, then nineteen, accompanied his father, John, to Michigan, settling in Detroit, the largest habitation of consequence in the Lower Peninsula. There, he helped his father in performance of duties and, in so doing, impressed both Cass and Jackson. However, Democrat John T. Mason found frontier politics not to his liking and, after a year, resigned his post to, as we would say today, "pursue other opportunities."

In 1831, George B. Porter of Pennsylvania was named Cass's successor as governor of the Michigan Territory. But in mid-July of that year, Old Hickory surprised everyone by naming Stevens T. Mason, also called Tom, to the secretaryship position his father had vacated, so that by the time Porter arrived in Detroit in September, young Mason was already serving as acting governor. What was Jackson thinking when he tapped wet-behind-the-ears Stevens T. Mason for the secretaryship? Mason's biographer, Lawton Hemans, says Jackson took to Stevens like a doting father to a son. Jackson perceived administrative qualities in the young man that warranted elevating him as the new secretary although

Stevens T. Mason, Michigan's "Boy Governor." Mason led the fight for statehood and maintained Michigan's right to control of the Toledo Strip. (Courtesy of the Historical Society of Michigan.)

he was not yet twenty-one. For his part, "Tom" Mason had adapted quickly to his new surroundings and became a popular figure in Detroit.

Governor Porter was often absent from the territory during the next three years. It is unclear where he went or what he did that prompted these departures, but Mason put the times to good use. As acting governor, he gained experience in dealing with the territory's politicians and newspaper moguls. When Porter died, in July 1834, in the cholera epidemic of that year, Mason once more became acting governor, at the young age of twenty-two. He developed into a canny, smart politician with a passion for his new state. His zeal in promoting Michigan's interests during the Toledo War led Jackson to label him "that Hotspur governor." However, mentor and mentee were destined to have a falling out.

After Porter's death, Jackson and the U.S. Senate deadlocked on a successor, with the result that Mason stayed on as the territory's chief executive. That is where things stood in 1835 when the Toledo War erupted. But before hostilities began, statehood for Michigan had long been on the front burner. Ohio had begun to take note of Michigan's preparations to establish a state government, and at some time prior to 1835, the northern counties of Williams, Wood, and Henry had attempted to levy taxes on the inhabitants of the disputed territory. The people living there, however, spurned this action. Nothing more came of it until early 1835, when Ohio governor Robert Lucas sent to his leg-islature a message asserting jurisdiction over the lands south of the mouth of Maumee Bay, urging legislation to control this territory.

After several quiescent years during which Michigan's territorial laws were extended over the disputed territory, the Toledo Strip contro-versy boiled over. In 1831, it was clear to state and territory that a speedy settlement of the border dispute was badly needed. The dispute, so localized that it only involved 468 square miles of mostly forgettable terrain, now slowly seeped into national consciousness. Some technical deficiencies were found in the Fulton survey, so in 1832, Congress or-dered yet another marking of the line, with a sunset date of December 31, 1835.

This time, the job was entrusted to Captain Andrew Talcott, who was aided in the project by a brilliant young graduate from West Point. Robert E. Lee, future Confederate war hero and military strategist in the Civil War, assisted Talcott in running a line that coincided with the Fulton line in placing the Toledo Strip clearly in the Michigan Terri-tory. A letter from Lieutenant Lee (then twenty-eight), written while he was on Turtle Island in Lake Erie, near Toledo, and directed to George Washington Cullum, a young assistant in the chief engineer's office in Washington, refers to Toledo residents' hostility toward the engineer-ing party and to the "cordiality" of Detroit. Lee writes, "The country around savors marvellously of bilious fevers and seems to be productive of nothing more plentifully than of mosquitoes and snakes. We hear that about Toledo they speak hardly of us. Hood [a fellow engineer] and myself are in high preparation for a trip up the Maumee river to make a survey from a little above its intersection with the due East line—from the S. bend of Lake Michigan to this place—it is some 12 miles off, the boat and men are ready, it is a long pull and we then have to establish ourselves for the night, and among enemies, too."[1]

The Talcott survey was reported to Congress in 1834 but was ig-nored. It simply joined the thousands of reports that, over the years, have gathered dust on shelves on Capitol Hill. For the record, the Tal-cott line and the Fulton line intersected the Maumee not more than three hundred yards apart.

In the territory, statehood fever first found expression in June 1832, when the territorial legislature provided for taking a vote in October on the question "whether it be expedient for the people of the territory to form a state government." The result of that vote was that the yeas car-

ried the day over the nays, but just barely. However, the seeming lack of
enthusiasm for statehood did not deter advocates.

The next year, the legislature followed regular prestatehood procedures and formally requested that Congress pass enabling legislation.
On January 8, 1833, the legislature adopted a memorial, or resolution,
to Congress requesting an act that would give the people the privilege
of drafting a constitution for a state that would have for its southern
boundary the line cited in the Northwest Ordinance of 1787 and in the
1805 act establishing the Michigan Territory. Congress took the matter
under advisement but showed no disposition to act on the statehood
proposal.

The year was coming to a close when, on December 11, 1833, Lucius Lyon, Michigan's territorial delegate to Congress, presented the
first formal petition of Michigan for admission as a state. He strongly
urged passage of enabling legislation. Later, Lyon submitted an exhaus-
tive argument on the boundary question to the House committee in
charge of the bill for the admission of Michigan. According to Lawton
Hemans, Lyon made arguments "which for perspicuity and logical de-
ductions could not have been surpassed, and which from the standpoint
of legal right remain unanswered."[2]

Lucius Lyon, born the eldest of eight children in February 1800 on
a farm near Shelburne Falls, Vermont, trained as a civil engineer and, in
1821, went to Michigan to survey public lands. He surveyed much of
the Lower Peninsula and came to own extensive tracts of land in Michigan and Wisconsin. He traveled with Lewis Cass and may have been in
love with Cass's daughter, although at one time he courted the sister of
Governor Mason. Throughout his life, he was interested in a variety of
internal improvements, including the Detroit waterworks; the lead
mines in Galena, Illinois; and the development of St. Joseph Harbor.
Lyon was part of a group that built the first water system in Detroit, and
he pioneered in sinking salt wells near Grand Rapids. He was among the
founding fathers of many settlements, including Ypsilanti and Kalamazoo. A consistent Democrat, Lyon was a land speculator and builder of
mills, dams, canals, and bridges. For Lyon, silk culture, railroads, and
banks came in for special notice. He raised sugar beets on one of his
farms and was informed on new agricultural methods. His interest also
extended to educational movements, Indian affairs, and lumbering. He
served as appointed Indian commissioner, working to settle problems
arising from misunderstandings with Indians.

But it was in public service to his adopted state that Lyon made his mark. His family motto was "Labor to be useful," and Lucius Lyon certainly was useful to the new state. The 1833 territorial Democratic convention elected Lyon its representative in Congress while the candidate himself was off on a surveying trip in the western portion of the territory. He won election on July 8 and took his seat in Washington as delegate to Congress from the Michigan Territory in December 1833, at the age of thirty-three. His career as a territorial delegate found him sponsoring legislation for internal improvements that would benefit the territory. On March 6, 1834, Lyon presented a resolution to establish a separate territorial government (Wisconsin) west of Lake Michigan and to recognize the line established as the southern boundary of Michigan by Article V of the Northwest Ordinance. He later was an influential member of Michigan's first constitutional convention, in 1835, and he took the finished document of that convention to Washington as the first U.S. senator from Michigan. Before he could take his seat, however, Lyon had to work for the adjustment of the boundary with Ohio and the admission of Michigan to the Union.

Lyon was an exceptionally qualified public servant with a high sense of calling, but in 1834, his hands were tied. By now, the bid for admission of Michigan as a state had become inextricably linked with the Toledo Strip controversy. The political forces arrayed against Michigan's bid for statehood were led by Ohio. Its representatives appealed to the "plenary, equitable and political discretion"[3] of Congress, knowing that the outcome there would be favorable. One Ohio congressman argued that Michigan would always be a third- or fourth-rate power because of population and geography and that there was therefore no need to discuss the boundary issue at all.

Michigan could read the handwriting on the wall. In 1834, the territorial legislature addressed another memorial to Congress, reminding that body that the people of the territory had voted in 1832 on the expediency of forming a state government. The legislature's main point was that the boundaries created by the Northwest Ordinance of 1787 could be changed only by mutual consent. Ohio wanted resolution of the Toledo Strip dispute before Michigan attained statehood, because as a territory, Michigan had no legal status, but as a state, it could take its case to the Supreme Court. For his part, President Jackson tried to take a hands-off approach, on the grounds that the boundary dispute was a problem for Congress to sort out.

A month before the 1834 Talcott survey reinforced Michigan's claim to the Toledo Strip, Congress dealt Michigan a harsh blow by rejecting its petition for statehood. A report of March 1834 by the Committee on Territories in the House of Representatives stated that it was "not expedient" to admit Michigan at present. If one were to keep track of these things, this was rejection number one. On the other side of the Capitol, an enabling bill introduced in the Senate to authorize the people of Michigan to form a state government was debated during May 9–12, 1834, and then tabled by a vote of 17–14. This was rejection number two. Rejection number three was provided by the Senate Judiciary Committee, chaired by John M. Clayton of Delaware. That committee, ostensibly debating whether Congress had the power to change the boundary lines that had been provided in the Northwest Ordinance, was reported by its chairman to be "unanimously of the opinion that Congress has the power to establish the Northern Boundary of Ohio as proposed in her constitution, and that it is expedient to do so."[4]

Lyon was furious. He wrote to his friend John P. Sheldon, a former Detroit newspaper editor, "The committee do not say the State of Ohio has the least claim to the tract of country which it is proposed to give her, but that it is *expedient* to fix the boundary as she asks it. The committee also say in their report that they 'have carefully examined the arguments and papers on both sides of the question,' when it is now well known that they never looked into a book, or a single document on the subject, but adopted a report which Mr. Ewing wrote for them, on a subject which not one of them knew anything at all."[5] Thomas Ewing was a senator from Ohio.

Since Lyon was not permitted to speak in the Senate, he went on the offensive in writing. He sent each senator a written message pointing out Michigan's reasons to oppose the bill, namely, that Ohio's northern boundary would deprive Michigan of 468 square miles of area; that it would cost Michigan a port on Lake Erie and increase Michigan's insularity; that it would be contrary to the Northwest Ordinance of 1787; and, finally, that it would reverse years of Michigan jurisdiction in the area. He enclosed a pamphlet stating that the proposed northern boundary of Ohio had not been adopted in any of the five times the proposal had been introduced to Congress since 1802.

Lyon's work was to no avail. The Judiciary Committee reported a bill that upheld Ohio's claim, delineating the Harris line as the official boundary. The Senate voted in favor of the Ohio claim. The same bill encountered heavy opposition in the House; it was referred to a committee, remaining there until Congress adjourned.

Stevens T. Mason had staked his future and political capital on immediate statehood for Michigan, yet more than two years had passed since the territorial legislature first got the wheels rolling on statehood. Seemingly, there was no good reason for Congress to reject Michigan's bid. Mason's sister, Emily, shared some of her brother's frustration, but on other matters. Writing from New York City on September 20, 1834, Emily says, "The ignorance of these people, New Yorkers, of Michigan and our affairs is certainly most astonishing."[6]

In September 1834, in view of the failure of Congress to pass enabling legislation, Governor Mason proposed to the legislature that provision should be made for a census. He argued that if the census showed the territory to contain more than sixty thousand inhabitants, a convention should be called to frame a constitution. The legislature complied with his request, and a census was taken the following October in each county of the territory. The head count showed more than eighty-seven thousand free inhabitants.

By circumventing Congress, Mason thought he could bring statehood to Michigan after the manner of Tennessee in 1796. Statehood, said Mason, hinged not on following proper procedures but on right. When Tennessee ascertained that its population exceeded sixty thousand free inhabitants, it framed a constitution without waiting for an enabling act from Congress. It then demanded statehood as a right that Congress could not deny. The result was a big argument over the propriety of this procedure. Naturally, politics was involved. A congressman and two senators were elected by the people of Tennessee and dispatched to Philadelphia (then the seat of the federal government), where they presented their credentials. The Federalists opposed the admission of Tennessee, as they were certain the state would favor the rival Democratic-Republican Party. However, they were outvoted, and Tennessee was granted statehood. Although Tennessee was not part of the Northwest Territory, its claim to statehood rested on a census showing that Tennessee had more than the sixty thousand people set forth in the Northwest Ordinance as a prerequisite for statehood.

In citing the "Tennessee precedent," the Boy Governor believed he was on solid ground, and Michigan would proceed without waiting for congressional authorization. Mason recommended to territorial lawmakers that provision be made for the election of delegates to a constitutional convention to frame a government for a state "with boundaries as fixed by the Ordinance of 1787 and the territorial lines drawn by the act of 1805."[7] Like Pizarro three hundred years before, this was Mason drawing a line in the sand with his sword. Only this time, the line was the Fulton line, reinforced by the Talcott survey. And instead of confronting the Inca in his Andean domain, Mason was challenging the governor of Ohio, Robert Lucas.

On November 19, 1834, Mason sent a message to the Michigan Legislative Council, stressing the importance of retaining the Toledo Strip. He did not want Congress acting on the issue, because Congress voted down admission proposals as long as Michigan refused to back down on the boundary matter. Once a state, he reasoned, Michigan could appeal the boundary question to the Supreme Court if necessary.

In his message, Mason set forth the need to appeal to Congress to establish a separate government for the contemplated territory of Wisconsin. Michigan's choices, he said, were to immediately call a convention to form a Constitution and state government or to petition Congress at their next session to admit Michigan into the Union as an independent state. Mason explained:

> Under ordinary circumstances, the latter course would be most preferable. But when the dispute with Ohio is called into question, we have but one course to pursue. We need to prevent all legislation whatever on the part of Congress. If brought to the test, Congress will decide against us. Our only hope of success is to delay their action until we become a state, when we can appeal for justice to the supreme judicial tribunal of the country, and maintain the rights that are secured to us by the Ordinance of July 13, 1787.
>
> If we petition Congress to pass a law for our admission into the Union, we can only succeed in it with the condition of bringing upon ourselves the oppression of an act of that body, admitting us into the union, but robbing us of one of the fairest portions of our country and establishing through the influence of the Ohio delegation the boundaries of our state, as are now demanded by an already too powerful neighbor.
>
> Our policy is to prevent all action on the part of the general government. We should urge Congress to establish . . . the territory of Wisconsin under a separate territorial government. In the event of the measure succeeding, Michigan will then be left with her boundaries unencroached upon. She will be admitted into the

U.S. at the commencement of their session in 1835, with full and ample power as an independent state to contend successfully with Ohio.[8]

Two months before Mason addressed the Legislative Council, his father, John, had written from New York, "We have seen several persons from Detroit lately and hear of 'wars and rumors of wars.' We are very anxious to know what is going on for if reports be true this Ohio business is becoming quite a serious affair."[9]

A month after Mason's message, the Legislative Council passed an act appointing three commissioners whose marching orders were to treat with Ohio on all matters concerning the southern boundary. Michigan was being conciliatory. Governor Robert Lucas did not address the matter directly, referring it instead to his legislature. He persuaded the Ohio legislature to pass an act stating in effect that the boundary is where they dictated it should be. Mason and the statehood advocates were more than a little upset by Lucas's response.

At the next session of Congress, beginning in December 1834, Ohio's senators revived the boundary bill, adding a section confirming the northern boundaries of Illinois and Indiana. Ohio argued that if Michigan won the boundary case with Ohio, it might put in jeopardy the rights to the land Indiana and Illinois had received north of the 1787 line when they became states. The Senate again passed the bill establishing the Harris line, with the additional provision confirming the northern boundaries of Illinois and Indiana. But again the House failed to uphold the Senate action.

As the sun set on the year 1834, Michigan was in limbo. Thirteen months into the future, Mason would still be referring to Michigan as "that of a people claiming and exercising all the privileges of an American State, and yet excluded from the bonds of the Union."[10] Various writers have commented on the state of affairs, one saying, "Michigan in 1834 was in the embarrassing position, nationally, of being an illegitimate child in the sisterhood of states. The minimum conditions for statehood had been met and exceeded, but Ohio blocked Michigan. And Congress played Ohio's game because Ohio had the votes and representation."[11] Annah May Soule, one of the best of the chroniclers of the Michigan-Ohio border dispute, said, "Here was a most embarrassing state of affairs. A Territory [Michigan] being refused permission to do so was about to make a state government for itself. A State [Ohio] which

was asking Congress to fix one of its boundaries had declared that
boundary to be already fixed, and was preparing to exercise authority
over the desired tract. No wonder the powers stood aghast at this im-
broglio."[12]

Of course, more was at work here than just a minor border dispute
between two political subdivisions in the wilderness of the Northwest
Territory. It was true that Ohio wanted to make absolutely sure that if
Michigan entered the Union, it would do so without the Toledo Strip.
At the same time, Southerners in Congress opposed Michigan's entry as
a free state, since it would upset the balance of power between slave and
free states. Since the Missouri Compromise of 1820, it was the practice
to admit a free state and a slave state simultaneously; that way, a balance
was kept in the Senate, thus preventing any action on the slavery issue.
Accordingly, Indiana was paired with Mississippi, Illinois with Alabama,
and Maine with Missouri. An equilibrium was preserved, but national
unity was a fiction. The slavery issue was destined to tear the country
apart, and no amount of compromising and prevaricating could forever
prevent the eruption that was the War between the States.

When both Arkansas, seeking admission as a slave state, and Michigan were ready for statehood, Michigan was involved with Ohio over
the Toledo Strip. President Jackson, a Southerner himself, did not want
to deal with slavery, and he also did not want his Democratic Party split
by the bad blood between fellow Democrats Stevens T. Mason and
Robert Lucas. In other words, Jackson wanted to ensure that the presidential election of 1836, with his protégé Martin Van Buren as the party
standard-bearer, would go Democratic.

For four long years, Congress would debate, off and on, the conditions under which Michigan would enter the Union. The argument
dragged on, to Michigan's detriment, until finally the politicians worked
out a compromise: if Michigan gave up its claim to the Toledo Strip and
agreed to cede Toledo as a condition of statehood, then Arkansas, a slave
state, could be admitted at the same time. Ironically, Michigan's petition
for statehood would have Southern support in Congress, since Michigan's pairing with Arkansas would mean that the Missouri Compromise
was still working and would postpone the showdown over slavery. On
June 15, 1836, "in air perfumed," to quote John Quincy Adams, "with
the 35 electoral votes of Ohio, Indiana and Illinois,"[13] Jackson signed
enabling legislation for Michigan's statehood, contingent upon Michigan ceding the Toledo Strip. Arkansas was admitted as a state, but

Michigan was being forced to give its assent officially to cession of the Toledo Strip as a condition of statehood.

It may well be said that the first call to arms of the Toledo Strip War was Governor Lucas's snub of the offer by Michigan commissioners to negotiate a settlement of the boundary dispute in December 1834. Already, Congress's refusal to authorize Michigan to proceed in applying for statehood had young Mason's blood up. On January 12, 1835, Mason announced to the Michigan Legislative Council that Congress had rejected Michigan's request for an enabling act and that he would use the "Tennessee precedent" to put Michigan on the fast track to statehood.

Accordingly, on January 26, 1835, after lengthy discussion in the Legislative Council, an act to authorize the people of Michigan to form a constitution and state government was signed into law by the acting territorial governor. Where Congress was unable in this matter of enabling legislation, Michigan was able. On April 4, 1835, with Michigan still going its own lonely way, Michigan residents voted to elect delegates to a constitutional convention. This body would begin its work in Detroit on May 11. By that time, the first shots were fired in the Toledo War.

CHAPTER SIX

A WAR OF WORDS OPENS THE CURTAIN
EVENTS OF FEBRUARY AND MARCH 1835

Let him get on our soil, arrest him, strike the blow at once, disgrace him and his state, and end the controversy.

> —GOVERNOR STEVENS T. MASON TO GENERAL JOSEPH W.
> BROWN OF THE MICHIGAN MILITIA, REFERRING TO
> GOVERNOR ROBERT LUCAS OF OHIO

With Michigan we have nothing to do. She has no chartering rights. We cannot notice her.

> —THOMAS L. HAMER, OHIO LEGISLATOR,
> TO GOVERNOR LUCAS

The curtain opens on 1835, a decisive year in Michigan history, with the state's bid for admission into the Union still stalled in Washington and with anger in Detroit over Ohio governor Robert Lucas's summary rejection of an offer by Michigan to negotiate a settlement of the boundary dispute in December 1834. Lucas's position was that Michigan as a territory did not possess the rights of established states and that the Toledo Strip was a national problem to be addressed by Congress.

His strategy of referring the issue to Congress was well thought out, as Ohio had votes there, while Michigan had none.

Acting governor Stevens T. Mason of Michigan had staked his political fortunes to statehood now, by any means necessary. However, Lucas did not want Michigan to become a state, with elected representatives in Congress and on an equal footing with other states in the eyes of the law. A trusted colleague of the governor was Thomas L. Hamer, who represented Ohio in Congress. Hamer wrote to Lucas from Washington on February 14, 1835, on the subject of a new state on the Michigan peninsula. "Michigan claims by a right—an absolute right—to seats in Congress whether we will or not," began Hamer, explaining,

> This right is claimed under the Ordinance of 1787—a document with them as sacred as the Magna Charta of Great Britain or the Constitution of the U.S.
>
> In forming this [the state of Michigan's] Constitution they will describe the boundaries of their state and take special care to include the disputed territory—a part of Ohio! She will become a state with this territory in possession. One of two things will then occur: either she will be admitted into the Union in this condition, and leave us to litigate in the Supreme Court for 10 or 20 years, and perhaps lose our rights at last, or she will not be admitted into the Union, and will remain an independent state on our borders, like Mexico, or any other foreign power.[1]

Hamer's strategy would become Lucas's own. "With Michigan we have nothing to do," continued Hamer, claiming, "She has no chartering rights. We cannot notice her. Our controversy is with the general government. . . . I do not doubt the People will sustain you in any measures, however strong, which may be necessary to preserve the integrity and inviolability of the territory and sovereignty of the State of Ohio."[2] So on January 26, when the Michigan territorial legislature voted, at Mason's instigation, for an April 4 election to choose delegates to a constitutional convention and form a state government, Lucas was alarmed.

One can take one's pick which was the immediate cause of the Toledo War. Residents of Michigan cite Governor Lucas's blunt refusal to negotiate in December 1834. More to the point, a Michiganian might also say that the stated intention by Ohio to mark and survey the line described in its constitution as its northern boundary was an act of provocation that made hostilities inevitable. If one's loyalties lie with

Robert Lucas, two-term governor of Ohio, in 1832. Lucas defended the Ohio territories against Michigan in the border dispute. (Courtesy of the Capitol Square Review and Advisory Board.)

Ohio, one could dispute Governor Mason's plan to bulldoze Michigan into the Union by calling a vote on a constitutional convention for which he had no congressional authorization. Additionally, the Pains and Penalties Act did not go down well in Ohio, nor did it win Mason any points in Washington. To Michiganians, Mason was fired with zeal, with a missionary's sense of what was right; but for Ohioans, he was a young Hotspur badly in need of a little discipline, and Robert Lucas was just the man to administer a lesson or two.

The Toledo War, not yet a shooting contest across a disputed line, heated up in earnest in February 1835. The first move belonged to Governor Lucas, who, on February 6, recommended to his legislature the passage of an act extending the boundaries of Ohio's northern counties: "All counties bordering on the northern boundary of the state shall extend to and be bounded by the line running from Lake Michigan to the most northern cape of Maumee Bay." He added, "We cannot admit that the Legislative Council of the territory of Michigan had any right to authorize a negotiation on the subject of boundary. Neither can we admit that there is any question of boundary existing between the state of Ohio and that territory."[3] Lucas then recommended that the northern counties bordering on the boundary line be organized into townships and exercise jurisdiction. His legislature passed a law in conformity with that recommendation, extending Ohio's jurisdiction over a part of Michigan. He then appointed a commission to place permanent markers all along the Harris line.

That determination to dig in despite Michigan's occupancy of the Toledo Strip meant that the surveyors who were marking the line eastward from the Indiana boundary had to cross Lenawee and Monroe counties in the Michigan Territory to complete their job. Michigan was not about to let that happen. Passage of the Pains and Penalties Act on February 12, 1835, amounted to some serious flexing of muscle by the Michigan Legislative Council, or territorial legislature. The power of arrest and stiff penalties were a strong sign that Michigan meant business. A week after he signed the Pains and Penalties Act, Mason authorized General Joseph Brown to take any necessary measures to prevent Ohio officials from acting in the disputed area. Mason mobilized the territorial militia and asked for volunteers, while placing himself at the head of these forces.

There is often a tendency to depict the Toledo Strip fracas as just so much bluff, comic incidents, and vain posturing. There was much of this, to be sure, but the Toledo War also threatened serious results. In Washington, President Jackson was vexed by the prospect of a civil war over the Michigan/Ohio frontier. He was upset that his friendship with Mason was being strained by the latter's headstrong tendencies. The presence of Lewis Cass, a Michiganian, in his cabinet as secretary of war was not helping Old Hickory, as Cass was trying to maintain neutrality about the boundary dispute while discreetly supporting Michigan's claim. The Toledo Strip dispute was being played up in the national press, with young Mason benefiting from a perceived underdog role.

Above all, Jackson was a politician who was eyeing the next election. If he came down on Michigan's side in support of his appointee Mason, he might lose the votes of Ohio, Illinois, and Indiana. Imagine the conundrum Jackson faced when he asked his attorney general for a ruling on the boundary matter and that worthy came back saying Michigan's title to the Toledo Strip was valid.

It is also true, as we shall see, that the Toledo War followed a "boys

will be boys," "anything you can do I can do better" pattern. For example, at one time in that summer of 1835, the Ohio legislature voted a
sum of money to defend the Toledo Strip, and the Michigan Legislative
Council quickly followed suit with an appropriation barely exceeding
Ohio's. Likewise, the war of words between Lucas and Mason escalated
to a point where it was hard to say who was looking more foolish. But
each believed there were principles to follow and territory to be fought
for, in the name of honor, right, and duty.

On February 23, the Ohio legislature, following its governor's lead,
extended the northern boundaries of Wood, Henry, and Williams counties to the Harris line and created two townships in the disputed territory. Lawmakers also authorized re-marking the Harris line, stating, "It
ill becomes a million of freemen to humbly petition, year after year, for
what justly belongs to them, and is completely within their control."[4]
The use here of the term *million of freemen* is worth remembering, as
Michigan would reference it time and again, unflatteringly.

The area annexed by Ohio had been under Michigan law for the
past thirty years. On February 24, Lucas appointed Jonathan Taylor of
Licking, John Patterson of Adams, and Uri Seely of Geauga as commissioners to retrace and establish monuments on the Harris line. They
agreed to meet at Perrysburg on April 1. Before that date, both Mason
and Lucas had received letters from John Forsyth, U.S. secretary of
state, cautioning them to avoid armed conflict. Cass also tried to help.
The involvement of the secretary of state, the secretary of war, and,
later, the attorney general of the United States showed the extent to
which the Toledo Strip dispute had captured national attention.

Eight days after enacting the Pains and Penalties Act, Mason wrote
a letter to Forsyth explaining the Michigan Territory's position. The letter concerned Michigan's boundary dispute with Ohio and set forth
Michigan's claims against Ohio, while warning of serious consequences
from the actions of Governor Lucas. "Ohio has determined upon taking
forcible possession of the territory claimed by her by extending her jurisdiction over it, without waiting for the final action of Congress upon
the subject," wrote Mason.[5]

In December 1834, the Michigan Legislative Council had passed an
act providing for the appointment of commissioners to adjust the
boundary between the state or states, to be formed north of an east-west
line drawn through the southerly extreme of Lake Michigan and the
states of Ohio, Indiana, and Illinois. This law had been communicated

to the governor of Ohio with the belief that the conciliatory disposition manifested by Michigan would be matched by Ohio. About that communication, Mason now wrote to Forsyth, "I have never received the cold formality of an answer, although strange as it may seem, it is made the singular pretext of a recommendation of the governor to the Legislature, urging the passage of a law, extending their jurisdiction over part of the Territory of Michigan claimed by Ohio. He [Lucas] in his communication to the Legislature, assumes that Michigan has no right to authorize a negotiation on the subject of boundary, and denies that any arrangement entered into with Commissioners appointed under her authority would be binding on Michigan herself, after she becomes an independent state. This position I entirely dissent from."[6]

Mason then provided Forsyth a history lesson with a Michigan spin. He cited Article V of the Northwest Ordinance, "if Congress shall find it expedient, they shall have authority to form one or two states in that part of the said territory which lies north of an east and west line drawn through the southerly bend or extreme of Lake Michigan." Mason argued, "This article is fixed and determinate. No provision is given Congress to alter or amend it. It is expressly declared that this part of the Ordinance 'shall be considered articles of compact between the original states, and the people and states in the said territory and forever to remain unalterable except by common consent.'" It is on this provision that Michigan based its right to the territory claimed by Ohio. Mason contended that if Congress could take from Michigan this right, Michigan might be deprived of every other right that it possessed under the ordinance. He wrote to Forsyth, "Will it be contended, then, that Michigan is not a party to that compact, or that it can be altered without the consent of the people within her territory, or the state soon to be formed within her boundaries? With this view of the subject, it is left for the nation to determine whether Ohio has not evinced a disposition to disregard the fundamental laws of the country in her attempt at seizing upon a portion of country justly belonging to Michigan."[7]

Mason concluded his letter with fighting words. Writing that Governor Lucas "declares that the question of boundary, if it exists at all, is between Ohio and the United States," Mason responded, "I would respectfully ask if his Excellency had not overlooked the fact that the delegation of Ohio in Congress when urging her claim upon the general government, at the very time when he recommends, that she should take the remedy in her own hands and seize possession of the territory in dispute. I mention this to show that Ohio is governed by no fixed rules of justice, but by an eager and greedy disposition to grasp after territory."[8] If that is bellicose in tone, consider the note Mason sent at about this time to General Brown, commander of the militia then posted at Tecumseh. Mason, spoiling for a fight, said a collision between Ohio and Michigan was inevitable and told Brown to be prepared to meet the crisis. Directing Brown to "obtain the earliest information of the military movements of our adversary," Mason wrote, "I shall assume responsibility of sending you such arms, etc., as may be necessary for your successful operations, without waiting for an order from the Secretary of War."[9] For his part, on March 20, 1835, Lucas wrote to Forsyth, "We have never anticipated a collision, we have given Michigan no cause of offence [but] Ohio has taken her stand in this matter. Her forbearance heretofore has been tortured into a doubt of her right. We cannot permit them [Michigan] to intrude upon the rights of Ohio, under any pretext whatever."[10]

On February 28, Brown was given a commission as brigadier general of the territorial militia. Mason issued a circular to the brigade commanders, ordering them to hold themselves in readiness to obey the orders of Brigadier General Brown. "Your only course is to assume a bold attitude, and to let your intentions be known," wrote Mason to Brown, adding, "The attitude assumed by that state [Ohio] makes it probable that the military force of this Territory may immediately be called into the field."[11]

The war of words now erupted into a blizzard of memorials, resolutions, letters, and legislative acts. A meeting of Detroit citizens at the courthouse on March 6 produced a memorial to President Jackson saying, "We shall not be deterred by the disparity of strength from opposing by force the lawless aggression of Ohio." This piece of paper was signed by such substantial citizens as John R. Williams, John Biddle, and B. F. H. Witherell, as reported in the *National Intelligencer* of March 26, 1835. Also in March, Robert Jackson of Greene County, Ohio, wrote to Lucas and offered the aid of one company of cavalry and one rifle company in protection of the northern border. Some citizens of Port Lawrence Township, which then occupied ground on which Toledo stands today, wrote to Governor Mason to say that they thought trouble was brewing, maybe even a riot on the occasion of the township meeting in April.

Both states prepared for a shooting conflict. Thomas Hamer wrote to Lucas again in March, just after he had talked with President Jackson about the boundary dispute. "I told Jackson," he wrote, "that we had waited until forbearance was no longer a virtue."[12] Neither Lucas nor Mason had any intention of backing down. On March 5, Mason urged Secretary of War Cass to send two companies of U.S. regulars from Fort Gratiot to occupy the border area. He also placed the Michigan militia on alert. And later, when too few men responded to a call for volunteers, he found means to muster five hundred men whom he planned to place under General Brown's command.

On two consecutive days, March 5 and March 6, Mason dashed off notes to Forsyth asking for "the views and determination of the President, on this unfortunate and unpleasant controversy." Mason noted the action of Ohio to extend jurisdiction over the disputed territory and requested the federal government's views on the dispute "before the parties in controversy proceed to extremities."[13] Puzzled by developments, Jackson did not reply. At least not yet. But as February slid into March, the president, who did not want to take sides in this seemingly inevitable frontier war, passed the buck to his attorney general, Benjamin F. Butler. Mason wrote to Forsyth on March 15, "It is now certain beyond a doubt that this collision must take place before or by the first of April. I shall without hesitation arrest Governor Lucas, as a citizen of Ohio, violating our laws, and in so doing, will meet his force by a force of like character."[14] April 1 was the date Lucas and his boundary commissioners were to meet at Perrysburg, a town on the Maumee just outside Toledo.

Forsyth was having a lively correspondence with Lucas, too. On March 14, the secretary of state counseled "mutual forbearance and prudence," saying the problem should be left to Congress to decide. Three days later, Forsyth told Lucas that "military force should not be used."[15] In his reply on March 20, Lucas assured Forsyth of Ohio's position: "We have not even taken notice of the inflammatory speech of the acting Governor of Michigan to the Legislative Council on the 12th of January, 1835."[16]

The day before Butler ruled on the dispute, Lucas was telling Forsyth, "Ohio has taken her stand in this matter. She has determined to be no longer baffled."[17] In today's world of e-mail, fax, and instant communication, it is hard to remember that in 1835, even the telephone had not been invented yet. The messages that flew back and forth be-

tween Mason and his commander in the field, General Brown, and between the territorial capital of Detroit and Washington City, as it was
then known, took days to reach their destination.

It was Brown's job to stand up to Lucas and call his bluff. It was
Brown, fully supported by Mason, who was daring Lucas to enter disputed territory with his commissioners and their guard. Once the commissioners were on Michigan soil, the Michigan civil officers could arrest them as trespassers, and no military action would be necessary.

In reply to a letter from General Brown, Mason, on March 17, suggested a strategy for dealing with Ohio's forthcoming attempt to exercise civil functions in the disputed territory. He repeated his audacious
plan to arrest Lucas if he strayed into the Toledo Strip: "He may dare to
enter the disputed territory with a small escort and thereby enable you
to arrest with the posse and civil officers of the county. Indeed he should
have time to commence some official function before our law can reach
him. Nothing but necessity should compel us to abandon a civil for a
military procedure. I think you will agree with me that an exhibition of
military force by us would induce him if he be serious to delay crossing
the line until he could reinforce. Let him get on our soil, arrest him,
strike the blow at once, disgrace him and his state, and end the controversy." Mason concluded his instructions by telling Brown to confine
his movements to Monroe County: "We may soon ascertain the force of
Ohio. If a battle is to be fought, let it be after the enemy is fairly in our
own territory. Then remove them."[18]

On March 20, Mason had more intelligence to share with Brown. "I
have just been informed that Governor Lucas for the present will not
use more than the Maumee Regiment. Such a force you can doubtlessly
resist successfully with the Monroe Regiment. So soon as a ministerial
officer is resisted by a force from Ohio, too strong for the posse of the
County to contend against, let him report the facts to you, and ask assistance. You will then take the field in your military capacity and order
out any force you think may be required. This course will protect us
from censure, and place us within the strict pale of all laws. Called on for
assistance to protect the civil authorities, you had better march a force
to Toledo or some other part of the disputed territory and make it your
headquarters."[19]

Mason then wrote to President Jackson, attaching a resolution of
the Legislative Council, calling attention to Ohio "extending her laws
over a district of country belonging to Michigan, and thus usurping the

rightful jurisdiction of the United States." He asked the president to protect Michigan from "the encroachments and usurpations of a powerful neighboring state."[20] It might be a good idea, Mason said, for U.S. troops to proceed from Fort Gratiot to Toledo to keep the peace there.

While he had the presidential ear, Mason promised to execute the "valid" laws of his Legislative Council to the utmost of his power. Mason wrote, "The Governor of Ohio will personally attempt to enforce the law of his State. He brings with him a regiment of militia. He has assigned the first of April as the day when he will meet his commissioners at Perrysburg for the purpose of running the northern boundary of his state. He has also issued orders to the militia of the northern counties bordering on Michigan, to hold themselves in readiness, subject to his orders." Mason said he would use all "honorable exertions" to prevent a collision, but he added, "If driven from pacific measures I feel bound to protect the territory from invasion. I feel confident such is the spirit by which Ohio is governed that nothing but submission by Michigan will satisfy her."[21]

As the chief legal officer of the United States, Benjamin F. Butler carried a lot of weight. His opinions did not have the force of law, of course, as only Congress can make the laws, but any ruling he would make after studying the legal ramifications of an issue would bear the stamp of authority. It could be argued that any chance the Toledo War had of being settled by peaceful negotiation was lost when Butler issued his report on March 21, 1835.

The report, couched in the language of legalese, said basically that Congress did not give its assent to the extension of Ohio's northern boundary. Butler wrote, "Until this last mentioned assent shall have been given by Congress, the tract in dispute must be considered as forming, legally, a part of the Territory of Michigan. If I am correct in this view, it will be the duty of the President to consider it as the boundary of the Territory of Michigan." He added, "The act of Michigan [the Pains and Penalties Act] is deemed a valid law. While it is true that Congress have the power to annul any law of the Territory, but until so annulled, it will be obligatory on all persons within the limits of the Territory. In whatever form an encroachment may be made on the jurisdiction of the U.S. in the Territory of Michigan, the only proper mode of resisting and correcting it is through the instrumentality of the judicial tribunals."[22] Pulling no punches, Butler used the word *repugnant*

to describe the act of the legislature of Ohio extending the jurisdiction
over a part of the territory of Michigan. Here was President Jackson's
legal adviser saying not only that the strip of land between the Harris
and Fulton lines legally belonged to Michigan but also that the far-
reaching Pains and Penalties Act was constitutional. Butler saw the
Toledo Strip controversy as "a web of paradoxes,"[23] and the opinion he
reached reflected that point of view. Butler said that Michigan's acts and
actions were legal and that Ohio's were not, but he also left the door
open for all three branches of government to resolve the issue.

Congress could act to accept the provision in the Ohio Constitution that ran the boundary "to the most northerly cape of Maumee Bay."
Congress had acted legally in not dealing with the boundary when Ohio
had been admitted, he said. The disputed territory could also be taken
up "through the instrumentality" of the proper judicial tribunals. And
most important, the chief executive had the duty to see federal laws
faithfully enforced. Butler opined that Jackson had jurisdiction over territorial officials and could remove them if they proved uncooperative.

The latter was the trump card Jackson held over Mason. Butler said
Jackson could try to persuade both governors to settle the dispute but
could not directly interfere. If force was resorted to, said Butler, the president could intervene. In the meantime, only Congress could annul legislation passed by the Michigan Territory, and until it did so, the Michigan
act of February 12 was legal, and any attempt by Ohio to increase its jurisdiction without congressional or judicial approval was illegal.

In Ohio, it was the Michiganian Lewis Cass, not Butler, who drew
down the fire. Cass never shied at promoting the interests of Michigan,
and it would be clear where he stood on the Toledo Strip controversy.
Still, as a cabinet officer, he tried to maintain a hands-off attitude. But in
Ohio, he was accused of using his position as secretary of war to aid his
own locality and of being the actual author of Butler's opinion. And as if
Cass's alleged complicity was not enough, Ohioans gave vent to outrage
over the fact that the offensive Pains and Penalties Act was deemed to be
valid law.

A short time after Butler gave his opinion, Cass wrote a confidential
letter to Mason, asking him to understand that as a member of the president's cabinet, he could not express his true sentiments as freely as he
would like in regard to the dispute between Ohio and his own state of
Michigan. Good team player that he was, Cass then commented on

Jackson's fairness and said that Jackson would act with "a single eye to his duty."[24] But Jackson was really in a bind. The question was how to uphold what is right but not lose the votes of Ohio in the next election. Earlier, he had said, "It is the President's opinion that without further legislation by Congress, the country in dispute was to be considered as forming, legally, a part of the Territory of Michigan; and that the ordinary and usual jurisdiction over it should be exercised by Michigan."[25] But what was he to do now? Should he bring young Mason up short and demand his resignation, or should he stall for time in hopes of pounding sense into Lucas and Mason? Jackson chose the latter course.

Michigan, naturally, used the Butler opinion as ammunition. On March 23, writing from the executive office in Detroit, Mason replied to a letter of Forsyth. Noting regrets at the president's failure to communicate his wishes (beyond urging forbearance) in the controversy with Ohio, Mason wrote, "I declare . . . that nothing but self defense will drive the authorities of this territory to acts of violence. Michigan is the injured party. When the powerful by force attempt to trample upon the weak and defenceless, such considerations must be abandoned in the fixed determination of freemen to resist aggression. I shall remain on the disputed territory that the wishes of the President may be realized if possible; although I fear I shall be foiled in my attempt by the stubborn determination of Ohio to carry her law into effect by physical force." Mason wrote again to Jackson that same day, enclosing a Legislative Council memorial calling Jackson's attention to recent actions of Ohio usurping part of the Michigan Territory. "I need not add," wrote Mason, "that the magnitude of the subject, and the consequences involved, will readily ensure your immediate attention."[26] The Michigan Legislative Council was not far behind their leader in importuning Jackson for a favorable course of action, writing, "We appeal to a Chief Magistrate, who during a long life devoted to public service, has, by splendid examples of patriotism and firmness, shown that he shrinks from no duty . . . and satisfied that if our cause is right, you will look to an impartial performance of the high functions committed to you."[27]

Jackson did not wait long after receiving Butler's opinion to take action. On March 24, he named Richard Rush and Benjamin C. Howard as official U.S. commissioners to deal with the boundary problem. Howard was a congressman from Maryland; he would serve in Congress until 1839, when he retired to become a member of the Maryland Senate. In 1843, he resigned to accept an appointment as reporter of the

U.S. Supreme Court. Richard Rush was a Pennsylvanian who had negotiated the 1817 Rush-Bagot Treaty, which limited armaments between Great Britain and the United States on the Great Lakes following the War of 1812. He had been minister to England in 1817–25 and was secretary of the treasury in 1825–28. Rush must have considered this assignment to be small game indeed. The errand to settle the Michigan-Ohio boundary dispute was a trifling incident in a career of international significance.

As mediators between the contending parties, Rush and Howard were to arrive in Toledo in early April. They informed Mason that the president did not want the act of February 12 enforced. But Mason wrote to Forsyth on March 27, "Our law is of course subject to the revisions of Congress, but does this render it less obligatory upon the civil authorities of Michigan to carry it fully into effect? The exercise of a jurisdiction which has already been attempted, the act of running the Ohio state line, by commissioners of Ohio, holding their appointment under Ohio and protected by the governor of Ohio, all within the limits of Michigan I fear to be too palpable a violation of the rights and laws of Michigan to admit of hesitation as to the course to be pursued by the authorities of this territory."[28]

Things were fast coming to a boil. Lucas ordered Commissioners Taylor, Seely, and Patterson to start marking the line; that in itself was guaranteed to provoke Michigan. The outsiders Howard and Rush believed that the real problem lay with the Pains and Penalties Act, which Mason said he would enforce. General Brown, meanwhile, was on horseback, drumming up recruits for a war with Ohio. Michigan courts, over which Mason claimed to have no control, found indictments against Ohio partisans in the disputed territory.

The Rush-Howard mission proved to be a miserable failure in that it failed to prevent hostilities and only hardened the hearts of Lucas and Mason. The latter in effect told the commissioners to tell the boss (Jackson) where to get off. Mason and General Brown mustered all the militia troops they could and marched to Toledo, allegedly with a thousand men under arms, ready to counter any aggressive act from Ohio. Governor Lucas, his commissioners, and six hundred armed men met General John Bell, commander of the Seventeenth Division of the Ohio militia, at Perrysburg. So there they were, on opposite sides of the Maumee River, within musket range of each other, with only an act of provocation needed to get the Toledo War started.

CHAPTER SEVEN

ACTS OF PROVOCATION

*I cannot obey his directions. . . . It pains me to think I may be pursu-
ing a course of policy contrary to his wishes.*

> —GOVERNOR MASON TO SECRETARY OF STATE JOHN
> FORSYTH, REFERRING TO ANDREW JACKSON

*Arrest the Ohio survey team the moment they stick the first stake in
Michigan soil.*

> —GOVERNOR MASON TO GENERAL BROWN,
> MICHIGAN MILITIA

Run that line peaceably if possible, forcibly if necessary.

> —GOVERNOR ROBERT LUCAS

Moves and countermoves, the imminent arrival of two federal emis-
saries, and the real threat of armed clashes between militia and law enforcement agents of the Michigan and Ohio governments set the scene
for the outbreak of the Toledo War. In Washington, President Jackson
made it plain to congressional leadership that nothing must be done to
endanger the party's chances of carrying Ohio, Indiana, and Illinois in
the next presidential election. To this politically charged atmosphere
was added fiery public opinion stoked by politicians and press. On
March 18, 1835, the *Cleveland Whig* wrote, "It is to be regretted that at
such a crisis the government of Michigan is in the hands of a boy just out
of his teens." On April 8, the same newspaper would recall, "It was
through the influence of Governor Cass that the jurisdiction of Michigan was first extended over the disputed territory, and Ohio will probably have occasion to repent of her thoughtlessness in permitting it, although at the time it seemed a matter of little moment."

In Detroit, Governor Mason ordered General Brown to arrest the

Ohio survey team "the moment they stick the first stake in Michigan soil."[1] In Columbus, Governor Lucas issued his own directive: "Run that line peaceably if possible, forcibly if necessary."[2] In late March 1835, Michigan territorial legislator James Doty stopped in Columbus to see Lucas. Doty reminded Lucas that the Toledo Strip was an area under territorial—hence federal government—jurisdiction, so if Ohio opposed Michigan, it actually opposed the federal government. According to Doty, Lucas retorted that Ohio would just as soon meet the United States as Michigan.

The man in the street was getting worked up as well. An anonymous Ohioan from Philadelphia wrote to Lucas reminding him of his responsibility: "Never let it be said that a Buckeye received an insult with impunity." A mass meeting at the Zanesville courthouse denounced Michigan's activities and declared the opinion of Jackson's attorney general "an impertinent interference with the rights of the state."[3] The *Western Courier* of Ravenna, Ohio, counseled delay, but Lucas's party organ in Columbus thundered, "no angry blasts from the North could shake the purpose of our unterrified commonwealth. Michigan must be taught to understand that even the lion, in the nobleness of his nature, can be provoked to the assumption of his rights. Our cause is the cause of human justice."[4]

Early in April, Mason sent a missive to Secretary of State Forsyth saying that public opinion in Michigan would not accept submission to Ohio. He claimed it was not the intention of Governor Lucas to listen to the mediation of the U.S. government. Mason said, "Here no military force has been contemplated. No measures, other than precautions and preparation, have been adopted. No militia have been called into service, and the order of General Brown although made public was intended but as one of preparation. I will refrain from all 'rash movements.'"[5]

Mason was fudging the truth. His informants must have told him that Governor Lucas was in receipt of a letter from Forsyth, dated March 14 and received on March 20, relating that Jackson had been told by Mason that a collision was likely to take place "between that Territory and Ohio, relative to the extension of our jurisdiction." Lucas wrote back, "As far as Ohio is concerned, we have never anticipated a collision, and in no case would it occur, unless resistance were made to our civil authority."[6] Mason, of course, had said that a collision was inevitable. On March 15, in a letter to Forsyth, Mason said, "It is now certain beyond a doubt that this collision must take place before or by the first of April." He promised to arrest Governor Lucas as a citizen of Ohio and to "meet his force by a force of like character."[7]

At this point, it is worth putting the Toledo War into some kind of perspective. It played out as a "war" for the residents but only as a "boundary dispute" for those farther removed. It was serious enough to get official Washington in a dither and the White House in a state of vexation. That the events of that summer of 1835 were accompanied with so much ludicrousness and lowbrow carryings-on does not diminish its historical character and significance.

Mason's biographer, Lawton T. Hemans, wrote, "It was the Toledo War, of course, which gave to the boy governor his first great popularity. Feelings were tense and earnest, and nobody voiced those feelings in Michigan with more zeal and fervor than did 'Tom' Mason, as he was familiarly called. Had a man of less energy and less insistence occupied the position as chief executive of the territory, we may well presume that Michigan would have been admitted without the upper peninsula as a territorial compensation for the wrong she suffered."[8] Many years after the Toledo Strip War, Clarence Burton, the Detroiter who gathered original source material on the history of Michigan and the Old Northwest, would say, "We traded a piece of poverty-stricken mud land for the Upper Peninsula and acquired hundreds of thousands of dollars. The Toledo War was a war without bloodshed, and one that is frequently referred to with a smile of derision, but it resulted in greater gains to the State of Michigan than the wisest statesman of that day could foretell."[9] The Toledo War was a campaign of process servings, bellicose rhetoric on both sides, and much bluster. But it was also a campaign of skirmishes, military preparations, recruiting drives, and deployment of militia. If any of this suggests actual warfare, that is precisely what caused anxiety in Washington.

Mention must also be made of this war's fighting men. The soldiers were a sorry sight to see. Soldiers are generally synonymous with training, weapons, and an army. None of that applies, except in a loose sense, to the Toledo War. Training was whatever the men picked up on the run; it would best be called improvisation. Weapons often included broomsticks and pitchforks. Moreover, the war had to be carried on, if at all, by the volunteer militia of the two contestants. The call for volunteers by both Mason and Lucas got a mixed bag of fighting men. When, on March 5, Mason asked for two companies of U.S. regulars

Map by David H. Burr, c. 1830, exhibiting the "relative positions of Lake Erie and Michigan according to recent surveys." This map clearly shows Toledo in Michigan Territory under the line mandated by the Northwest Ordinance. (Courtesy of William L. Clements Library, University of Michigan.)

from Fort Gratiot, it may have been partly because he could not depend on enough homegrown "talent" to rise to the occasion. And when too few volunteered for the first call to arms, he still managed to muster five hundred men to take the field. Accounts of the day refer to "sharp-shooters" and "armed posses," but it is pointless to think of snappy uniforms, marching in drill, and well-disciplined men. Volunteers for the

Toledo War came forward, a few hundred from either side, with sticks, clubs, pitchforks, pistols, and homemade weapons.

All was not well with the Ohio militia, either. For the most part, the people of Ohio stood behind their governor, though when he called out the militia, there was no enthusiastic response in many sections of the state. The militia muster was a failure in many counties where the people were either indifferent or opposed to an appeal to arms. In Adams County, only twenty-one men volunteered, leading to the comment that "this caused the Tree of Liberty to blush in Adams County."[10] It was reported in the *Morning Courier* and *New York Enquirer* of May 15, 1835, that of 275 Ohio militia assembled at Maumee, all but 30 refused to advance into the disputed territory. On May 18, the *Detroit Free Press* jeered the Ohio militia as "heroes in imagination" who had been "shaken to pieces by the Fever and Ague in the Black Swamp."

An amusing story has come down about recruiting tactics. For many years after the war, the citizens of Perrysburg would recall one stirring episode. It seems the commander of the Ohio militia sent a drummer and a flag-bearer to Perrysburg to enlist recruits. The drummer was a man of gargantuan girth by the name of Big Odle, who was togged out in a green cloth coat and bark-dyed trousers, each trimmed in black lace. The drummer took his job seriously and marched up and down the streets of Perrysburg, creating a fearsome racket and drawing attention to himself and to the cause of Ohio. It so happened that court was in session in town, presided over by a judge of somewhat testy character. Big Odle's drumming set the judge's teeth on edge, and he ordered the sheriff to silence the drummer. Big Odle replied that he was under orders to "drum for recruits for the war." He was arrested, and his captain was summoned. The captain stated that the drumming had been approved by Governor Lucas of Ohio. This appeared to carry no weight, as both he and Big Odle were ordered to jail. The captain immediately threatened to impose martial law and arrest the court. This had the desired effect—the judge continued his case, and the drummer resumed his drumming.

On March 31, Governor Lucas, his party, and Major General John Bell of the Seventeenth Division of the Ohio militia neared Perrysburg. This was where Lucas had promised to meet his three commissioners (who were re-marking the Harris line). There, they proceeded to muster a force of about six hundred volunteers, who were organized and went into camp nearby to await the governor's orders.

The next seven days were crucial to Michigan's bid for statehood and for its prosecution of the Toledo War. On the first of April, Michigan held elections for township officials in the disputed area. This was Michigan reasserting its rights to an area it had organized and administered under territorial law many years before.

On the next day, Mason, who was at Monroe (preferring to be near the scene of potential conflict), addressed a letter to Robert Lucas at Perrysburg, as Mason had been informed that Lucas was camped there. This six-page letter at one point flattered Lucas for his "national reputation" and service during the War of 1812. Mason appealed to Lucas's patriotism and sense of justice. But just in case Lucas should fail to see which way the wind was blowing, Mason warned him that Michigan would not surrender any of the disputed territory: "My duty under the instructions of the Legislative Council is a brief though painful one. It is to say to you, Sir, in temperate and respectful but firm and decisive language, that no portion of the rightful jurisdiction of Michigan will be surrendered until the competent tribunal shall have decided the question." Mason went on, "I feel confident you know the character of the people of Michigan."[11] Mason ended by expressing his hope that the dispute would be settled to the satisfaction of both sides. To that end, he proposed that all operations should be suspended by Ohio until the arrival of the promised federal mediators.

Lucas and his entourage arrived in Perrysburg on April 2. On the next day, he received a note from federal commissioners Richard Rush and Benjamin Howard, who had just reached Toledo and were requesting an interview with the governor. Lucas agreed to meet with the commissioners on April 7 on the subject of conflicting jurisdiction, and at that meeting, they gave Lucas a document stating the opinion of the U.S. attorney general. Lucas complained that "all the proceedings in Washington were dictated under feelings highly excited and unfavorable to Ohio."[12] On April 4, the people of Michigan voted to elect delegates to a constitutional convention, the purpose of which was to draw up a constitution acceptable to Congress, thus moving the territory nearer to statehood. This act by his northern neighbor made Lucas more determined than ever to block statehood until the dispute over the Toledo Strip was settled—in Ohio's favor.

As excitement mounted, on April 6, Ohio held its own elections in the new townships of Sylvania and Port Lawrence within the Toledo Strip. Major Benjamin F. Stickney, Platt Card, and John T. Baldwin acted as judges of election. That act of provocation gave Michigan the opportunity to enforce the Pains and Penalties Act. There were now two points of potential confrontation and provocation: the re-running of the Harris line by the Ohio commissioners and the illegal elections of April 6. The question on everyone's minds was whether the Ohio officers elected would try to exercise their duties and, if they did, what the Michigan authorities would do. Mason believed that Michigan's cause had been aided by the attorney general's opinion of March 21, and he wrote to Secretary of State Forsyth to discuss the opinion of the attorney general on the powers of Congress over the question of boundary. "I find that his views of the powers of Congress over the question of boundary between Ohio and Michigan do not yield to Congress the right to interfere with the boundary line as proscribed in the fifth article of the Ordinance of 1787," stated Mason.[13]

Howard, one of the two peace commissioners sent from Washington, wrote to his wife of his experiences on the frontier. In a letter postmarked April 4, he began, "My dearest wife, we are midway between the two governors [Lucas and Mason], and our difficulties are rather increased by the news we learn here; for the governor of Michigan has brought with him a thousand stand of arms and fifteen kegs of cartridges. But I think we can keep him quiet." On the next day, Howard wrote again from Monroe to say, "You will see by the above date, my dearest wife, where we have got to. We are on the Michigan side of the 'disputed ground' and in the same tavern with the Governor which throws us together so often that we have been able to establish a free and friendly intercourse with him. There is better hope of influencing him than the other Governor for many reasons. . . . The Governor of Ohio is coming to Toledo tomorrow and there we expect to meet him at night. I fear we cannot do much with him, as he is very firm in his character and though doing what nine-tenths of the nation will hereafter pronounce wrong, yet will listen to no argument upon the point, because he says his State has decided upon it and it is his duty to execute her laws."[14]

Howard got it right. Governor of Ohio from 1832–36, Lucas was fifty-four years old at the time of the Toledo War, roughly thirty years older than his opponent, Stevens T. Mason. Lucas was a veteran not only of the War of 1812 but of the political wars in his state. He was given to exaggeration when it suited his purposes and was a bit of a demagogue. On the matter of re-marking his state's northern boundary and of treating with his territorial neighbor, Lucas dug in his heels. According to John C. Parish, author of a book on the Ohio governor, "Robert Lucas was a man of practical political sense rather than of formulated political theories. He cared little for the abstractions of governmental philosophy. A shrewd common sense added to years of experience gave him a knowledge of political affairs and a judgment that was fundamentally solid. It is important to remember that Lucas held that it was only with the U.S. that the state of Ohio could carry on negotiations and that with the Territory he had nothing to do. The Territorial officers were appointed by the federal government and amenable only to the authority of that government. With this view in mind, Lucas believed that an agreement entered into with the commissioners Rush and Howard appointed by Jackson was perfectly legal and binding, regardless of what action the Territory of Michigan might take in regard to the matter."[15]

Howard found time to dash off one more letter to his wife, on April 10, by which time he wrote, "Things have got dreadfully worse." Howard explained, "The court is sitting and has ordered some men in the disputed district to be arrested—and the sheriff has gone out with his *Posse Comitatus* (meaning everybody he can pick up) to arrest them. The village has been alive and in the afternoon the spectacle quite animating, notwithstanding the bad cause. Men galloping about—guns getting ready—wagons being filled with people and hurrying off, and everybody in commotion."[16] In his talks with Rush and Howard, Mason was informed that President Jackson was urging restraint and that he did not want the February 12 act enforced. It may have been at this time that Mason received his first warning, that if he did not abide by the wishes of the president in this matter, he risked his removal from office. If those words were not actually uttered by Rush and Howard, the implication must have been there.

After meeting with both Mason and Lucas, the two federal commissioners made their way back east, but not before they submitted a proposition that was anything but balanced, as far as Michigan was concerned. These were the measures they considered necessary if Michigan and Ohio were to avoid war. First, the boundary line Ohio wanted should be surveyed and re-marked without Michigan doing anything to stop it. Second, residents of the disputed area would accept concurrent jurisdiction; that is, they would be allowed to use officials of either Ohio or Michigan. Third, Michigan would agree not to enforce the provisions of the Pains and Penalties Act until Congress had a chance to act. The cover letter urged moderation on the part of Mason and the Ohio authorities with respect to the border dispute. The commissioners said that Jackson would express "no opinion at the present moment," as he considered the dispute a question to be determined by Congress. "It becomes the duty of the undersigned," they explained, "to make known to his Excellency the wish of the federal government that under no state of excitement should resort be made to force under this Territorial law until an opportunity shall be afforded to Congress to consider if that Act [of February 12] requires to be disapproved."[17]

When he learned the news, Mason was apoplectic, wondering whether Lucas himself had crafted the "compromise." Lucas readily agreed to the Rush-Howard plan, and he agreed to maintain peace so long as no prosecutions were made under the Pains and Penalties Act. In Lucas's view, Ohio's commissioners should be allowed to finish remarking the Harris line because, as Lucas himself said, the state had "an indisputable right to run out and designate her northern boundary, in accordance with the provisions of her constitution." He maintained that "commissioners appointed for that purpose would have instructions to run and remark the same from the most southerly extreme of Lake Michigan, to the most northerly cape of the Maumee Bay."[18] Lucas even disbanded his forces in the field.

With all the conditions of the Rush-Howard proposition seemingly favoring Ohio, Mason hotly rejected all three. He saw it as an arrangement that appeared satisfactory to only two parties in the dispute, Ohio and the United States. How could the president and his commissioners ask moderation and forbearance of him while allowing Lucas to extend jurisdiction over an area that, according to the national attorney general's declaration, belonged to Michigan? Mason said he could not suspend the Pains and Penalties Act, because it was an act of the legislature to which Congress had assented. Further, he could not interfere with the courts for those who were apprehended under the act, lest he himself would be labeled a usurper. Mason would uphold Michigan's law in the disputed territory, and that was that.

While his anger was still high, Mason put his case to Forsyth, stating his awareness of Governor Lucas's decision to occupy the Michigan Territory peaceably or with force. Mason wrote, "We are happy to have in our possession the able opinion of the attorney general declaring the resistance of the laws and authorities of Michigan gave offense not only punishable under our territorial act, but also under the act of Congress of 1790. Upon his opinion, Michigan will stake her case, and from it she can never recede. I am required not to proceed by force under the territorial law. To this command I have but one word to say. I constitute but one department of the territorial government, and can have no right to interfere with the other departments." "I cannot obey his directions," continued Mason, referring to President Jackson's instructions not to proceed by force and to "supersede the commissioners of every officer in the territory." "Such an act of tyranny and executive usurpation I cannot attempt," Mason argued, "nor can I conceive that the President will either expect or desire me to."[19]

By saying, "I cannot obey his direction," Mason, protégé of the president, was saying to Old Hickory that he was prepared to go it alone and that even presidential authority would have to take a backseat to territorial law, or at least to Mason's interpretation of it. Is it any wonder that Ohio partisans were outraged at the Pains and Penalties Act requested by this youthful chief executive or that Jackson regarded Mason's latest act of defiance as a dare to fire him? If it took a lot of nerve on Mason's part to defy the White House, it may be that he felt strong enough, both in the state's legal rights to the Toledo Strip and in terms of personal popularity, to stand up to Washington. As events were to prove, this was a grievous error in judgment on Mason's part, and if he felt he could rely on his personal friendship with the president, Mason erred again. He failed to consider how it would look to have a territorial governor showing up the president with a national election in the offing.

Annah May Soule writes, in *The Southern and Western Boundaries of Michigan*, that Mason did at one time express willingness to let the line be run.[20] As it was, Attorney General Butler's ruling added that the line might be surveyed without necessarily involving the exercise of jurisdiction in the disputed tract. Forsyth, Jackson, and, of course, Lucas agreed with this opinion. Secretary of War Cass wrote to Mason on May 9, 1835, "The remarking of the line claimed by Ohio does not seem to be such an exercise of jurisdiction as necessarily to require resistance on the part of Michigan."[21] But Mason could not stomach the presence of an Ohio survey team in the Michigan Territory, marking a line that was, from the beginning, calculated to cost Michigan valuable land.

At one point, Cass traveled to Detroit to cool Mason's ardor. There, too, Mason felt on strong enough ground to reject Cass's advice. Jackson also passed word to Mason, through Forsyth, to calm down and be reasonable. Mason would not, and eventually it would cost him dearly. Meanwhile, the men elected under the Ohio act assumed office, and civil processes against them were issued under Michigan's Pains and Penalties Act. As the Toledo Strip War played out in the summer of 1835, posses from Monroe made repeated raids to arrest Ohio officials deemed to be guilty of violating the February 12 act. Michigan, bent on upholding the law, arrested Ohio sympathizers in Toledo and hauled them up to Monroe for sentencing.

Despite his frequent correspondence with Forsyth and the access of his well-placed mentor, Cass, to the presidential ear, Mason underestimated Lucas's political skill and cunning. Lucas worked the levers of power in Washington, reporting regularly to the White House. He sent three of his friends, all supporters of Vice President Martin Van Buren, to confer with Jackson and to explain Lucas's policy. The Lucas trio, consisting of William Allen, David T. Disney, and Noah H. Swayne, wanted to avoid further embarrassment and a party split. According to former Governor Ethan Allen Brown, a prominent Ohio Democrat, it was widely stated in Ohio, Indiana, and Illinois that the Jackson administration had taken the side of Michigan. As incredible as that seems given the recommendations of Rush and Howard, there may be an inkling of truth to it. Along that line of thought, the Rush-Howard proposal ran counter to the wishes of Jackson, who, mindful of his attorney general's ruling, may have wanted Ohio out of the disputed strip until Congress decided the matter. But then the actual hostilities, Mason's zeal in pushing Michigan's cause, and Lucas's clever diplomacy nudged Jackson away from any pretense of neutrality.

The mission of Rush and Howard succeeded in muddying already troubled waters. The commissioners were perceived, in the Michigan Territory, as tools of the Lucas administration, which was currying favor with Jackson. As Michigan had long suspected, the president gave private assurances to Lucas's representatives in Washington that Mason would be removed if he refused to acquiesce in the compromise the president's commission had suggested. Jackson assured Lucas he would veto a bill for Michigan statehood if Congress passed one before the boundary was settled.

Sometime in early July, Jackson struck a deal with Messrs. Disney, Swayne, and Allen. We have it on the authority of Allen himself, who later served as governor of Ohio and provided an account of events. In a speech he delivered in 1874, giving Andrew Jackson the credit for settling the Michigan-Ohio border war, Allen said that the determining factor in the Ohio victory was the endorsement by President Jackson of the position presented to him by an Ohio delegation sent to Washington by Governor Lucas at the height of hostilities. Ohio, relates Allen, "retaliated to the Pains and Penalties Act by legislative acts creating Lucas County and appropriating money to support the militia called out by Governor Lucas."22

The departure of Rush and Howard from the disputed area saw an increase in activities that presaged war. When he learned of the Ohio-sponsored election (on April 6) of local officers in the disputed strip, the sheriff of Monroe County, Nathan Hubble, formed a posse and proceeded to Toledo on April 8, to arrest alleged violators of the Pains and Penalties Act. According to Hubble, Toledo erupted with gunfire and blowing horns. Nathan Goodsell and George McKay fell into the net and were later released on bail. According to one source, McKay's person bore the marks of violence. One report has Hubble arresting him after wrestling a gun from him. Goodsell said he was overcome by force "and treated very roughly as was also my wife."23

Emboldened with success, Sheriff Hubble, on April 10, again led a foray to Toledo to arrest Ohio partisans who were thumbing their noses at the Pains and Penalties Act. This time, Hubble got wind that a hundred armed men were waiting in Toledo to resist the Michiganians' effort to enforce the law, so he formed a posse of about 160 men who were under orders to fire their weapons only in self-defense. The raid came to nought, as the Hubble party found that the men they were seeking had fled Toledo. In the town of Defiance, Lucas received intelligence of the "outrages committed at Toledo by a body of armed men, under pretense of serving civil process issued against our fellow citizens for acting in obedience to the laws of Ohio." He also learned of preparations in Michigan to "arrest our commissioners."24

During these events—rival elections, raids and arrests, promises of stout resistance—commissioners Rush and Howard traveled between Monroe, where Mason was, and Perrysburg, where Lucas was encamped. There, the federals found two equally determined executives. According to Howard, Mason agreed not to take "any step that will lead to a broil," as long as Ohio did not try to establish jurisdiction over the territory, which, of course, it was attempting with the election of April

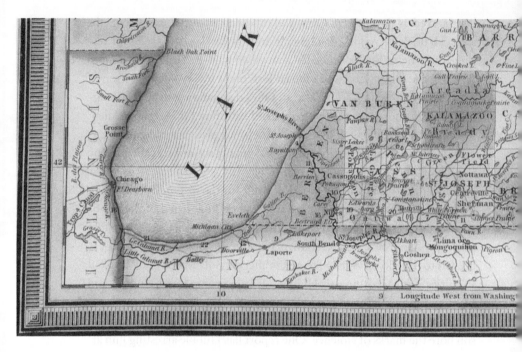

6. And when Mason held out an olive branch to Lucas, urging an end to "sectional divisions," Lucas did not even bother to respond, because, he said, Mason's letter was filled with menaces and threats.[25]

The arrests of Goodsell and McKay and the threat of more arrests forced the Ohio officials elected on April 6 to beat a prudent retreat. Nearby, the Ohio commissioners chosen to resurvey the Harris line sized up the situation. "We shall certainly be made prisoners," one of them wrote from Maumee on April 11. They informed Lucas that their supplies were exhausted, the roads were bad, and there were rumors that General Brown was gathering a force at Adrian.

Sebried Dodge was an engineer on the line of the Wabash and Erie Canal. He wrote from Maumee on April 10 to say that the governor of Ohio would not be able to run the survey line without a strong militia force, since Michigan had three hundred men under arms at Monroe, six hundred soon to come, and "1,500 stands of arms from the U.S. arsenal at White Pigeon."[26] Dodge's letter was to Samuel Farrer, one of the canal commissioners of Ohio. Lucas advised his line commissioners to move as rapidly as possible, to exercise caution, and to keep a sharp lookout. He warned, "do not suffer yourselves to be surprised."[27] That

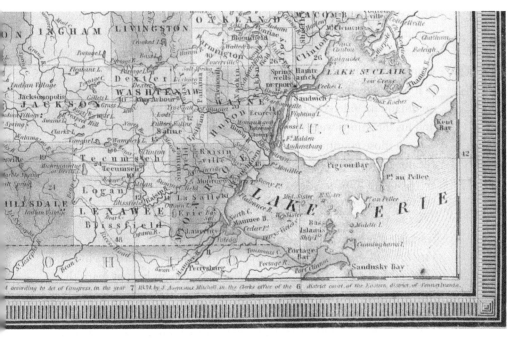

Close-up of a "tourist's map" of Michigan by J. H. Young, published by S. Augustus Mitchell in 1834, showing Toledo in Monroe County, Michigan. (Courtesy of the William L. Clements Library, University of Michigan.)

they were taken by surprise at Phillips Corners must have annoyed the Ohio governor.

Mason sent Rush and Howard on their way, stating he would enforce the Pains and Penalties Act. He said that under the opinion of the U.S. attorney general, "Michigan is in the exercise of a jurisdiction she has held for 30 years"; that the disputed territory belonged to Michigan; and that until the assent of Congress was given to the claim of Ohio, "the tract in dispute must be considered as forming legally a part of the Territory of Michigan."[28] This is becoming old stuff, of course, but here we have a territorial governor, who serves at the pleasure of the president, telling the latter's mediators that they have wasted their time and that they may also inform His Excellency in the White House that Michigan will repulse any show of force by Ohio.

Robert Lucas's survey team re-marked the line, starting at the Indiana border and working their way east. These men clearly qualified for hazard pay; they must have known that long before they glimpsed the welcoming waters of Maumee Bay, they would be in an armed stare-down with the Michigan militia. But Lucas thought of that angle; he ordered a small guard for their protection, drawn from the ranks of Major General John Bell's Seventeenth Division of the Ohio militia. Bell's area of command included the border counties of Wood, Henry, and Williams, and his directions were to extend his command to the northern boundaries of those counties. The Ohio line drawers were told to proceed until met by a force of resistance, and if such force should appear, they were to withdraw to Maumee, well within Ohio territory, "until a guard sufficient to protect them should be collected."[29]

On the other side of the border, Governor Mason issued a stern warning: "In anticipation that the Governor of Ohio may order a military force to sustain the [boundary] commissioners and officers of Ohio, General Brown is further commanded, the moment he may learn that a military force of any description, ordered out by the authorities of Ohio, is about to approach the disputed territory, to place himself, with a sufficient force of a like character, on the ground in contestation and to fire upon the first military officer or man who persists in crossing the boundary as at present claimed by Michigan."[30] Brown sent out scouts to report any attempts by Ohio to re-mark the line as the two presidential commissioners had proposed. Before they left the area to report to President Jackson, Rush and Howard wrote to Mason from Toledo, urging that force not be used against the Ohio authorities. They reported, "We have found an apprehension existing in this quarter, that forcible obstruction will be interposed by the authorities of Michigan, in case of attempts by the commissioners of Ohio to run the line." They said they were not doing their duty if they did not make it known that President Jackson wished to avoid violence.[31] In reply, Mason regretted he could not more fully cooperate with the two U.S. commissioners but that he was thwarted by circumstances beyond his control—namely, that as chief executive, he had no authority to suspend the operations of the law. He argued that it was Ohio, not Michigan, that was the aggressor. "Ohio in her encroachment is only met with gentle forbearance and moderation," said Mason.[32]

On April 18, Mason penned a remarkable letter to his mentor, Lewis Cass, who was in Washington. Citing his disagreement with commissioners Rush and Howard, Mason expressed fears that his stand to uphold Michigan's rights could ruin his political future. He said that he was pained that he might be in pursuit of a policy course contrary to President Jackson's wishes. But he complained that the federal commissioners were so prejudiced against the rights and honor of Michigan that "I AM INDUCED TO LOOK FORWARD TO MY REMOVAL FROM OFFICE." Mason, it seems, grasped the peril of his position—that of angering the president. Perhaps he was making a play for sympathy or stronger intervention on Cass's part. He wrote, "Should my removal take place, I shall surrender my charge without one sigh of regret, save that produced by the wounded feelings which bind me to the President. If he should deem it important to carry out the views of Messrs. Rush and Howard, I will submit to my fate without a murmur, and indeed even be gratified with the result. No compromise of rights can be made. Ohio has none in question. Her whole course is based upon usurpation. Public sentiment in this territory rejects the proposition of the commissioners, and as a young man commencing life I must sacrifice present interests to the permanent good will and opinion of my fellow citizens."[33]

On the same day Mason wrote to Cass, he explained his position to Rush and Howard. He said he would like to cooperate but just could not see it their way. "It is with regret that the authorities of Michigan conceive themselves called upon to make further and additional concessions to their powerful but ungenerous neighbors," Mason stated in repeating his intention to enforce the act of February 12.[34] He yielded to the "high legal authority" of the nation's attorney general. Time and again, Mason and the Michigan forces would use Butler's opinion as legal tender.

The Ohio commissioners and the survey party were in the field, painstakingly marking the Harris line eastward. They were accompanied by an armed force, reported to be about forty men, and their movements were reported to Mason and to General Brown. Brown, in Tecumseh, wrote to Governor Mason on April 18 to say he had spent the previous day at Adrian, adding, "and if I have nothing posative [sic] soon shall go there on Monday with the Sheriff and make our final arrangements that we may be ready when the time arrives, for us to act with promptness." He went on to relate that he had received a letter from Balden, "who informs me that some man from Ohio and a citizen from our county by the name of Hoadely? in the interest of Ohio have torn and marked Harrisses line." Clearly not a good speller, Brown tells Mason, "I have directed him [Hoadely?] to loose no time, and meet the

Officers of Ohio as far West as he can that we may be prepaired when they arrive in our county to receive them with Suitable Honors. I have also directed Hubble [sheriff of Monroe County] to send one of his best deputies to Whiteford, that if they should get by us, they may be nabed in that County."[35]

Clearly, Brown was relishing the chance to break up the survey team and put Ohio on the defensive. Mason again pleaded for federal action "to protect the territory and jurisdiction of the United States."[36] He suspected this was one sticky situation the national government did not want to touch. Mason informed Cass that the sheriff of Lenawee County was instituting proceedings in accordance with the Pains and Penalties Act.

All was in readiness for the "Michigan-Ohio border dispute" to become the Toledo War—for the war of words to become a conflict of weapons. Phillips Corners will never make the history books as a decisive battle in the military/strategic sense, but it is where Michigan chose to defend its sovereignty and to repel an invasion of its soil. And the soil was indeed Michigan's, until the courts or Congress said otherwise.

CHAPTER EIGHT

EVENTS OF APRIL–JUNE 1835

We are fast advancing to a horrid border war. The generous Ohioans will restrain the savage barbarity of the hordes of the North.

— BENJAMIN F. STICKNEY, OHIO PARTISAN

We promise you hospitable graves.

— GOVERNOR MASON TO OHIO INVADERS

When we last encountered the armed posse of Undersheriff William McNair of Lenawee County, his men were in hot pursuit of the Ohio survey commissioners and their military escort. The Battle of Phillips Corners on April 26 had ended with the arrests of several Ohioans who were considered to be in violation of the Pains and Penalties Act. A chastened remnant of the survey party hightailed it through the Black Swamp for the safety of Perrysburg on the Maumee River. Undersheriff McNair made a jocular report, setting forth how his action was a civil process, issued by a justice of the peace; that under it, he had arrested nine persons, without bloodshed or trouble; and, closing with a tongue-in-cheek statement, that the commissioners "had made very good time," reaching Perrysburg with nothing more serious than the loss of their hats and their clothing.

It was at Phillips Corners that name-calling between Ohio and Michigan first took on the Wolverines/Buckeyes coloration. Stories had circulated in Ohio depicting the Michiganians as wolverines, known to be vicious and ornery critters with disgusting eating habits. Michiganians gleefully took to the epithet and turned it around, saying the wolverine was tough, cunning, and a fearless predator. Engagements subsequent to

Phillips Corners found more usage of *wolverines* as a term of contempt among the Ohioans. The nickname stuck, and eventually the state university in Ann Arbor assumed title to the name for its athletic teams.

Many years later, an account of the Battle of Phillips Corners was given by Dr. M. A. Patterson of Tecumseh to the Raisin Valley Historical Society. He mentioned "40 armed men who surprised a division of the survey party of Ohio, with their military escort, while comfortably refreshing themselves in a house owned by a man named Phillips." Patterson continued, "They had not the least suspicion that the Wolverines were on their trail. The Ohio commissioners, in another house, heard the report of firearms and fled, not to be found. Colonel Hawkins of the Ohio party had fiercely demanded by what authority they presumed to arrest the legal officers of the powerful state of Ohio. McNair replied, 'By virtue of the posse of Wolverines here presented we will arrest you.' The Ohioans leveled their pieces and threatened to shoot. Ohio did give us the nickname Wolverines around this time, thinking it a derogatory name. But Michiganians liked it, thinking of it as mean, ornery and unafraid."[1]

After the fusillade of musket fire at Phillips Corners died away, the press got into the act. On May 9, the *Detroit Free Press* headlined the story "The First Blow Struck!" This account had Charles Hewitt, a magistrate of Michigan, issuing an arrest warrant for the survey party and other persons engaged in violating the laws of the territory: "The warrant was given to the sheriff of Lenawee, who summoned a posse of 30 or 40 respectable persons of that county, and with them proceeded to the place where he understood the Ohio commissioners were stationed. On arriving near the house of Phillips, 7 miles within the Michigan line, they found 9 or 10 armed men, ascertained to be a portion of the Ohio party, and demanded their surrender, which the latter refused to do, but leveled their arms and very coolly threatened to shoot up the gentleman sheriff of Michigan. But the latter, nothing daunted, pressed hard upon their Ohio neighbors and, in obedience to orders, fired over their heads—a maneuver which instantly caused them to take to their heels. They were, however, chased by the Michiganians, and captured. Col. Hawkins, the Ohio surveyor, and seven armed persons were made prisoners and brought to Tecumseh for examination. The Governor of Ohio has issued orders for the raising and marching of 10,000 men, declaring the boundary lines shall be run, and the jurisdiction of Ohio extended over that portion of the territory she claims."[2]

The breakup of the survey party created intense excitement throughout Ohio. Charles R. Tuttle writes, "It was evident that Ohio was aroused and that state pride was wounded. The idea that the young territory of Michigan, with its stripling governor, should successfully defy the great state of Ohio, with a million inhabitants and an aged governor, was one that the authorities could not endure with any degree of patience or equanimity."[3] The *Columbus Hemisphere*, in a story reprinted in the *National Intelligencer* of May 12, 1835, quoted Otis Parrish as saying, "Gen. Brown made an attack upon the commissioners and their party who were stopped during the Sabbath with some private families. Brown and some 80 armed men made captive nine of our Ohio corps. Gov. Lucas postpones further active measures for 2–3 days. Gen. Andy Jackson will veto the proceedings of the Hotspur of Michigan." Parrish adds, "When the attempt was made to arrest the chainmen, etc., some of them run, and Brown's men fired upon them, and they all gave up."

In early May, Lucas disbanded his militia because of a lack of provisions and to signify his compliance with the Rush-Howard plan. The Michigan militia left the area but stationed a military force in Adrian under Brown. Writing from Monroe on May 1, Mason promised commissioners Rush and Howard that Michigan would cooperate with the proper courts in resolving the controversy with Ohio. Two days later, Mason wrote again to refuse any solution short of an exclusive jurisdiction over the disputed territory. Anything less, he argued, would be "an act of dishonor on my part degrading to the people over whom I preside as chief magistrate."[4]

The pullback of armed forces only served to relocate the hostilities. The battle of resolutions and newsprint went back and forth. Ohio newspapers proclaimed its "million of freemen" would have what was rightfully theirs. One reported, "Outrage has been added to insult. Gen. Brown performed another of his exploits in making prisoners of Col. Hawkins and others of his assistants. The commissioners escaped the fangs of the captors, and made their way to Perrysburg, where they joined Governor Lucas."[5] Two weeks after Phillips Corners, the *Cleveland Whig* would say, "There is now a suspension of hostilities between our state and Michigan; and we hope it will not prove to be the calm which precedes a more dreadful tempest. We earnestly hope that the President will take measures to restrain the youngster who controls the government of the territory."[6] Newspapers on both sides continued to report grossly exaggerated rumors of "outrages" perpetrated by partisans of the opposition. The Ohio legislature pledged to protect its citizens who had been persecuted by Michigan "with a degree of reckless vengeance rarely paralleled in the history of civilized nations." The Michigan legislators replied that Michigan would resist "all attempts to rob her of her soil," and Governor Mason promised "hospitable graves" to any invaders.[7]

A civil war of some magnitude threatened. In Washington, Jackson was disturbed that the dispute had gotten so out of hand. From the War Department, Cass, on May 9, advised Mason, "A resort to force would be a serious calamity. The offenses against the laws of Michigan in relation to this business are what may be termed political offenses, not involving moral turpitude." Cass wanted the territory to "keep right on her side."[8] As the attorney general weighed in with an opinion favorable to Michigan and as Cass tried to rein in Mason, Jackson's cabinet became more and more involved in the Toledo Strip controversy. On May 11, an angry Governor Lucas wrote a letter to Secretary of State Forsyth saying, "The outrage against the commissioners running the line was made in the most unprovoked manner, on the Sabbath, by a party of armed men, headed by a judge of the court, a sheriff, and a brigadier general. This outrage . . . has impressed upon me the necessity of convening the Legislature . . . that this whole subject matter may be laid before them."[9]

Cass privately wrote to Mason on May 9, admitting his own belief that Michigan's claims were correct, but expressing concern "lest possible civil war" erupt between Michigan and Ohio. He stated that Old Hickory hoped the conflict would be resolved without his interference beyond "advice and remonstrance." Cass then warned Mason to "temper the firmness of the community with a due show of moderation." He argued, "The proceedings instituted under her [Ohio's] authority to obtain forcible possession of what I believe to be a part of Michigan are among the most unjustifiable executive and legislative acts which have taken place in our country during my time. Still . . . the remarking of the line claimed by Ohio does not seem to me such an exercise of jurisdiction as necessarily to require resistance on the part of Michigan."[10] Was Cass here suggesting that Jackson would not hesitate to remove Mason from office if he failed to pull in his horns? Could Mason count on Cass being in his corner to the bitter end? Cass was the wiser head, to be sure, with access to the president to boot. By continuing to forcefully press the issue for Michigan, Mason was going against both his mentor and the chief executive. Throughout the summer of 1835, the headstrong but principled Mason would receive both hints and warnings that his head was on the block.

At about this time, a poem appeared that presented Michigan with another rallying point. Attributed to George B. Catlin, "The New Cock Robin" saw the light of day in the *Detroit Journal and Courier* on May 6, 1835. Read today, it does not sound like anything that would stir passion or draw more than a chuckle, but it managed to stoke the flames of war on the Michigan side of the Fulton line. It went as follows:

> And who would cut up Michigan
> "I," says Governor Lucas
> "What I undertook is
> To cut up little Michigan."
>
> And who has bid him do it?
> A million freemen,
> (Counting women and children)
> 'Tis Ohio bids him do it.
>
> And who rings the bells of war
> "I," says General Bell
> " 'Tis I that rings the bell,
> Ding, dong goes my bell of war.
>
> And what is all this pother for?
> For Port Lawrence? No
> For Vistula? No
> Both died of ague last year.
>
> But out of their graves did spring
> A little mushroom
> Of sickliest bloom
> Which botanists call Toledo
>
> The flower is Ohio, no doubt
> 'Tis Buckeye in breed
> She scattered the seed:
> Then let Gov. Lucas transplant it
>
> But the swamp where it grew is not here
> Then let him beware

How he runs up a fence there
He will find other stings than mosquitoes."[11]

The Ohioans were cowed neither by bad poetry nor by Michigan bravado. A Geauga County meeting of citizens on May 7 had adopted a resolution declaring that if the "general government permit the authorities of Michigan to hold possession of said territory [the Toledo Strip], it places the United States IN A STATE OF WAR with Ohio." Thomas L. Hamer wrote to Lucas to say that if President Jackson had intimated that force would be used, "I should have told him to his teeth—that if an armed man dared to pollute the soil of Ohio, he should be blotted from the face of the earth, and that the first crack of a rifle would bring 200,000 freemen to the border!"[12]

Back in Detroit, Mason worried, in a letter to Cass, that his Ohio counterpart would, with an inflammatory message, induce his legislature to appropriate five hundred thousand dollars with which to prosecute the next campaign. Mason continued, "Should Gov. Lucas be sustained by his Legislature, we will expect the strong arm of the general government to be interposed at once. If this does not happen, Michigan will assume the guardianship of her own rights, for I should deem it a deadly blow at our mission, if Ohio is permitted to pursue unchecked her concept of nullification."[13] Mason's use of the words *interpose* and *nullification* was highly purposeful. They were hot-button words because the doctrine of nullification was still a lively topic in 1835. Nullification was a states' rights issue advocated by former vice president John Calhoun of South Carolina and other prominent South Carolina politicians, especially on the issue of national tariffs.

In 1832, Vice President Calhoun was a busy man, explaining for South Carolina legislators his doctrine that no state could be bound by a federal law it believed to be unconstitutional. When Congress renewed high tariffs that year, South Carolina declared them void (nullification). A compromise bill brought relief. But any perceived right to nullify federal law was dead because President Andrew Jackson had rallied public opinion against the doctrine of nullification. The Union had withstood a serious challenge and emerged supreme. Interposition trumped nullification.

In taking a strong stand against nullification, Robert Lucas was echoing the sentiments of his party leader and the nation's chief executive, Andrew Jackson. But in making a point of denouncing nullification, Lucas fell into a trap of his own making. And Mason cheerfully helped to push Lucas into his snare. By drawing the Harris line to its own advantage in altering its northern boundary and by demanding territory (the Toledo Strip) to which it had no legal claim, Ohio was in essence seeking to nullify an act of the federal government when it created the Michigan Territory with its southern boundary as stipulated in the Northwest Ordinance. Ohio was, then, "pulling a South Carolina," and Democrat Lucas stood with the thoroughly discredited Calhoun in riding the dead horse of nullification.

Some Whigs in Ohio made no bones about opposing Lucas. Benjamin Wade, later to become a notable U.S. senator, wrote, in May 1835, that "the good people of Ohio had become nullifiers to all intents." He said that the same principle (the doctrine of nullification) that Ohioans had denounced in South Carolina had been accepted by Ohioans now "because it was in their interest."[14] Many Whigs, along with Taylor Webster, Democratic congressman from Hamilton, believed that Lucas and the Ohio legislature were acting unreasonably in the boundary dispute. Webster wrote a letter to the editor of the *Columbus Hemisphere*, dated June 6, 1835, in which he said, "remarking the survey lines is useless and a waste of public expense. The question is the right of jurisdiction to the territory between those lines. Directing Harris's line to be remarked must be viewed now as a useless labor."

Lucas was, in fact, receiving much gratuitous advice at this time. Some of his friends advised him to go slowly, to put the blame on Michigan, and to remember that prudence is the better part of valor. On June 11, Secretary of State Forsyth warned Lucas that if he renewed the running of the line without regard for the feelings of Michigan, he would create a crisis demanding presidential interference.

Michigan tried to portray Lucas as "the Great Nullifier." After Jackson had initiated an aggressive policy toward the South Carolina nullifiers, Michigan suggested that he deal equally vigorously with the Ohio nullifiers. In August, the cheeky Michigan legislature stood foursquare by Governor Mason in his conduct of the boundary dispute and, in its report to the president, chided him for not applying the same stalwart approach to Ohio as he had to South Carolina when it threatened secession. So the question was whether Old Hickory, who had successfully squelched the attempt to nullify federal tariff laws in 1832, would turn a blind eye to an armed clash between a state and a territory. Twenty-six years later, states' rights and the secession issue resurfaced with the formation of the Confederate States of America and the Civil War (1861–65).

Remember, too, that Lucas's mantra was that the Toledo Strip dispute was not a quarrel with Michigan at all, because Michigan was only a territory. To Lucas, Ohio's dispute was with the United States. As a territory, Michigan had no rights other than what it was given by the federal government (i.e., Congress), and therefore Ohio was treating with the United States when it wanted its boundary dispute settled. Ohio was staking all on winning its case in Congress, rather than the Supreme Court, which likely would side with the attorney general in ruling for Michigan.

Mason told Cass that federal commissioners Rush and Howard meant well but "have closed the doors against compromise with the People of Michigan." He explained, "In securing Ohio for the next presidency, they have given a sad blow to the Democratic Party in Michigan, and if their views meet the approbation of the administration, it will not leave twenty Van Buren men in Michigan."[15] Mason was saying that Michigan would not vote for Jackson's man, Martin Van Buren, in the next presidential election if Ohio got its way in the boundary matter. Mason was convinced Rush and Howard were in Ohio's corner. Why else would they propose the "compromise" they crafted, with terms so favorable to Ohio?

Many newspapers in Ohio continued to support Lucas. The *Columbus Western Hemisphere* said, "One heart, one mind is here, as to the right of Ohio to the soil." The Whig organ at Columbus agreed: "All party lines are obliterated. We go hand in hand in the assertion of our rights and in the maintaining of the sovereignty of Ohio over her legitimate domain."[16]

On May 11, Michigan opened its constitutional convention. If Congress continued to drag its heels on the statehood issue, Michigan would go it alone, without the consent of Congress. While the Toledo War raged, delegates to the convention went about the serious business of drafting a charter for the budding state.

Of all the colorful characters in the Toledo War (and there were many), the standout was Benjamin Franklin Stickney. He was known as Major Stickney, though the origin of the military rank is not clear. A contemporary described him as "a queer compound of a man, a bundle of inconsistencies."[17] Partisans of Ohio saw him as a fine patriot in the cause of Ohio, while partisans of Michigan viewed him as a turncoat, verbose hypocrite, and instigator.

Tana Mosier Porter writes that Stickney evidently was well respected in the Toledo area, despite his eccentricities. "As an independent thinker," Porter writes, "Stickney often experienced problems in getting along with people."[18] Toledo historian John M. Killets said, "It seemed to be his ambition to be as different as possible from everybody else." Believing that children should be allowed to choose their own names when they were old enough, Stickney named his sons One and Two, in birth order. Apparently, they never replaced their birth names. The story goes that soon after the family moved to the Maumee Valley, while they were living in a house near the landing at the mouth of Swan Creek, Mrs. Stickney came one morning to the bank of the stream, where a vessel lay at anchor, and called to her younger son, "Two, call One for breakfast." A sailor aboard the vessel reportedly looked up and said, "Is this Maumee? It is a terribly hard country when it takes two to call one for breakfast." Stickney also named a daughter Indiana.

Born in Pembroke, New Hampshire, in 1775, Stickney married Mary Stark, the daughter of Revolutionary War general John Stark. Not much is known about Stickney's early life, but in 1812, President James Monroe appointed him Indian agent at Fort Wayne, in the Indiana Territory. Monroe had had a difference of opinion with General Stark and may have appointed Stickney as a favor to regain the general's friendship.

At some point, Stickney bought a large tract of land near the mouth of the Maumee River, which came to be known as Vistula. He had deduced that the eastern terminus of the Wabash and Erie Canal that the state of Ohio was planning to build would be near the mouth of the Maumee, which was, of course, part of the Michigan Territory. In 1832, Vistula was "boomed" by Stickney and Captain Samuel Allen of Lockport, New York. Port Lawrence had grown up alongside Vistula, and the two merged in 1833. By this time, Ohio had begun asserting its rights to the strip of land that contained the future town of Toledo. As the canal project became a certainty and work began, new towns were platted along the Maumee River, and settlers began moving in. Engineers had already determined that just below Toledo would be the best place for the canal to enter the Maumee River, and since Ohio was to build the canal, Toledo would have to become a part of the state of Ohio.

At first, Stickney persuaded his neighbors that it was to their advantage to swear allegiance to the Michigan Territory, because then they would not be subject to Ohio state taxes. Michigan even appointed Stickney a justice of the peace to defend residents against Ohio's attempt to collect taxes in the area. But when it became obvious that Ohio would not pay for a canal with its terminus in a Michigan port, Stickney turned opportunist and decided it was in everyone's best interest to belong to Ohio. He gathered his neighbors again, and according to an account in the *Courier & Monroe Ad-Venture*, they adopted resolutions to the effect that they considered themselves to be part of the state of Ohio. From then on, Stickney's fortunes were linked with Ohio, and he remains a hero, if a somewhat odd choice, to Buckeye partisans. Today, a major thoroughfare in Toledo carries his name.

Throughout the spring and summer of 1835, Michigan process servers, acting under the terms of the Pains and Penalties Act, raided Toledo, arresting Ohio sympathizers and carrying them away to jail in Monroe. On April 8, sometime between midnight and 3 a.m., a Monroe contingent of thirty-five or forty persons entered Stickney's house in Toledo and drove out his two guests, George McKay and Nathan Goodsell. The two victims were forcibly carried to Monroe, given a mock trial, and released at bail, their crime being "obstruction of justice and interference with the arrest of Toledoans loyal to Ohio."[19] Stickney reported, "30 or more ruffians from Monroe in a ferocious manner demolished the door to my house, seized Mr. Goodsell and treated my daughter with brutish violence. When my daughter gave out the cry of murder, she was seized by the throat and shaken with monstrous violence, and the prints of a man's hand in purple was strongly marked, with many other contusions."[20] In a May 23, 1835, letter to Governor Lucas of Ohio, Goodsell said, "I was treated very roughly, as was also my wife, who had left the house to alarm the neighbors; but was overtaken by the kidnappers and treated with violence and insolence. My journey [to Monroe] was rendered unpleasant by the insolence of some of the party, and my life jeopardized by being obliged to ride upon a horse without a bridle."[21] The *Columbus Hemisphere*, in its issue of May 2, published a letter from Maumee, dated April 11, in which the writer stated, "On the 8th instant at a late hour between 12 and 3 o'clock, a posse, attended by the sheriff of Monroe, went to Toledo, broke open the house of Major Stickney, in his absence, and after abusing the family and using the females quite rudely, succeeded in taking away Mr.

Goodsell, and at the same time broke open the office of Mr. McKay, seized him and made their way to Monroe."

Benjamin F. Stickney himself managed to get arrested several times during the summer of 1835, all of which he wore as a badge of honor. The first time, after the Battle of Phillips Corners, found Stickney and his family "fighting valiantly" but overpowered by numbers and transported to jail in Monroe. During another of his arrests, he was requested to mount a horse but flatly refused. He would not walk or ride in the Michiganians' custody. He was put on the horse by force, but still he balked at sitting astride the animal. Finally, two men were detailed to walk beside him and hold his legs, while a third led the horse. After making half the distance in this manner and with Stickney still protesting, they tied his legs under the horse and got him to jail in Monroe. He was charged with disobedience to the laws of Michigan.

From his jail cell in Monroe, Stickney wrote to Governor Lucas, "Here I am, peeping through the gates of a loathsome prison, for the monstrous crime of having acted as the judge of an election within the state of Ohio. The officer who first took me treated me in a very uncivil manner, dragging me about as a criminal through the streets of Monroe."[22] Stickney wrote that he had been "14 hours without refreshments" and that "these bands of ruffians . . . require chastisement."[23] The major was right in one respect—he had acted as a judge of an election. On April 6, five days after Michigan held elections for township officials in the disputed area, Ohio held its own elections. Stickney had, like others, undergone a change of mind. He was transformed from a justice of the peace for Michigan to an officer favorable to Ohio. So, at Monroe, Stickney was arrested and imprisoned for acting as a judge at the Ohio election of local officers. He was considered an important prisoner, and many gibes were made regarding him. On April 13, Stickney was quoted in the *Toledo Gazette* stating, "We are fast advancing to a horrid border war. The generous Ohioans . . . will restrain the savage barbarity of the hordes of the north."

In June, Governor Lucas called a special session of the Ohio legislature to address the boundary dispute with Michigan. On June 8, in his message to the second session of the Thirty-third General Assembly, Lucas could barely contain his anger at being shown up by Stevens T. Mason and the upstart Michigan Territory. He recounted the incidents leading up to Phillips Corners and how the authorities of Michigan commenced prosecutions against the citizens of Ohio, in opposition to the advice of the U.S. commissioners, "with a degree of reckless vengeance scarcely paralleled in the history of civilized nations." A portion of his address is worth repeating here.

> It appears to me, the honor and faith of the State is pledged in the most solemn manner, to protect these people [residents of the Toledo Strip] in their rights, and to defend them against all outrages. They claim to be citizens of Ohio. The Legislature, by a solemn act, has declared them to be such, and has required them to obey the laws of Ohio, which, as good citizens they have done; and for which they have been persecuted, prosecuted, assaulted, arrested, abducted and imprisoned. Some of them have been driven from their houses in dread and terror, while others are menaced by the authorities of Michigan. . . .
>
> Our Commissioners, appointed in obedience to the Act of the 23rd February, while in discharge of the duty assigned them, were assaulted, while resting on the Sabbath day, by an armed force from Michigan. Some of the hands were fired on, others arrested, and one of them, Col. Fletcher, is now incarcerated in Tecumseh, and for what? Is it for crime? No, but for faithfully discharging his duty, as a good citizen of Ohio, in obedience to our laws. These outrageous transgressions demand your most serious consideration; and I earnestly recommend, and confidently hope, that such measures may be adopted as will afford protection to our citizens; provide for the relief of those who have been arrested, and bound under recognizances; and for the liberation of those who are imprisoned; as also for the indemnity of those who have suffered loss in consequence of their obedience to the laws of Ohio; and in an especial manner, for the more prompt execution of our laws, and the punishment of those who have violated them.

At this point in his speech, His Excellency was just warming up. On the subject of the state's northern boundary, he said that the national press was creating an atmosphere of public opinion hostile to Ohio. His state, Lucas lamented, was portrayed as a great and powerful entity, while Michigan was cast as a small and weak territory. He complained, "This appears to be the substance of every argument, from the beginning to the end of this controversy; we also find it in the arguments of the ex-President [John Quincy Adams] in the last Congress." Lucas then continued,

> But what is the true state of the case? Ohio has oppressed no-
> body—she claims no territory more than what is defined in her
> Constitution while, on the other hand, we find the territory of
> Michigan (who can have no legitimate claim to sovereignty, as her
> government, at any time, may be dissolved by Congress, and the
> territory, north of Ohio, attached to this State) exerting all the
> power of her temporary or territorial Government, to oppress the
> small village of Toledo, punishing its inhabitants, not for crime,
> but for claiming their constitutional rights. But the true parties in
> the controversy are the United States and the State of Ohio; and
> let me ask which is the weaker party in this controversy? Surely it
> will not be contended that the great and gigantic State of Ohio (as
> she has been tauntingly called) is about to weaken the United
> States, by claiming her constitutional rights; or that, by enforcing
> these her just claims, she would be making the weak weaker, and
> the strong still more powerful, according to the arguments of our
> opponents. Is not Ohio a member of the Union? Will not any
> measure calculated to promote the prosperity of Ohio, also pro-
> mote the prosperity of the United States? Why the extreme exer-
> tions of many editors of newspapers, and other individuals, in
> some of the States, to forestall public opinion, and make impres-
> sions unfavorable to Ohio, without examining the justness of our
> cause? Is this course liberal? Is it just? We think not.[24]

Stormy applause greeted Governor Lucas's remarkable speech.
There is nothing like war fever to unite an assembly of lawmakers, and
the group that was gathered at Columbus in June 1835 was happy to do
Lucas's bidding. For them, there would not be another Phillips Corners,
with fleeing Buckeyes showing their backsides to the Michigan militia.
When Lucas had finished speaking, the legislators got down to some serious business.

First off, a new county was created from the northern part of Wood
County and given the name Lucas; the county seat would be at Toledo.
Provisions were made for a court of common pleas to meet at Toledo on
September 7 (a date that would live in infamy for Michigan), and official
business would then be transacted to validate the legitimacy of Lucas
County. The bill to create the county of Lucas passed the House 41–26

and the Senate without a division of the vote. Laws were approved enforcing the state's jurisdiction over the Toledo area; one law provided three to seven years of hard labor for anyone guilty of "the forcible abduction of the citizens of Ohio."[25]

To complete their business, the Ohio lawmakers endorsed the proposition put forth by federal commissioners Rush and Howard and appropriated the sum of three hundred thousand dollars—with the authorization to borrow a similar amount—to support the militia and teach Michigan a lesson or two. The appropriations bill passed the Senate 26–7 and the House 41–26. The record shows that there was, throughout the discussion over thirteen days, divided opinion as to the policy to be pursued but virtual unanimity as to the rights of Ohio in the case.

Anticipating what effect these actions might have on Old Hickory in Washington, Lucas named a three-man delegation to meet with Jackson. They were William Allen, David T. Disney, and Noah H. Swayne. (Disney was speaker of the Ohio Senate.) These smooth-talking Ohioans, working through Secretary of State Forsyth and unbothered by any Michiganians nearby to provide a counterweight to their arguments, carried the day with Jackson. Lucas had the good public relations sense to oil the gears in Washington, whereas Mason naively believed right would triumph in the end.

Jackson acceded to all the Buckeye trio asked for—namely, the Rush-Howard proposition. In late June, Lucas took the additional step of writing to advise other states "on the subject of the controversy between the United States and the State of Ohio, relative to the boundary line between Ohio and Michigan Territory."[26] Lucas was singularly determined not to recognize Michigan as a state and therefore as a coequal. He intended to block Michigan's statehood bid with all the means at his disposal.

The *Detroit Journal* of June 19 said, "Gov. Lucas narrates the course of events between that state and Michigan about the boundary line. His accounts are filled with exaggerations and false conclusions. With such an opponent our governor can well measure skill and wisdom." On June 27, the *Ohio Journal* put the case another way: "The olive branch of peace is held out, on the one hand, while on the other, if spurned, Ohio is prepared with but one feeling to step forward in the maintenance of her rights. Our own feelings would have gone in favor of more energetic action." The *Ohio Journal* concluded that both branches of the assembly acted with unanimity.

The *Ohio Journal* was not joking about Ohio's preparations for armed conflict. The adjutant general of the state reported to Lucas that ten thousand troops were ready for action. Governor Mason had used that same figure in the days just before the Battle of Phillips Corners. The belligerent conduct of Governor Lucas and the truculent nature of his address to the special session created much discussion and considerable anxiety in Washington and throughout the country.

As June gave way to July, the Toledo Strip War morphed into a series of minor skirmishes and harassment of Ohio partisans by Michigan process servers. The people of Monroe County in particular were occupied with assisting the sheriff in executing his processes and making arrests in Toledo. Many of the Ohio partisans were then taken to the jail of Monroe County. The *Toledo Gazette*, an outspoken proponent of the Ohio cause, reported that the Michigan militia was an invading army "composed of the lowest and most miserable dregs of the community—foreigners and aliens, low drunken frequenters of grog shops, who had been hired at a dollar a day." For its pains, the *Gazette* had its presses smashed that summer by "an armed mob" in an action the newspaper characterized as "worse than Algerine robbery or Turkish persecution."[27] The colorful prose it employed marked it as a potential target for the next invasion by "low drunken frequenters of grog shops."

CHAPTER NINE

BLOODSHED IN TOLEDO

There, damn you, you have got it now!

— TWO STICKNEY, ON STABBING DEPUTY SHERIFF
JOSEPH WOOD

*How long will the President permit a reckless wayward youth to com-
mit his savage depredations against our unoffending citizens, under
the official sanction of a post he is so little qualified to fill?*

— *Toledo Blade*

War fever was fanned in the summer of 1835 by the press of both sides
and by the politicians. In Washington, the presidential ear was being
bent by the Ohio trio of Disney, Swayne, and Allen. It was becoming increasingly clear that the electoral vote of 1836 meant more to President
Jackson than did Michigan's plight.

In Detroit, Governor Stevens T. Mason was a man marching to the
guillotine. Already warned in May by Secretary of War Lewis Cass to
show moderation or risk removal from office, Mason nevertheless
matched moves with Governor Robert Lucas of Ohio and ignored the
"compromise" proposition advanced by federal mediators Richard Rush
and Benjamin Howard. The territory's constitutional convention had
wrapped up its work and was prepared to present the voters with their
first charter. Michigan was prepared to present Congress with a package
that included a constitution approved by the voters, the requisite population, and fulfillment of all other terms required for statehood. It did
not matter to Michigan that it was proceeding on its own, without congressional authorization.

Ohio was prepared to go the last mile to block Michigan's statehood
in Congress until Ohio's northern boundary was set as defined in the
Ohio Constitution of 1805. On July 4, Independence Day, there was a

parade of Sunday school teachers and their children at Newark, Ohio.

An observer said they made an excellent appearance. "If Gov. Lucas was
to march with this company, he could run a line, in spite of the Wolverines," it was proudly reported. That same day, President Jackson wrote
to Lucas, "It is certainly greatly to be desired that any measure now
taken should be calculated to avoid forcible hostile collision, and to induce the parties to wait peaceably for the action of the next Congress
upon the subject."[1]

When Governor Lucas's remarks at the special session of the Ohio
legislature in June reached Mason, they were more than he could stand.
He said that the right of control followed the right of ownership and
that the public opinion supported him. On July 11, he called for a special session of the Michigan Legislative Council. Cass wrote to Mason
offering to come to Monroe, near the scene of action, if it would be
helpful in averting a collision. Mason informed Secretary of State John
Forsyth that he had convened the Legislative Council and that he would
submit the Rush-Howard proposition to the members. Mason said that
his views were "unalterable" on the proposed compromise proposition
but that he would appeal to the wisdom of the legislature, knowing full
well that the legislators would reject the Rush-Howard plan. In a postscript, he added, "It may not be unimportant to suggest to the secretary
of state that the County of Lucas has been formed out of the disputed
territory, and a court directed to be held at Toledo as the seat of justice
on the first Monday of September."[2] But before the Michigan legislature had time to act, fighting broke out.

On July 14, William L. Riggs, a justice of the peace in Monroe County,
commissioned the deputy sheriff of Monroe County, Joseph Wood, to
arrest Two Stickney of Toledo, Benjamin F. Stickney's second son, for
allegedly resisting two Michigan officers by force. Riggs pleaded for a
strong armed force in anticipation of "the forcible resistance of the inhabitants of the village of Toledo."[3] Two Stickney informed Wood that
"the day you set foot in Toledo, your life will be in danger." On July 15,
Wood called Stickney's bluff and went to Toledo to serve a warrant on
him and on George McKay, another prominent Ohio partisan.

Lyman Hurd, a constable of Monroe County, said that he and
Wood went unarmed to the hotel of J. Baron Davis, a hotbed of Ohio
partisans, looking for Stickney and McKay. They evidently knew where
to look, as both were on the premises. As the parties sized each other up,

Two Stickney, made bold by the comforting presence of so many of his compatriots and also perhaps by liquor, refused to accept the warrant unless it was served under Ohio authority. For his part, Hurd made an attempt to arrest McKay, but McKay, apparently the more agile of the two, jumped out of the way, grabbed a chair, and told Hurd to desist or he would "split him down."

Wood then made an attempt to arrest Stickney, laying his hand on Stickney's shoulder. A scuffle ensued. Two Stickney drew a knife and stabbed Wood between the second and third ribs in his left side, exclaiming, "There, damn you, you have got it now!"[4] Wood released his grasp of Stickney and grabbed his side. With blood staining his hand and uniform, Wood staggered to the door, saying he had been stabbed. In the uproar that followed, Two Stickney and McKay escaped.

A physician by the name of Jacob Clark was summoned to examine the wounded Wood. Wood was astonished to learn from Clark that he was not mortally injured. However, suspecting the doctor's Ohio proclivities, Wood sent to Monroe for a surgeon, who confirmed Doctor Clark's diagnosis. Upon examination, Wood had suffered a deep wound from which he bled copiously. The knife had cut a longish gash but had not penetrated the lungs. Still, the loss of blood may have led Wood to conclude that his life was ebbing away, and the case did appear a little precarious at first.

"There, damn you, you have got it now!" may not live among history's greatest declamations—alongside John Wilkes Booth's "Sic semper tyrannis!"—but it was the best Two Stickney could come up with in the heat of the moment. As it was, the shedding of Joseph Wood's blood by Two Stickney in the close battle conditions of a hotel bar was the only real bloodshed of the Toledo War. A report was filed the day after the stabbing by the district attorney's office in Monroe and sent to Governor Mason. J. L. Adams, the district attorney, and Nathan Hubble, sheriff of Monroe County, wrote, "Your Excellency will receive affidavits detailing a series of outrages recently perpetrated at Toledo in this County. . . . Joseph Wood yesterday afternoon while endeavoring to arrest Two Stickney under a warrant issued by one of the magistrates of our village, was stabbed in the side by Two Stickney with a dirk, inflicting such a wound that his life is despaired of, and in all probability he is not at this time living."[5] Adams and Hubble requested a military force to aid the civil authorities in the execution of the law.

Two eyewitnesses provide an account of the hotel fight. In an

Two Stickney, son of Major Benjamin Franklin Stickney. Two was responsible for the only bloodshed of the Toledo War, when he stabbed a deputy sheriff in Toledo in July 1835. (Courtesy of the Michigan Historical Commission.)

affidavit signed on July 16, 1835, at Monroe, Henry Clark Jr. says, "I saw Joseph Wood come from Davis's tavern to Smith's tavern and [he] was very feint. We took off his coat and laid him on a bed. He bled at one of his sides and I examined his side and it had the appearance of being stabbed with a dirk or knife. The wound appeared to be deep and Wood appeared to be very feint."[6] According to another affidavit of the same date, from Franklin Johnson of Monroe, Wood rode to Smith's Inn. Johnson explained, "I found Mr. Wood sitting in an armchair. The wound was about one half inch broad and the cut a full half inch which, with the copious flow of blood, and the distention of the flesh, were the only means which I have of judging of the depth or direction of the wound. Mr. Wood was pale and very weak from loss of blood. He said he was not in much pain."[7]

Informed of events at the executive office in Detroit, Mason fired off a note to the Secretary of State in Washington: "I regret to inform you that an encounter has taken place in Toledo in which the sheriff of Monroe County is said to have been mortally wounded. The sheriff was engaged in the peaceable exercise of the duties of his office, and you can readily conceive the excitement prevailing amongst our citizens."[8] At nine o'clock on the morning of July 16, Wood felt well enough to leave Toledo for the safety of Monroe. He asked Mason for armed aid against two hundred Toledo malcontents. On the next day, Mason, who had hurried to Monroe to meet Wood again, wrote to Forsyth, "Wood the sheriff who was wounded is still living, and I think he will recover. The excitement here is exceedingly great, but the circumstances which have given rise to it constitutes its justification. I will use my individual exertions to temper public feeling, although I fear it will have its sway." Mason reaffirmed "the utter impracticality of recognizing a concurrent jurisdiction with Ohio over the disputed territory."[9]

The spilling of Wolverine blood by Buckeyes enraged Michigan partisans. Governor Mason ordered out a large posse of armed men, rather than militia units, to seize the wanted men in Toledo. About fifty to seventy-five leading Toledo citizens, including Nathan Goodsell and George McKay, gathered to pledge resistance against any further Michigan arrests, "as long," they said, "as we have a drop of blood left."[10] Informed of this, Mason ordered a Monroe posse of two hundred men into Toledo to arrest Two Stickney.

The posse reached Toledo on July 17, only to find that most of the wanted men had left. However, the instigators, McKay and Major Stickney, were found in the major's cellar. These men, along with several others, were brought back to Monroe and jailed. As often as the major was arrested that summer, the Monroe jail surely must have had a "Stickney Suite" set aside for him.

When they sighted the armed force from the north, the other Toledoans fled across the Maumee River. A shooting match ensued, though the combatants were out of range of each other. The Battle of the Maumee, if it can be so called, was full of sound, fury, and wildly inaccurate gunfire. As many as a thousand Wolverines and Buckeyes exchanged hundreds of shots. It was a "feel-good" fracas with plenty of hostility worked out on both sides. It remains for historians to record whether the vigorous but indiscriminate swapping of gunfire across the Maumee should be designated a naval battle.

On the evening of July 18, the sheriff of Monroe County returned to Toledo, with a posse of about 250 armed men, and made seven or eight arrests, chiefly for individual grievances. When newspaper accounts related that two or three hundred Michigan horsemen, armed with guns and bayonets, had moved into Toledo and dishonored the Ohio flag by dragging it through the streets on the tail of a horse, Major Stickney was moved to avenge the outrage in print: "There cannot be a doubt Ohioans will turn out en masse to protect their northern border and restrain the savage barbarity of the hordes of the north."[11] The ultimate insult, however, was when the Michigan posse broke into the offices of the *Toledo Gazette* and proceeded to trash the place.

Apoplectic with rage, the *Gazette* spluttered against violent acts committed by troops from Michigan who broke into the *Gazette* office, where the type was "thrown into confusion." The headlines read: "RENEWED HOSTILITIES, upon the disputed ground, and unparalleled outrages upon the citizens of Toledo, by the Michigan authorities." The editors said,

> We have barely type and materials enough saved from the outrages we are about to relate, to lay the following facts before the public.
> On Saturday last, a large body of armed men, headed by the sheriff of Monroe County, Michigan Territory, . . . proceeded to this place for the ostensible purpose of serving some civil processes upon a number of our citizens. After arresting and making prisoners, among them Benj. F. Stickney and George McKay, they proceeded to the printing office of the *Toledo Gazette* and forthwith commenced an attack upon the Press.[12]

Brothers in Buckeye journalism, the *Toledo Blade* joined the *Gazette* in amping up the hyperbole: "The transactions [at the *Gazette*] are a disgrace to civilization, and in perfect character with barbarians of a bygone century. Not content with putting law, order and decency at defiance, the ruffians who do the bidding of the Michigan autocrat level their fury at the press that dares to record their deeds. How long will the President permit a reckless, wayward youth to commit his savage depredations against our unoffending citizens, under the official sanction of a post he is so little qualified to fill?"[13]

Two Stickney, who, during the fracas, had escaped for parts unknown, was indicted by a grand jury. Now he had a price on his head of five hundred dollars. Governor Mason demanded that he be apprehended and delivered to the authorities of Michigan, but Governor Lucas coolly refused to extradite him, on the grounds that Ohio had jurisdiction over the area.

So matters stood after the Battle of the Maumee removed the border controversy one step further from an amicable settlement. For a time, however, both sides broke off additional hostilities, and things actually calmed down a bit. On the Michigan side, George R. Griswold, captain of the Detroit Rifle Corps, wrote to Mason, "Should the crisis arrive in which it would be deemed necessary for the maintenance of our laws and protection of our citizens to require military aid from the arrogant encroachments of Ohio, be pleased to accept in the name and behalf of the members of the Detroit Rifle Corps their undivided services of defence of our rights."[14] In Ohio, the *Cleveland Whig*, in its editions of July 22, huffed, "All the anxiety, trouble and expense which this unpleasant controversy has occasioned would probably have been averted if there had been a man of experience and judgment in the executive chair of the territory."

In a private letter to Cass dated July 22, Forsyth criticized Mason for not accepting the recommendations of the president in bringing about a temporary arrangement pending final solution to the boundary dispute. "His call of the Legislative Council," Forsyth said, "is more likely to make trouble than prevent it."[15] The president, alarmed by the knife attack on Deputy Sheriff Wood and by the allegation that Governor Lucas was protecting Stickney the Stabber, recommended to Governor Mason that no obstructions should be made to the re-marking of the Harris line, that all prosecutions under the Pains and Penalties Act should be discontinued, and that no others should commence until the next session of Congress. These recommendations had no effect on Mason; to his own peril, he ignored the president, and prosecutions went on as before.

Forsyth pleaded for calm, saying Governor Lucas "was content to abide by the arrangement made." Forsyth said Jackson had no desire for Michigan to surrender anything. But in fact, the fix was in. Old Hickory was in the pocket of the trio of Ohioans Lucas had dispatched earlier to inform him of boundary goings-on. And it may be that now, in late July, Jackson already had determined to sack Mason.

The Legislative Council met in Detroit and predictably rejected the Rush-Howard proposal as accepted by Ohio. It authorized Mason to borrow up to $310,000 on the credit of Michigan to prevent Ohio operations in the Michigan Territory. (This bit of monetary one-upmanship was in response to the $300,000 Lucas requested from the Ohio legislature.) On July 20, Lucas ordered the marking of the Harris line resumed. For his part, Mason said the laws of the territory would be enforced, adding, "and although I have every disposition to avoid a collision, it is beyond my power to effect it. Delay will only bring about a renewal of hostile maneuvers."[16]

That summer, one of the Cleveland newspapers reported, "Gov.

Lucas has issued orders . . . for volunteers, who shall be ready at a moment's notice to march against the governor of Michigan and his forces. This may be too serious a matter to joke upon, but really, we hardly know whether its gravity or ridiculousness predominates."[17] The newspaper had it right; it was that kind of war. Public sentiment in Michigan was kept as belligerent as possible during these days, as the state was determined to prevent the Ohio court's planned September 7 session in Toledo. Lucas was just as determined to hold that court, so he could show the world, by the official record, that he had executed the laws of Ohio over the disputed territory.

CHAPTER TEN

THE CASE FOR OHIO

The question of boundary of one of the states of this union is not a legal but a political question.

— THOMAS HAMER, SENATOR FROM OHIO

Before examining the Toledo War's conclusion, we should consider each principal's case for ownership to that wedge of land between the Harris and the Fulton lines. Who had the stronger claim? Who had the goods from a strictly legal point of view? And why, in the end, did it not matter at all; that is, why, when Congress took possession of the dispute, was it a given that politics and who commanded the most votes would settle the issue?

A politician of that era put it best. Writing to two members of the Ohio legislature, the Honorable Thomas Hamer, senator from Ohio, said, "The question of boundary of one of the states of this union is not a legal but a political question." He went on to claim that it was the intention of Congress in 1802 that Ohio should have the margin of Lake Erie for its northern landmark and the territorial line in the center of that lake for the limit of its jurisdiction. Ohio's strategy was then set forth. "It would be a sound policy," Hamer wrote, "for us, I mean the Ohio delegation in Congress, to vote against admission of Michigan until our northern boundary be permanently settled, and the justice of our claim admitted."[1]

To recapitulate local history, on January 29, 1818, the Ohio legislature ratified and adopted the Harris line as its northern boundary. In explaining its actions, Ohio said the northern boundary line as fixed by the Northwest Ordinance was based on imprecise geographical knowledge. Furthermore, it was an "impossible" line, because instead of intersecting Lake Erie, it would actually pass several miles south of the lake and divide what is now Cuyahoga, Lake, and Geauga counties. Congress, reasoned Ohio, never intended such a boundary line and always recog- nized Lake Erie as the northern limit of Ohio.

In the eighteenth century, all the states that had western land claims except Virginia ceded their titles to the general government without conditions. Virginia said that in the creation of new states in the North-west Territory, attention should be paid to lakes, rivers, and natural boundaries. Ohio's claim to the mouth of the Maumee River, given that state's interest in canals and subsequent internal improvements, makes sense under the reasons stated by Congress for asking that attention be paid to the course of rivers and facilities for navigation.

The frame of reference in that day was Mitchell's map of 1755, er-roneous as to the true placement of the most southerly end of Lake Michigan. The framers of the 1787 ordinance did not leave a copious written record of their deliberations. They did not write in their diaries what they may have envisioned for the states of the Northwest Ordi-nance. It may be that they meant for such states as Indiana and Illinois to have frontage on Lake Michigan to assist in navigation and com-merce.

The case for Ohio's claim to the Toledo Strip can be made utilizing the following points of law and practical considerations:

1. Congress neither confirmed nor rejected Ohio's revision of its northern boundary as described in the Ohio Constitution. Ohio in-terpreted this as implied consent.
2. Ohio was a sovereign state with influence in Congress. Ohio said maps were faulty and that this was reason enough to accept Ohio's version of a northern boundary. Because early maps were confusing, Ohio could legitimately claim it was impossible to be absolutely certain that using the northern border would deprive Ohio of the mouth of the Maumee River.
3. One could read or interpret Article V of the Northwest Ordinance in different ways. Ohio said it should be read in the light of the in-tention of its framers and not by the letter of the document. The evident intention of the framers was to make the new states of con-venient size and with equal commercial facilities. Boundaries should be made to conform to the intention of the ordinance, not its letter.

4. The theory of inalienable rights bestowed by an inviolable contract, as maintained by Michigan, is untenable. Today, all agree that one Congress cannot bind another.

5. Since the terms of the ordinance of 1787 were not embodied in the Constitution of the United States, its terms are not binding on the government. Thus Congress had a perfect right to divide the public domain regardless of the ordinance and, having this right, had given to Ohio a northern boundary line extending from the foot of Lake Michigan to the north cape of Maumee Bay. In other words, Congress had the undoubted right to adjust boundaries under the federal Constitution as the supreme legislative authority of the Union, whatever one might think of the ordinance as a compact.

6. The parties to the compact did give their consent to any changes that had been made in Article V. The old states that gave the land agreed silently to the boundaries of Illinois and Indiana, and by silent acceptance, they consented to the change in the Ohio boundary.

7. The purpose of the ordinance makers in naming the line running through the southern extremity of Lake Michigan was to prevent the northern states from pushing down below that line and encroaching on the southern states, making them smaller. Article V meant that the southern tier of states might be extended as far north as Congress chose, but the northern tier could not be extended farther south than this fundamental line.

8. Precedent favored Ohio. Congress had admitted Indiana and Illinois as states and, in each instance, had accepted their northern boundaries well north of the east-west line specified in the ordinance. Since both Illinois and Indiana had encroached on the original southern boundary of Michigan, Ohio had right on its side in adjusting its boundary.

9. Equity and expediency also favored Ohio. The limits Michigan claimed would have made the state much larger than Ohio, with a long coastline. The commercial interests of Ohio demanded that Ohio, the key to the west, should have lake ports as terminuses for canals. In 1835, canals trumped railroads (Michigan's commercial interest).

10. In terms of its electoral votes in the 1836 presidential sweepstakes, Ohio was a desirable political plum. With state and eastern capi-

talists on its side, Ohio curried favor politically because it was a
doubtful state electorally speaking, whereas Michigan was believed
to be safely Democratic.

Ohio's politicians in Congress, the state's allies in that body, and
scholars of government made forceful arguments for the state's right to
the Toledo Strip. When it came time to call in its chips and submit its
case in the national legislature, Ohio found a sympathetic jury in Congress. It was the expedient thing to acknowledge the claim of an established state, with important electoral votes in the balance, and to offer
the loser a consolation prize—in this case, about nine thousand square
miles of poor country.

L. G. Stuart, in a paper read before the Michigan Political Science
Association in Grand Rapids on April 3–4, 1896, put the case for Ohio.
Stuart said that the Northwest Ordinance was not irrevocable but an ordinary act of Congress, subject to amendment; and in fact, it was
amended. It was not submitted to the people of the thirteen states for
ratification. Another scholar, John Fiske, in his *The Critical Period of
American History*, said that the ordinance "was simply the thirteen states,
through their delegates in Congress, dealing with the unoccupied national domain as if it were the common land of a stupendous township."

As for Article V of the ordinance, Stuart asks what is meant by the
term *common consent*? In the Continental Congress, the vote of nine
states was sufficient to carry an important measure. Did Congress propose in the ordinance, Stuart asks, to make *common consent* mean unanimous consent or the consent of the majority? Did it mean the consent
of all or a majority of the states to be created out of the western country,
of all or the larger portion of the people living in the vast domain? Ohio,
Indiana, and Illinois preceded Michigan in gaining statehood. If the ordinance were a compact and if it, along with its east-west line, were irrevocable, argued Stuart, then the consent of Ohio, Illinois, and Indiana, with their million and a half population, was "common consent"
against the Michigan Territory, with its lesser population, and would be
sufficient for its change. Should three states or one territory rule? Pur-
porting to be a compact between the original states, on the one hand,
and the people and states in the said territory, on the other, it lacked the
very first and most important principle of a compact. It had no party of
the second part agreeing to it.

Also, Stuart said, the east-west line established in the Northwest

Ordinance was not a true boundary, nor was it absolutely fixed and positive. It was purposely indefinite, so that injustice might not be done to any of the states created in the Northwest Territory. Finally, Stuart applies the crusher: "I have been unable to discover who conferred upon the Continental Congress an attribute so divine in its nature as the power to make an immutable law. Where or how or when it [the ordinance] acquired its immutability does not appear; how it was made sacred from amendment or change for all time to come cannot be found."[2]

From Ohio's point of view, Governor Mason and his legislature overstepped their bounds in taking military measures against Ohio. As officials of a territorial government, they were beholden to Congress and the federal government. Beyond the specifics of territorial law, Michigan had no authority for independent action. Ohio's alleged encroachment on federal territory was a matter with which the U.S. government perforce had to deal. In the absence of instruction or advice from the federals, Governor Mason had acted illegally in sending out his militia to repulse the "invaders."

Six months after the Toledo War wound to its conclusion, Senator John M. Clayton, chairman of the Senate Judiciary Committee, made a report to his committee. He traced the history of the boundary dispute to the Northwest Ordinance, which, in Clayton's opinion, "carefully reserves to Congress the exercise of reasonable discretionary power, both in reference to the boundaries of the districts of which the territory might be composed, and the limits of the states which were to be formed out of it." Congress, Clayton said, sought the discretionary power to adapt the boundaries of these states to the "situation and future circumstances of the country." Thus, when Indiana drew its northern boundary ten miles north of the southern extreme of Lake Michigan, it was to gain access to this "vast sheet of water" for commercial activity and for its canals, railroads, and other avenues to the lake.[3]

It was thus the intent of Congress, in passing the Northwest Ordinance, that future Congresses, should they find it expedient, could adjust boundaries of the states to be formed within the Northwest Ordinance. In the case of Indiana and Illinois, the latter of which fixed its northern boundary by a line drawn west from the middle of Lake Michigan, Congress consented to their claims. "If the construction of the Ordinance of 1787, contended for by Michigan, be the *true* con-

struction, then Congress had no discretionary power to adjust boundaries," Clayton said. His report continued,

> while both states must yield their own most important facilities for
> commercial intercourse through the lake, to a new state [Michi-
> gan], nearly surrounded on all sides by vast sheets of water being
> everywhere except on her southern border, bounded by lakes and
> streams which connect them. To the judgment of your committee,
> nothing is more apparent than the correctness of the principle
> which Congress has thus twice decided.
>
> By the terms of the 5th Article of the Ordinance of 1787, three
> states designated as the western, middle and eastern were to extend
> north to the territorial line, but there is an express reservation of
> authority to Congress to alter their boundaries so far as to form
> one or two states in that part of the said territory, which lies north
> of an east-west line drawn through the southerly bend of Lake
> Michigan.
>
> The territory of Ohio was within the eastern state. Congress
> then had the power to extend Ohio to the territorial or Canada
> line, the ordinance provided that it should be so extended, unless
> Congress should find it expedient to alter this provision. Illinois,
> Indiana and Ohio were all thus laid out by the Ordinance as States
> to extend to the territorial line, but it was also provided that Con-
> gress might lay out one or two States "in" [not, as the Ordinance
> has sometimes been misquoted, "out of"] that part of the territory
> north of the east and west line referred to.[4]

Clayton cited the state of Virginia, which altered its deed of cession
to lands in the western country to allow the division of territory into
states "as the situation of that country and future circumstances might
require." This language was taken from the journal of the proceedings
of the old Congress of July 7, 1786. Clayton took this to mean that the
east-west line drawn from the most southern part of Lake Michigan as
an unalterable boundary between the states north and south of it was
voted down by that Congress on the date given. He said that the framers
rejected a motion to make it an instrument that, on the part of Michigan, it is now claimed to be—that is, an unalterable boundary.

> Now, after the lapse of nearly 50 years, we look back upon the vote
> of this day in consequence of which the arbitrary line was rejected,

and the discretionary powers of Congress over this very boundary was obtained, as an evidence of wisdom in that Congress which is entitled to our highest admiration. Their general prediction that circumstances would be pointed out by a more perfect knowledge of the country, requiring the power to change the boundary, has been completely fulfilled by the discovery within the last 20 years of the true location of the southern limit of Lake Michigan, which entirely changes the actual position of the principal line which they had, and we have now, under consideration.

Clayton then applied the clincher:

> Michigan claimed a vested right to territory given to them by the act of Congress 31 years ago. The act referred to is January 11, 1805, "to divide the Indiana territory into two separate governments." But a vested right is an irrepealable right, and it would have been not only inconsistent with the design of a territorial government which was expressly declared to be temporary. The very section in that act which prescribes these boundaries declares that they are marked out for the mere purpose of temporary government.
>
> There is nothing, either in the Ordinance or any law of Congress, to prevent Congress from annexing the whole territory [of Michigan] to Indiana and Ohio at any moment before the assent of Congress to a state Constitution proposed for Michigan by the people of the territory. The language of the Ordinance clearly confers this right upon Congress. . . . Michigan has no cause for disagreement with Indiana that cannot be adjusted by Congress. Can there be any similar cause of disagreement between Ohio and Michigan which cannot be adjusted by Congress?[5]

Earlier, in a letter to Clayton dated December 7, 1835, Senator Thomas Ewing of Ohio had made it very clear that Michigan had no "vested" right of any kind. "If anyone can find in the clause of the 1787 Ordinance," Ewing wrote, "a vested right in this territory [Michigan] which is not formed by the Ordinance or by act of Congress into a State to come into the Union when its inhabitants shall be 60,000, or to hold fast, permanently, against the will of Congress, to the boundaries fixed for it as a territory, for the express purpose of temporary government, he must have a perception and reasoning faculties of a different order from those which are possessed by the rest of mankind."[6] Ewing argued

that Congress had asked for discretion for the purpose of adjusting the
boundaries of the contemplated states to suit the natural features of the
country. He said that Congress had the right to create territorial governments and to modify them at pleasure, including their boundaries.

On December 21, 1835, Ewing rose on the floor of the U.S. Senate
to introduce a bill to settle and determine the northern boundary line of
Ohio. He said that the resolution of Congress dated October 10, 1780,
asked for authority to change nothing relative to the contemplated
states in the Northwest Territory, except the extent and boundaries, and
that Congress "asked for discretion for the purpose of adjusting their
boundaries to suit the natural features of the country." Ewing cited Article V of the Northwest Ordinance, stating that "the boundaries of
these three states [Illinois, Indiana, and Ohio] shall be subject to be so
far altered, that, if Congress shall hereafter find it expedient, they shall
have authority to form one or two states in that territory which lies
north of an east-west line drawn through the southerly bend of Lake
Michigan."[7]

Why should the proposed adjustment of boundary be made? "Congress intended," argued Ewing, "that the new states should secure to
each such natural advantages of navigation as most properly pertained
to it." He explained,

> The intent of Congress in 1802 in the act under which Ohio joined
> the Union was that the line designated as her northern boundary
> shall run due east from the southern extreme of Lake Michigan
> until it intersects Lake Erie or the territorial line; thence with the
> same, through Lake Erie, to the Pennsylvania line. But that line
> does not touch the northern boundary line of the U.S. at any point
> in Lake Erie.
>
> This boundary is based on the assumption that that east and
> west line will touch the territorial line [which is the northern
> boundary of the United States] in Lake Erie or north of it; other-
> wise it could not, without changing its direction, run with it,
> through Lake Erie to the Pennsylvania line. It is an impossible
> boundary.

Next, Ewing put the rubber to the road. He argued that Ohio's claims
to the boundary as delineated in that state's constitution were based on
the fact there was no official objection to it by Congress; that Ohio's
claim conformed with the resolution of Congress of July 7, 1786, which

Close-up of a map by John Farmer published in 1836, clearly
showing Toledo and the mouth of the Maumee River in Monroe
County, Michigan. Ohio claimed all along that the mouth of the
Maumee River (and Toledo) belonged in the state of Ohio.
(Courtesy of the Local History and Genealogy Department,
Toledo-Lucas County Public Library.)

asked of Virginia a modification of its deed of cession, with a view to regard terrain, natural features, and the commercial relations of the contemplated states; and that Ohio's claim accorded with the view of the
framers of the ordinance of 1787, "as appears by the map of their day,
showing their opinion of the law which should bound the contemplated
states." Ewing said that Congress gave its implied consent to the boundary proviso when it accepted Ohio into the Union.[8]

As for the rights of Michigan, Ewing was dismissive: "That Territory has no right to any particular boundary, either by virtue of the Ordinance of 1787, or any of the Acts of Congress. Michigan is a temporary, territorial government. So long as it continues a territory, it is

subject to be changed and modified, as to boundary and extent, at the pleasure of the same power in that it was called into existence by an act of Congress." (Michigan was, at the time of Ewing's speech, a fully functioning state, with elected representatives and the required population standard, even though not officially recognized as a state by Congress.) "Is it expedient," Ewing asked, "that that state [Michigan] should hold the mouth of the Miami [Maumee], which has its whole navigable course in Ohio and Indiana, and control its entrance to Lake Erie?" He argued, "Indiana and Ohio are constructing a canal connecting the Miami River with the Wabash River, and that grand work is now delayed, awaiting the decision of this question. I ask, is it expedient that a State, which you are to form hereafter north of these two states, should hold the outlet of the vast region intersected by this canal—that this new state should have delivered to her the key, and be the sole keeper of the entrance to the noble edifice erected by the industry and enterprise of her neighbor? It is not right."[9]

In 1819, Ohio started building a series of canals. The canal referenced by Ewing was to traverse his state, with the Maumee Bay as its northern outlet. To Ohio, the Toledo War was an inconvenience and a potential source of embarrassment in that summer of 1835. But it became the vehicle to hold Michigan statehood hostage and thus achieve for Ohio what it wanted all along.

CHAPTER ELEVEN

THE CASE FOR MICHIGAN

The tract in dispute must be considered as forming, legally, a part of the Territory of Michigan.

—U.S. ATTORNEY GENERAL BENJAMIN F. BUTLER

In its claim to the Toledo Strip, Michigan did not budge from its position that the language of the Northwest Ordinance of 1787 should be held as the highest standard and that a boundary description for the two contiguous states should be strictly interpreted. The great founding document rang with such words—monolithic in character and principle—as *irrevocable, inviolable, inalienable,* and *immutable.* Michigan clearly had the better legal and historical claim on the Toledo Strip; Ohio had strong geographical and political claims, as well as the benefit of a favorable interpretation of the Northwest Ordinance. In the end, political matters proved successful.

A recap of historical events puts Michigan's claim to the Toledo Strip in a proper perspective. The Continental Congress approved the Northwest Ordinance in 1787, establishing the southern border of the Michigan Territory, which was formed in 1805. The 1818 Fulton survey put the mouth of the Maumee River in the Michigan Territory. After Michigan presented its first formal petition for admission as a state, yet another survey was ordered. The federal Talcott line, named for Captain Andrew Talcott, was found to be nearly identical with the Fulton line.

The case for Michigan's ownership of the Toledo Strip can be made citing the following points of law and practical considerations:

1. Congress had never consented to any change in the boundary between Ohio and Michigan as originally fixed in the Northwest Ordinance. Ohio had desired—even applied—for the consent of Con-

gress to the proviso in its state constitution but had failed to obtain
it. Michigan said this was Congress's real intention all along.

2. One party to a compact may not annul it at its own pleasure. The language of the Northwest Ordinance said that boundaries could be changed only by mutual consent. The ordinance of 1787 was a compact that could be dissolved only by common consent of the contracting parties.

3. The southern boundary was inviolable because it was established in the ordinance of 1787, and Michigan's boundary claim predated the Ohio Constitution. Article V of the ordinance provides for the creation of one or two states north of an east-west line drawn through the southerly bend of Lake Michigan.

4. Possession is nine-tenths of the law. For nearly thirty years, Michigan had exercised jurisdiction over the disputed area. Territorial officers had governed the disputed area, county courts had sat there, and public land was sold through the Monroe land office in the Michigan Territory. For example, the plat map for Sylvania, Ohio, clearly in the Toledo Strip, was filed in the clerk's office in Monroe.

5. The 1834 Talcott line had the force of congressional authority. This survey, ordered by the federal government, was supposed to eliminate all doubt as to the true location of Ohio's northern border. The Talcott line was found to be nearly identical with the Fulton line.

6. When Congress created the Michigan Territory, Article V of the Northwest Ordinance was so far carried into effect as to vest in the people of that region an inalienable right of admission into the Union as soon as they should number sixty thousand inhabitants. Michigan's claim of a vested right may be disputed in a court of law, but no one could argue that its census showing eighty-seven thousand inhabitants was a miscount.

7. Inhabitants of the Toledo Strip had voted in territorial elections. Post offices were established for six Michigan villages. Government was fully in place, in all aspects, and Toledo Strip residents were Michiganians in terms of their votes and preferences. Every action Congress took in the matter, right up to the final settlement, confirmed the right of Michigan to exercise jurisdiction over the disputed tract.

8. It was necessary for the nation to have a strong state on the international border. This argument must be considered in the context of

the times. Lucius Lyon, Michigan's first elected senator, said that Michigan "must always remain in a very exposed situation on the frontier, and for a long time must be in the immediate vicinity of a powerful and warlike tribe of Indians."[1] In this context, "strong" meant that dismemberment was out of the question and that, by inference, Ohio, with its million of freemen, was already strong enough.

9. A strict interpretation of the law and the language of the ordinance was in Michigan's favor. If the letter of the law was to be enforced, Michigan clearly had the better claim to the Toledo Strip. The reality, however, is that not all jurists are strict constructionists, and not all politicians vote to support what is clearly in the right, as John Quincy Adams so eloquently lamented while arguing Michigan's case in the House of Representatives.

10. The attorney general of the United States had ruled in Michigan's favor. In March 1835, Benjamin F. Butler, after a request for a ruling from President Jackson, said that until the assent to the boundary proviso in the Ohio Constitution was given by Congress, the tract in dispute legally formed a part of the territory of Michigan.

Michigan's politicians gamely defended the territory's right to possession of the Toledo Strip, but they were not heard where it counted most: in the corridors of Congress and in the ear of Old Hickory in the White House. Although Attorney General Butler opined favorably for Michigan, his view was not shared by cabinet colleague John Forsyth, secretary of state. In Forsyth's view, Governor Mason had exceeded his authority in taking military measures against Ohio: Mason was a territorial official, responsible to Congress and the federal government, and he had no legal grounds for taking independent action. If Ohio was indeed the trespasser on federal territory, argued Forsyth, then the U.S. government should be prepared to handle the matter.

After Jackson's peace commissioners Rush and Howard weighed in with their recommendations, Forsyth followed with a letter written July 3, 1835, in which he urged that no obstruction be given to the remarking of the Harris line, that all proceedings begun after enactment of the Pains and Penalties Act be discontinued, and that all questions about disputed jurisdiction be referred to Congress. The trouble with Forsyth's view was that Congress, forced to choose between a sovereign

state and a feisty territory eager to become a state, knew a hot potato
when it saw one. It did what Congress often does best—temporize. And
with Michigan already rejecting Rush and Howard, it was not going to
have its mind changed by Forsyth's opinion. Michigan probably figured
one Butler was worth two or three Forsyths, even if the latter had Jackson's ear. Besides, Forsyth did Jackson's bidding: on August 29, the secretary of state communicated the decision of Old Hickory to dismiss
Mason as secretary and acting governor of the territory.

Before it was awarded the western two-thirds of the Upper Peninsula, Michigan considered itself fairly small in territory and therefore
unfairly diminished if it were forced to give up the Toledo Strip. Michigan portrayed itself as a weak state compared to its powerful southern
neighbor. Lucius Lyon, arguing for a strong state, suggested the propriety of strengthening Michigan as much as possible "instead of adopting
a measure which will tend so much to weaken it as the one now offered."[2] He was referring to the compromise brokered in Congress that
removed the Toledo Strip from Michigan jurisdiction and "replaced" it
with those lands of the frozen north.

Lyon may have been protesting a little too much. Consider the
lengthy letter of January 5, 1836, that Lyon, John Norvell, and Isaac E.
Crary wrote to the Honorable John M. Clayton, chair of the Senate Judiciary Committee. Lyon and his Michigan colleagues started out by
hailing the citizens of Ohio as "brethren of the same great social and political family," but they quickly got to the point, arguing, "To take from
Michigan a fertile and extensive tract of territory of which she has been
in possession for more than 30 years, to deprive her of the only port and
harbor she has, or can have, immediately upon Lake Erie, Ohio threatens to tear from her diadem the brightest jewel which adorns it." Michigan did not want to give up Toledo without a fight, and the Michigan
delegation to Congress (comprised of Lyon, Norvell, and Crary) was
bound by duty to make the territory's points. "The people of Michigan
have a vested right," Lyon continued, "to all that part of the Northwest
Territory which lies north of a line drawn east from the southerly bend
or extreme of Lake Michigan until it shall intersect Lake Erie, and west
of a line drawn from the said southerly bend through the middle of said
lake to its northern extremity, and thence due north to the northern
boundary of the United States." Lyon claimed, " These are the boundaries given to Michigan by the act of Congress, passed 31 years ago, establishing the Territorial Government of Michigan."[3]

As for the argument that in fixing the dimensions of the new states to be carved from the Northwest Territory, due attention ought to be paid to natural boundaries, Lyon said, "It is a self-evident truth that a line drawn due east from the southerly extreme of Lake Michigan is a far more natural boundary between Ohio and Michigan than the one running to the north cape of the Maumee Bay." Moreover, whatever proviso Ohio might have incorporated into her constitution in relation to a change of northern boundary, it would have become null and void, Lyon said, "the very moment her state government was formed." He explained why: "Because from that moment Congress had said, that *all* the country to the north of Ohio, as bounded in the act of 1802, should be attached to the Indiana Territory and should, at a future day, become a part of the one or two states which they were at liberty to form north of the east and west line."[4]

The framers of Michigan's first constitution in 1835 were not silent, either. In an appeal by the 1835 constitutional convention of Michigan to the people of the United States in relation to the boundary question between Michigan and Ohio, Mr. Norvell of Wayne said on June 1, 1835,

> The committee of Congress, of which the Honorable J. Q. Adams was the chairman, at the late session of that body, were, after a laborious investigation, unanimously of the opinion that Ohio had no just claim to the country she demands. . . .
>
> It will be most painful to this convention, and the people of Michigan, to be compelled to defend their rights by force. But if they are forcibly assailed, they must and will be forcibly protected.[5]

Unbeknownst to Norvell, statehood was still a year and a half away. He was speaking while the Toledo War was going on. Michigan's defense of its frontier was of equal importance as its bid for statehood. The Toledo War and territorial governor Stevens T. Mason's relentless push for admission to the Union consumed Michigan's interest in 1835.

Young though he was, Mason had a keen appreciation of the odds that were against the territory of Michigan in the contest with Ohio and of how the underdog role would play in the court of national public opinion. Illinois and Indiana were in sympathy with Ohio's cause. Mason had observed enough of politics to know that simply standing for the right was an unattractive reward in a contest of politics and expedi-

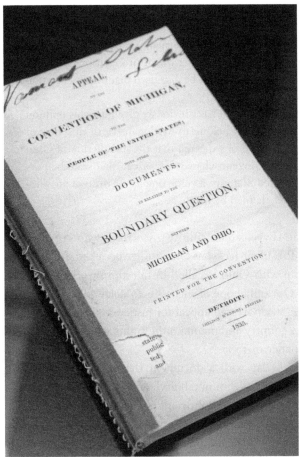

Appeal by the framers at Michigan's first constitutional convention in 1835 to the "people of the United States," in which Michigan presented to Congress the opinion that "Ohio had no just claim to the country she demands." (Courtesy of the Local History and Genealogy Department, Toledo-Lucas County Public Library.)

ency. Without electoral votes, political prestige, or voting members in Congress, Michigan had little more to offer than an appeal to conscience.

In a letter of April 10, 1835, to Washington's peace commissioners Rush and Howard, Mason cited the attorney general's opinion on the boundary dispute, which stated "That until this assent shall have been given by Congress, the tract in dispute must be considered as forming, legally, a part of the Territory of Michigan." Mason went on to state:

> She is disturbed in the exercise of that jurisdiction, her officers of justice have been resisted. An attempt, by a military force actually embodied, to suppress the jurisdiction of the Territorial officers,

acting as they do under the laws of the United States, in the disputed tract, and to maintain therein the exclusive jurisdiction of Ohio, would expose the parties concerned, if the region in dispute be legally a part of Michigan, to criminal prosecutions of a still more serious character. It cannot be disguised that this prosecution would be for treason.

He [the attorney general] has previously given it as his opinion that the tract does legally belong to Michigan. With this view of the case, can it be asked or expected that the jurisdiction of Ohio be recognized to any extent whatsoever, or can that state be permitted by the United States to assume one jot or tittle of jurisdiction over the tract claimed by her?[6]

This is Mason the lawyer addressing two worthies who are going to make a report to President Jackson. On another occasion, Mason said, "When the dispute with Ohio is called in question, we have but one course to pursue. Our only hope of success is to delay their action until we become a State, when we can appeal for justice to the supreme judicial tribunal of the country and maintain the rights which were secured to us by the Ordinance of 1787."[7]

Michigan's hopes lay with a document that was increasingly regarded as a dead letter. Its "immutability" and "inviolability" had already been badly compromised. Politicians being politicians, the men of Congress in 1835–36 did what was necessary to conduct the business of the day. They were men of the moment, not given to the long view or to the principled position, which makes them neither better nor worse than politicians of today.

CHAPTER TWELVE

GOVERNOR MASON IS FIRED

If you do not coincide in the views I suggested, you must be removed.

—SECRETARY OF WAR LEWIS CASS TO
GOVERNOR STEVENS T. MASON

No one has dared to impeach my moral character.

—GOVERNOR MASON TO PRESIDENT ANDREW JACKSON

The summer of 1835 simmered into August with Michigan continuing to prosecute officials deemed to be in violation of the Pains and Penalties Act. Like a poker player holding a fistful of winners, Governor Robert Lucas of Ohio bided his time. Before the month was out, his youthful opponent, Stevens T. Mason of Michigan, would be removed from his job by an order from President Jackson himself. Before bringing the Toledo War to its comic-opera conclusion, it is well to get a measure of this man Mason, who did so much for his adopted state and whose name lives on in its many corners.

Stevens Thomson Mason was born October 27, 1811, of the Masons of Virginia. His wealthy father, John T. Mason, owned a plantation in Loudon County, Virginia. His mother, Elizabeth Moir, came from a family of modest means. Stevens was christened at the Episcopal Church in Leesburg, where his father moved shortly after the boy's birth. Stevens had an older sister, Mary, and a younger sister, Emily, born when Stevens was nearly four. Emily lived to the ripe age of ninety-seven. Siblings Catherine, Laura, and Theodosia followed, to complete the family.

The Masons moved to Kentucky when Stevens was quite young. John T. Mason headed west to indulge his urge to explore and settle the frontier of the new nation. As a boy, Stevens, called Tom, was a precocious child and a quick learner. He attended a private school in Lexington, Kentucky, where he seems to have curbed his scholarship in favor of making himself popular. At Transylvania College, Tom Mason devoured the classics. Nearly six feet tall and skinny, he was an elegant dresser who appealed to the ladies. After he and his father moved to raw Detroit, he quickly found the territory's politics to his liking. While helping his father, who held the position of territorial secretary, young Tom caught the eye of both Cass and Jackson. He excelled as a stand-in in his father's job and was rewarded in mid-July 1831, when the president pulled a shocker by naming him to the position his father had vacated. Jackson may have made this appointment to annoy Detroit's Whigs and to position the state-to-be in the Democratic column. Young Mason had enough confidence in himself to accept with alacrity, and he had the wisdom to solicit advice from Detroit's seasoned political veterans.

On July 26, 1831, Mason wrote to President Jackson regarding local opposition to his appointment as secretary of the Michigan Territory, "I have been beset with a sort of inquisitorial scrutiny, and finding nothing to rest upon but the fact of my minority, I have been asked to relinquish my office. That it is designed to strike higher than one so unimportant as myself is clear. Their objection rests upon a fact that forms no disqualification, and is merely a computation of months and days as to my age. No one has dared to impeach my moral character."[1] Mason's youth was not a problem to him, but it clearly was to opposition Whigs and other doubters. In an 1831 letter to the U.S. Senate, Mason told the senators to "be forewarned, that an attempt will be made to prejudice me in your estimation. You should be apprised of the true estimate in which I am held by the best portion of society in this Territory. I believe a just expectation that where no crime has been committed, no condemnation will ensue; and that the crime of being a young man will be assuaged by the recollection that once you were young, and must now feel, how slender would have been your advancement in life without the protection and support of older men."[2] On August 1, Mason again wrote to Jackson, enclosing a paper "containing a remonstrance against my appointment [as territorial secretary] and my reply to it in a handbill." I feel a confidence, Mason wrote, "in being ultimately sustained by the good sense and correct sentiments of the community." He added, "I am assured a large fraction of the people are ready if called upon to sign a petition in my favor. I shall be enabled at a proper time to show you that my appointment is not of that obnoxious character which violent partisans represent."[3]

By the time George B. Porter arrived in Detroit to assume his post as territorial governor in September, Mason was already serving as acting governor. In February 1832, the Senate confirmed Porter's appointment. But no sooner had he arrived at his new assignment than he fell into a pattern that would mark his entire time as Michigan's territorial governor. Some say he did not want the appointment to begin with, others that he was appalled at what he found in Detroit. Porter, a man of wealth and eminent Pennsylvania stock, was a patrician in plebeian Detroit. So he found one excuse after another to stay away for long periods. He was an absentee governor whose duties devolved upon Mason.

Mason grew in stature and popularity and was getting friendly newspaper space. The people addressed him as "governor," and he signed appointments. The Whigs did as much as they could to discredit him in advance of his confirmation hearings in Washington, with the result that he became toughened for the job at hand. He even got a reputation for fisticuffs. When the *Ann Arbor Emigrant* coined the nickname "the Boy Governor" for the youthful Mason, the name stuck. Though Mason despised the label, it remained with him as long as he held office in Michigan. It so angered him that when he discovered the editor of the Ann Arbor newspaper on a Detroit street, Mason attacked him and gave him a beating with his fists. Then there is the story recounted in a letter from C. M. Bull of Detroit to his father, John Bull Jr., in New Lebanon, New York. "What shall we do with our young governor?" the younger Bull asks, explaining, "He had two or three fights within the last week and had to give bonds of $500. I think the people of Michigan are imposed upon very much. I should not wonder if the inhabitants serve him in a rough way if the Senate confirm his appointment."[4]

On May 22, 1832, John Norvell wrote from Washington regarding Mason's appointment as secretary of the Michigan Territory, "Your confirmation is not certain but probable. In the event of your rejection, my office [postmaster at Detroit] will be offered to you."[5] Mason was confirmed by the Senate in May, and by 1833, his star was on the rise. The Michigan Territory was booming in population, and statehood advocates took Mason as their champion. At only twenty-one years of age, he already had more discipline than his father and well reflected a robust young territory in the boldness of his actions. The task of building a state government fell on him, and he relished the prospect of leading Michigan out of the wilderness and into the federation of states.

In the summer of 1834, after a two-year absence, the dreaded Asiatic cholera made its appearance in the Michigan Territory, claiming the life of Governor Porter. It is hard not to appreciate the irony of a chief executive so often absent from his state returning for a rare appearance only to be struck down on his home turf. Porter's death made Stevens T. Mason acting governor again. He immediately called a special session of the Legislative Council to expedite Michigan's admission to the Union.

In a letter of September 10, 1834, to Governor Littleton W. Tazewell of Virginia, apparently a family friend, Mason transmitted the resolutions of the Legislative Council of the Michigan Territory, declaring the right of the territory to form a permanent constitution and state government as soon as there were sixty thousand free inhabitants within the territory. He also traced the history of Michigan's and Ohio's land claims. The defining events of Stevens T. Mason's years as secretary and acting governor of the Michigan Territory were his strong advocacy of statehood and his defense of the Toledo Strip as rightfully belonging to Michigan. Believing he had right on his side, he stuck to his guns on the Toledo question.

On August 3, 1835, General Joseph Brown of the Michigan militia informed Mason he had it on good authority that Governor Robert Lucas was raising an armed force "of some magnitude" in Toledo to protect the court to be held there. Brown wrote, "It is the most busy season of the year and it will be almost impossible for us to raise many troops, and to make the attempt and fail will be political death to you, and disgrace to Michigan. But I have found in every part of Michigan the proper sentiment, and if you think it better to meet him on the threshold with a military force, I am ready for I am sure that it will be for my individual benefit. I should say wait, at least a few days, and see how strong the force we shall have. . . . I shall be in Monroe tomorrow and will wait further orders."[6] Still spoiling for a good fight, Mason agreed on the need for a state of readiness. On the other side of the line, James Thompson of Carrolton, Ohio, wrote to Lucas to say Carroll County would furnish two hundred men to protect Ohio citizens at the border.

In Washington, it was clear to Mason's mentor, Cass, which way the breeze was blowing from the White House. President Jackson respected his war secretary, but politics came first. It is not known whether Jackson suspected Cass of surreptitiously helping Mason in the Toledo War; in all likelihood, Jackson knew of Cass's sympathies but trusted him, as a cabinet officer, to take a neutral position. On August

11, however, Cass took the opportunity to warn Mason by letter that his failure to coincide with Jackson's policies could bring about his removal by the president. This was not the first warning Mason received on the subject. But strengthened by popular opinion, his own sense of what was right, and the prosecution of the war to date, Mason persisted on his course. On August 16, Cass was even more forceful in a "confidential" letter to Mason. Writing that he had a long talk with the secretary of state, John Forsyth, he confided, "I find he considers the declaration in the letter to the Ohio commissioner that the President will exert his constitutional powers to give effect to the Ohio proposition, as intended to convey the distinct idea, THAT IF YOU DO NOT COINCIDE IN THE VIEWS I SUGGESTED, YOU MUST BE REMOVED. Forsyth's personal feelings toward you are of the warmest nature, but he says a person must be there who will give affect to the views of the President."[7]

On the next day, the Michigan Legislative Council met in Detroit. Mason yielded a bit by telling the lawmakers that he could permit a rerunning of the boundary but that he could not recognize that Ohio had equal claim to the disputed tract. The council reiterated its rejection of the Rush-Howard proposals as accepted by Ohio. In other words, the council stood firm behind Mason.

As the court date promised by Lucas neared, things heated up again. On August 21, Mason wrote from the executive office in Detroit to Forsyth saying Michigan would resist by force any attempt by Ohio to exercise jurisdiction. "The authorities of Ohio are now collecting a force to sustain and protect the court about to be held by them on the disputed territory," said Mason, adding, "The general government must expect a serious collision, as the attempt to exercise jurisdiction will be resisted by Michigan."[8]

Mason was given a big boost on August 24, when he was notified that Michigan Democrats had nominated him as their gubernatorial candidate under the new state constitution. This was a great honor that Mason was proud to accept. On the following day, he ordered up a force of two hundred volunteers or, if that was impossible, the territorial militia. His orders for mounted men in the counties of Oakland, Macomb, Wayne, Lenawee, Washtenaw, and Monroe were "to organize and march to the village of Toledo, on or before September 1, two hundred mounted men to assist the sheriff of Monroe County in the execution of civil process." Mason added, "Volunteers will be preferred, but if not to be obtained, you are vested with full powers to order out the military under your command."[9] At this time, the *Detroit Free Press* reported the Legislative Council's appropriation of $315,000 "to meet any emergency which may arise," adding, "we learn that every arrangement will be made to afford a warm reception to any portion of the 'million' of Ohio, that may visit our borders. Michigan defends her soil and her rights, and we would wish our fellow-citizens of Ohio to recollect that 'thrice armed is he who hath his quarrel just.'"

Throughout the summer of 1835, Mason must have known the ax was poised above his head. There had been hints from Forsyth that his boss was displeased. There was Old Hickory's support for the Rush-Howard proposals, with its clear message for Mason to yield ground. There were Cass's pleas to avoid angering the president. As early as May 9, Cass was telling Mason, "A resort to blood would be a serious calamity." But armed force was what Mason was prepared to throw against Lucas.

The blow fell on August 29. Secretary of State Forsyth wrote Mason that Jackson had dismissed the latter from office because of his truculent position toward Ohio: "The President having maturely considered your recent communication to the Legislative Council of Michigan, in connection with other proceedings on your part, is brought, with regret, to the conclusion that your zeal for what you deem the rights of Michigan, has overcome that spirit of moderation and forbearance which, in the present irritated state of feeling prevailing in Ohio and Michigan is necessary to the preservation of the public peace. He finds himself constrained, therefore, by his sense of duty, to supersede you as secretary of the Territory of Michigan, and has appointed Charles Shaler of Pennsylvania to be your successor."[10] Communications being what they were, it would be September 10 before Mason learned he had been fired.

Of course, the real reason for Mason's removal was that Jackson could not afford to antagonize Ohio and lose its electoral votes. But were Jackson's political instincts failing him? Why did he fail to appoint a successor to Governor George Porter, dead since the summer of 1834? Jackson did nominate Henry D. Gilpin of Pennsylvania to the office of governor of the territory, but the Senate rejected the nomination in a close vote. Was Jackson building up acting governor Stevens T. Mason as a comer in Democratic Party ranks, only to find the dog bit-ing its master? As for Shaler, he immediately declined the post of secretary, thus providing another embarrassment to Jackson.

Jackson simply had to fire Mason to indicate presidential firmness after a lot of waffling on the subject. Old Hickory knew that Mason was immensely popular in Michigan, that he would likely be elected governor in October, and that Jackson's putative successor, Martin Van Buren, would have to deal with him later. The firing was all in the timing; Jackson had tipped his hand earlier that summer in his meetings with the Ohio trio of Disney, Allen, and Swayne. Perhaps Jackson reasoned that if he removed Mason now, the incident would have blown over by the time the presidential election rolled around, even given Mason's sure election as governor.

Incredibly enough, Jackson's letter of dismissal contained the statement that he had supported Michigan's position from the beginning of the discussion. He claimed to have thought that without further legislation on the part of Congress, the country in dispute should be considered as forming, legally, a part of the territory of Michigan and that "the ordinary and usual jurisdiction over it should be exercised by Michigan." Jackson, said Forsyth, "has never admitted the right set up by Ohio." In this, the views of Lewis Cass and Jackson were identical. Cass, too, pleaded to refrain from violence and the use of force. But the cynical Jackson was trying to have it both ways. How would it play in Michigan to hear that the president had been in their corner all along, that he supported his attorney general in the legal aspects of Michigan's claim, that he had stuck by his boy Mason as long as possible?

How disturbing this dispute was to Jackson may be seen in the range of his reactions. At first, he counseled forbearance and then a laissez-faire approach. Usually, he was of the mind to let Congress deal with it. When his hand was forced, he tilted toward Ohio, which still leads some in that state to credit Jackson with "settling" the Toledo War. For example, the *Columbus Western Hemisphere* credited Jackson with the peaceful holding of elections in the Toledo area in April, while the *Cincinnati Daily Gazette* and the *Ohio Monitor* held that it was Jackson's "single ipse dixit that stayed the military ardor of the Veteran of Ohio and the Lad of Michigan." On the other side of the border, the *Detroit Journal and Courier* joked about the "Ministers Plenipotentiary and Extraordinary, from Andrew the First, of the Empire of Uncle Sam." But as we can see from his letter dismissing Mason, Andrew Jackson's mind was like that of *Omnia Gallia*—divided into three parts. One part favored the status quo, one part agreed with Ohio, and the third wished Congress would put an end to the business. On another matter, Jackson did not want to deal with the slavery issue, either.

When word reached Michigan that the Boy Governor had been sacked, the reaction was one of outrage. The *Monroe Sentinel* reported a great citizens meeting of two thousand freemen, with Austin E. Wing of Monroe serving as president, expressing regret at the removal of Mason and terming Robert Lucas "a misguided old man." Mason's dismissal intensified pro-Mason and anti-Mason feeling in the Michigan Territory. His supporters were determined to hold out against Jackson. The anti-Masons, especially the Whigs, viewed his removal as a blessing. They opposed Mason, standing, on principle, against any compromise. They believed that statehood should follow a congressional enabling act and that Mason's go-it-alone stand was wrong.

Although the pretext for removing Mason was his excessive zeal, he was actually removed to purchase political peace for this troubled region, and Jackson now believed he had Ohio's electoral votes safely in his pocket. On October 5, the people of Michigan elected Stevens T. Mason the state's first governor, prompting Emily Mason to write, "My brother was deposed from office for one month, and then elected governor of the state."[11] Vindication was not long in coming for Tom Mason.

The Ohio point of view portrays Mason as the "goat" of the Toledo Strip controversy because he was sacked by the president. This is Mason as "the young Hotspur," Mason as a wet-behind-the-ears youth, Mason in over his head as acting governor. But when Michigan adopted its constitution and rejected compromise with Ohio, its act of defiance, as personalized in Mason's leadership, was embedded into history. It shows in the Great Seal of the State of Michigan, which gives 1835, not 1837, as the true date of Michigan's statehood.

CHAPTER THIRTEEN

STATEHOOD IN THE BALANCE

Never in the course of my life have I known a controversy of which
all the right was so clearly on one side, and all the power so over-
whelmingly on the other; never a case where the temptation was so
intense to take the strongest side, and the duty of taking the weakest
so thankless.

  —JOHN QUINCY ADAMS TO THE
  U.S. HOUSE OF REPRESENTATIVES

We bow to the power but question the right.

  —JOHN R. WILLIAMS, DELEGATE TO THE SECOND
  CONVENTION OF ASSENT IN ANN ARBOR

At this point, it is necessary to briefly depart from the Toledo War to carry through the other important thread of our story. When we last visited the statehood issue, delegates to a constitutional convention unauthorized by Congress had begun its work in Detroit. The convention opened on May 11, 1835, and worked for thirty-eight days, producing a document remarkable for its time. All the while, the Toledo War was occupying the minds and hearts of the delegates. Governor Stevens T. Mason was ardently pushing statehood, but there could be no state without a fundamental charter to present to Congress.

Michigan framed a constitution that summer and elected state officials later in the year, without the usual enabling act from Congress. Lacking this crucial support, Michigan must have come off as a kind of troublesome child among legislators in the federal capital. Still, it had friends who were willing to stick their necks out on principle. One of these was John Quincy Adams of Massachusetts, the sixth president of the United States, who was extending his political life and public service to the nation in the House of Representatives. Adams did not always rub folks the right way, but because he was an Adams and a member of a handful of New England families who were presumed to talk directly to God, he was listened to and respected.

A new session of Congress had begun its duties in December 1834. Michigan was back knocking on the door, demanding enabling legislation. The difference now was that Governors Mason and Lucas were getting ready to put their militias on full alert in the Toledo Strip. In January 1835, the boundary bill, which had been before the Senate for two years already, was up for debate. The bill, which set the northern boundary of Ohio in favor of Ohio, was read for a third time and passed.

On the other side of the Capitol, the subject of boundaries was up for debate on February 9, when Adams rose in the House of Representatives as a defender of Michigan's rights. He said, "These are the terms [Article V of the Northwest Ordinance] of the compact—a compact as binding as any that was ratified by God in heaven. They [Ohio] call upon you to repeal this provision [southern boundary established by the Northwest Ordinance] to declare that it is not binding, to say that this shall not be the line and to establish a different one. And why? Because it suits their convenience, and the convenience of these states that the line should be altered."[1] One can imagine this pillar of New England public life, all rectitude and propriety, remonstrating his colleagues with rheumy eyes and then resuming his seat to polite applause. His remarks were published in the *National Intelligencer* newspaper. Published in Philadelphia, this publication was considered to be the house organ of President Andrew Jackson's National Democratic Party.

When Adams referred to "the convenience of these states," he was including Indiana and Illinois, because both had breached the southern boundary of the line established by the Northwest Ordinance. On April 19, 1816, Congress passed an enabling act for Indiana and set its northern boundary to include ten miles of Lake Michigan frontage, thus satisfying the state's desire for a lake port. No one in Congress cared about the subject, and Michigan was not yet represented. The resolution for admission of Indiana into the Union, as the nineteenth state, was approved by President James Madison on December 11, 1816. The area claimed by Indiana from the Michigan Territory had never been organized by Michigan and was in fact barren wilderness. Two years later, Illinois violated the ordinance line by moving it sixty miles north to include Fort Dearborn, now Chicago. The admission of Illinois into the Union in 1818 fulfilled one major provision of the Northwest Ordi-

nance, that of dividing the Old Northwest into "not less than three nor
more than five states." The vast region to the north of the three states of
Ohio, Indiana, and Illinois remained in territorial status until such time
as two more states would be created. Michigan's statehood would pre-
date that of Wisconsin, the last of five states to be created.

After his February argument before the House, Adams was not
finished with the boundary question. An entry in his diary on March 18,
1835, records his feelings on the issue: "Never in my life have I taken in
public controversies a part more suicidal to my own popularity than on
the present occasion. The people of Ohio, Indiana and Illinois will hate
me with perfect hatred for crossing their interests. The people of
Michigan may pass cold resolutions of approbation or of thanks to me
for espousing their cause, and then forget me. In its consequences I
have no compensation in prospect but the bare consciousness of having
done my duty."[2] At one point in Congress's slow deliberation of Michigan statehood, Adams successfully moved that the Michigan-Ohio
boundary question be referred to a select committee, with himself as
chairman. Other procedural moves worked against Michigan; at one
time, the House got tangled up on the question of abolishing slavery in
the District of Columbia when it should have been speeding Michigan's
application.

The former president was not alone in championing Michigan, but
he was among the most vocal and eloquent. He would remind his colleagues that a House committee in 1835 had voted 6–1 that the state of
Ohio had no right to the disputed territory. They had believed that
Michigan was entitled to it "by every law, human and divine."

In early 1835, Michigan's strong legal claim to the Toledo Strip,
buttressed by an opinion from the country's top legal officer, along with
votes Adams mentioned, did not sway Congress. Because of special interest lobbying, it was unwilling to consider statehood for Michigan
apart from the border issue. Statehood for Michigan clearly stood on its
merits, but right was no match for money and politics. Ohio and Indiana, with generous help from Washington, were carrying out plans for
the Wabash and Erie Canal, designed to link Lake Erie with the Ohio
River at Evansville, Indiana.

By the summer of 1835, Michigan's bid for statehood was in the cat-
egory of old news. What really got the nation's attention was the Toledo
War and Michigan's determination to press for statehood without pre-

liminary approval from Congress. The Toledo War landed on President Jackson's desk with a thud, and the eastern press started taking sides in the Michigan-Ohio dispute, with much of the opinion favorable to Michigan. The anti-Jackson newspapers delighted in Old Hickory's embarrassment at having two fellow Democrats (Lucas and Mason) roundly condemning each other. With a national election looming the next year, Jackson wanted his anointed successor, Martin Van Buren, to continue Jacksonian policies.

On October 5, 1835, the people of Michigan voted 6,299–1,359 to ratify the constitution put forth by the constitutional convention delegates. A full slate of state officials was elected, including Stevens T. Mason as governor. Isaac E. Crary was elected representative to Congress, and the state legislature picked Lucius Lyon of Kalamazoo and John Norvell of Detroit as U.S. senators. Lyon wrote to a friend, Edwin Crosswill, in Albany, New York, "I have the pleasure to inform you that I have been elected, by the unanimous vote of both houses of the legislature to a seat in the Senate of the United States, whenever Michigan may be admitted into the Union. John Norvell, postmaster of this city, has been elected my colleague."[3]

For all intents and purposes, Michigan was then a state. On November 1, the legislature convened to elect officers. Two weeks later, the legislature adjourned until February 1, 1836, in the hope that Congress would admit Michigan to the Union in the meantime. Although Michigan's official date of entry into the Union is given as January 26, 1837, the date rendered on the Great Seal of the State of Michigan is November 2, 1835. The seal was designed by Lewis Cass and presented to the constitutional convention for adoption on June 2, 1835. However, one writer, Alec R. Gilpin, dates statehood from July 18, 1836, when the Michigan Senate confirmed Governor Mason's nomination of Supreme Court justices. Chief Justice William A. Fletcher and associate justices George Morell and Epaphroditus Ransom were Mason's picks. According to Gilpin, "If Michigan had a legal government before admission in 1837," it dates to this day in 1836, "when the third branch of government was organized, not from November, 1835."[4]

In December 1835, the battle for statehood began again in the Twenty-fourth Congress which opened that month. Lyon, Norvell, and Crary were on hand to take their seats. President Jackson sent both houses a message including a copy of Michigan's freshly minted consti-

Lucius Lyon at age 50. Michigan's first U.S. senator, Lyon helped to get the western Upper Peninsula attached to Michigan to compensate for the loss of the Toledo Strip. (Courtesy of Bentley Historical Library, University of Michigan.)

tution and documents concerning the boundary controversy. An optimistic Lyon wrote to E. D. Ellis of Monroe, "I find the members of Congress as well as the cabinet as favorably disposed toward the admission of Michigan into the Union as could be expected. It will probably be made a party question, but I think the State will be recognized as early as February. Ex-president Adams will take charge of the matter in the House."[5] Lyon's upbeat mood was echoed in the territorial capital of Detroit. Michigan was a new state, with its representatives ready to partake in national business. Statehood seemed to be there for the taking. The young lion, Stevens T. Mason, was idolized throughout the territory for standing up to Robert Lucas in the border war and for being such a strong champion of statehood.

But disillusionment and despair soon set in. At the end of December, Lyon was singing a different tune from the cheerful ditty he had sung in his letter of December 6 to Ellis. Now he wrote to Allen Hutchins of Adrian, "I need not inform you that from present appearances Michigan will have to give way to the interests of Ohio and the two states [Illinois and Indiana] leagued with her. Mr. J. Q. Adams made yesterday in the House one of the best and most thrilling speeches I ever heard on the subject, but all to no purpose; the iron arm of power disposed of the matter, so as to best suit the 'millions of freemen.'"[6] Lyon here gets in a dig at Governor Lucas and his constituency. What happened in the short space of three weeks to alter Lyon's outlook?

On December 10, Senator Thomas Hart Benton of Missouri presented the credentials of Senators-elect Lyon and Norvell and moved that seats be given to them until Congress acted on admission. After considerable debate, the motion failed. Six days later, the motion again failed, with the opposition led by Henry Clay of Kentucky. The duly elected trio from Michigan, which included Crary in the House, was relegated to spectator status and compelled to listen, without any chance to reply, as an Ohio congressman set forth that state's claims to the Toledo Strip. Michigan's bid for statehood was off to a bad start.

At about this time (in all likelihood, early in 1836), a rumor started that Michigan might be forced to exchange the Toledo Strip for lands north of the Straits of Mackinac. In the Senate, the bill to admit Michigan was referred to a select committee chaired by Benton. From this committee emerged, in due time, the compromise, unpalatable to Michigan, giving Ohio its Harris line boundary and granting Michigan a large area of the Upper Peninsula.

One of Lyon's first acts as senator-elect was to address a letter to John M. Clayton of Delaware, chairman of the Senate Judiciary Committee, asking for the privilege of appearing before the committee. The Michigan position was argued by Lyon, the Ohio position by Representative Samuel F. Vinton from that state. When all the arguments were heard, Senator William Preston of South Carolina inquired how much territory lay west of Lake Michigan. He remarked that the peninsula of Michigan was an unequal division of the remaining territory and that the country west of the lake was too large for one state. He put his finger on a map that hung conveniently nearby and drew along it the line that now forms the boundary between Michigan and Wisconsin, remarking that he thought that would be a fair division of the country. Lyon protested strongly against that division of the territory. He said that Michigan did not wish to extend the state beyond the limits of the Lower Peninsula, arguing that "for a greater part of the year nature had separated the Upper and Lower Peninsulas by impassable barriers" and that "there never could be any identity of interest or community of feelings between them."[7]

Although history is sketchy on who first suggested that Michigan be given a huge chunk of the Upper Peninsula as a consolation prize for the Toledo Strip, it seems fairly certain that Preston suggested such a swap with either Lyon or Lewis Cass sometime in February 1836. And it was not so much a "suggestion" as an ultimatum. The hard reality was that Michigan was going to be stripped of the Toledo Strip.

Lyon was still taking a hard line as the new year dawned. "We shall never acknowledge the power of Congress to take from us the tract claimed by Ohio," he wrote to O. D. Richardson of Pontiac. That same day, in a letter to A. S. Schoolcraft of Detroit, he wrote, "The prospects of Michigan look dubious so far as relates to her southern boundary."[8] Epaphroditus Ransom, a future governor of Michigan, wrote to Lyon from Bronson on January 19, 1836, "If we are not admitted as a state, what follows? We should . . . go forward and organize our state government, fully, a sovereign and independent state, and if Congress does not decide it proper to receive us into the Union, let us go on by ourselves."[9] Lyon did not see things in quite those terms. "Flagrant as the wrong it is," he wrote to Charles C. Hascall of the Michigan State Senate, "it will probably be better to submit to it than attempt a revolution in which we must eventually be overpowered."[10]

In mid-January, Norvell and Crary wrote to Mason, saying their hopes for a rapid admission to the Union had disappeared. They wrote of the "spirit of avarice and territorial aggrandizement" that characterized the governments of Ohio and Indiana. It must have been a bitter series of disappointments for these two men to observe congressmen from Ohio and Indiana joining forces against Michigan. At one point, Indiana even suggested that Ohio press for a northern boundary parallel to Indiana's own, thereby potentially depriving Michigan of even more territory.

January 1836 found the admission bill locked in the judiciary committees of both houses of Congress. It was becoming a foregone conclusion that a compromise harmful to Michigan interests would be effected before the admission bill would pass. Michigan would have to cede the Toledo Strip if it were to enter the Union. In his address to the people of Michigan on February 1, 1836, Governor Mason said, "We have been deceived."[11] Reaction to the done deal was immediate and hostile, as Toledo was perceived as vital to Michigan's future growth, whereas territory north of the forty-fifth parallel was regarded as fit only for Eskimos and polar bears.

Meanwhile, Lyon was carrying on a vigorous correspondence on the subject. On February 4, he wrote to Colonel Daniel Goodwin of

Detroit, "The committee . . . will be willing to give us all the country west of Lake Michigan and north and east of the Menominee River of Green Bay and the Montreal river of Lake Superior, which may at some future time be valuable. If the southern boundary should be broken, I for one shall go in for all the country Congress will give us west of the lakes."[12] Writing to Colonel Andrew Mack of Detroit on February 21, Lyon repeated what he said to Goodwin about "going in for all the country we can get on Lake Superior and Michigan." Predicting that in a few days, the House Judiciary Committee would report "against us and in favor of Ohio" on the boundary question, Lyon wrote, "I understand Messrs. Norvell and Crary are opposed to this addition and will try to prevent it. My opinion is that within twenty years the addition here proposed will be valued by Michigan at more than forty millions of dollars, and that even after ten years the State would not think of selling it for that sum. When compelled by the strong arm of power most unjustly to give up and yield to the gigantic state of Ohio a part of our territory on the south, I can perceive no good reason why, under the circumstances, we should not receive all Congress are willing to give us elsewhere."[13]

Lyon was right on both scores: Michigan would soon come to value its frozen tundra north of the straits, and John Norvell and Isaac Crary were against giving up the Toledo Strip. So now the Michigan delegation in Congress was split on the issue of the land swap, which must have been cause for rejoicing in Ohio. Lyon caught a fair amount of criticism for his turnabout in position; back home, he was perceived by some as selling out Michigan's interests. But in this, Lyon proved to be far more of a statesman and visionary than his colleagues, who, not wanting to view themselves as traitors, merely went with the flow of popular opinion. Norvell and Crary found it easier to knuckle under to the incorporators and stockholders of the two Michigan railroads that were in the planning stages at the time. John Biddle, who had served as president of Michigan's constitutional convention, came right out and accused Lyon of selling out. But Lyon was the only one who demanded compensation for the loss of Toledo, and he is entitled to much of the credit for gaining the Upper Peninsula.

The proposition to give Michigan something for ceding Toledo may also have had Ohio origins. In any event, the idea must have come to the attention of Lyon's old friend Cass, who had visited the north

country and knew something of its nature and of its rich mineral re-
sources. He and Henry R. Schoolcraft, a noted geologist, had explored the Michigan Territory in 1820, and Schoolcraft knew the area thoroughly. During the statehood hearings, Schoolcraft appeared before a Senate committee to describe the region, expressing the opinion that it will be "found of far greater value and importance to the State than the seven mile strip surrendered."[14] Having visited portions of the Upper Peninsula as a surveyor, Lyon had undoubtedly heard of its mineral wealth, timber resources, and rich fisheries. Lyon's correspondence clearly indicated that he knew Michigan would lose on the south and that he was in favor of the northern addition. It would also give Michigan an imposing appearance on the map.

So Lyon "went in for all he could get on the north."[15] Doubtless, he was encouraged by Cass and Schoolcraft, particularly the former, who was anxious that the dispute should in some manner be adjusted as speedily as possible and who knew that Michigan would not regret the exchange of territory once the true value of the Upper Peninsula became known. Cass, former territorial governor, had influence in Congress as a cabinet officer, and it is easy to imagine him making the rounds in Washington City, working a congressman here and a senator there for an enlarged Michigan. Astute politicians in reading the tea leaves, both Lyon and Cass urged the exchange of the Toledo Strip for several thousand square miles of frozen north, because it was clear to them that statehood was dead in the water until Michigan consented to giving up Toledo.

By March, the respective committees in both Houses had done their work, and their reports went before Congress. On March 1, 1836, the Senate Judiciary Committee reported in favor of Ohio on the proposal of the Ohio boundary; the committee cited eleven maps of an earlier period to prove that Ohio's contention was correct. On March 12, writing to Zina Pitcher at Fort Monroe, Virginia, Lyon sent a copy of the report of the Judiciary Committee on the boundary question. "It agrees with the report of the committee of the House," Lyon said, "and both show beyond all question that practically there is no such thing as morality or honesty in politics." He explained, "All parties are courting the electoral votes of Ohio, Indiana and Illinois and poor Michigan must be sacrificed."[16] Michigan's position as the sacrificial lamb appears in another letter by Lyon, written to A. E. Wing of Monroe on March 19: "There is a fixed determination to sacrifice us by each party in a manner that shall be most acceptable to Ohio. It is really too bad. An honest man after looking on here a month or two would laugh at himself for having ever supposed that the merits of a question like this could have anything to do with the decision of Congress upon it."[17]

From March to June 1836, Congress reviewed committee reports that supported Ohio's claim to the Toledo Strip. The same arguments were set forth. What Congress did not study—nor did it need to—was the five-hundred-pound gorilla lurking just outside the door, in the form of Ohio's big bloc of electoral votes so important to the Democrats and Martin Van Buren. The debate on admission of Michigan dragged on, with Southern senators resorting to delaying tactics designed to postpone the admission of Michigan until Arkansas, a slave state, also was ready. A Senate bill to fix the boundary to suit Ohio, Illinois, and Indiana was defeated in the House, largely through the efforts of John Quincy Adams. The often tedious debate in the Senate came to a close on April 2, 1836, when the amended Benton compromise bill was passed.

Back in Michigan, the legislature convened on February 1, 1836. One of its acts before adjourning in March was to authorize payment of the militia that had been involved in the Toledo War. In his address to lawmakers, Governor Mason conveyed a great sense of bitterness and frustration over the statehood issue.

> It would have afforded me the highest satisfaction, fellow citizens, to have been able to communicate to you at this time the favorable result of our application for admission into the Union. The people of Michigan have been deceived. Their application remains without the final action of Congress.
>
> The position which Michigan now occupies is a peculiar although not a new one in the history of our government. It is that of a people claiming and exercising all the reserved rights and privileges of an American state, and yet excluded from the bonds of the federal Union. This state of things is deeply to be deplored and its continuation must lead to the most unfavorable results to our permanent welfare as a nation.[18]

In his address, Mason traced recent territorial history. In 1832, the Legislative Council passed a law seeking the judgment of the people on the expediency of forming a state government. The result was a vote in the affirmative. Mason explained, "Petitions were for several years, presented to Congress seeking approbation and support of the general government; asking for passage of enabling legislation for Michigan to form a permanent Constitution and state government. Their repeated applications were unsuccessful, not receiving the action of Congress." In 1834, the Legislative Council authorized a census. Nearly eighty-five thousand inhabitants were counted. Application to Congress was again renewed and again disregarded. Mason explained that the Legislative Council, weary of rejection and despairing of Congress, "in obedience to public sentiment and under the authority of the Ordinance of 1787," then passed an act on January 24, 1835, "to enable the people of Michigan to form a Constitution and state government."[19] A convention met in May 1835 and drafted a charter. The question now, said Mason, was whether the people had the right to adopt this constitution without the previous authority of Congress. In Michigan's defense, Mason brought up that in 1796, Tennessee formed a permanent constitution and state government without the previous authority of Congress and was admitted into the Union as an independent state.

After lamenting Indiana's successful raid on Michigan's lands, Mason made a pitch for settlement of boundaries by the Supreme Court, a restatement of an old position. As for Ohio, he said, "We have nothing to yield, but will endeavor to maintain our jurisdiction. If the territory in contestation does not legally belong to Ohio, the time has passed when Congress have a right to present it to her as a gift on the exclusive grounds of expediency." Michigan, concluded Mason, is "a state without a country."[20] He was fortified in his position by resolutions passed at a public meeting of the inhabitants of LaSalle Township in Monroe County on March 17, 1836, against any compromise seeking to resolve the boundary question by surrendering any of the rights of Michigan. A day later, in a resolution to Congress, 108 citizens of the township of Whiteford gave vent to their feelings about the land swap: "The proposed alteration would be robbing the poor and feeble to aggrandize the rich and powerful, for the State of Ohio, with its million of freemen, is large in territory and rich in resources, while Michigan has a population of but little more than 100,000, with one half of her territory sterile and comparatively worthless. Your memorialists are not willing to sell their birthright for a mess of pottage on the frozen and sterile shores of Lake Superior, which are not naturally connected with Michigan, and could be of no use to her as part of her State."[21]

In a letter to his friend E. D. Ellis of Monroe, Lucius Lyon wrote, "I have always said that I did not believe the legislature or the people of Michigan would consent to the change of boundary proposed by Congress; if, however, they should think it better to do so than forever to remain out of the Union either as a territory or an independent sovereignty, we ought to be well compensated for the injustice done us in compelling us to adopt so injurious and degrading an alternative."[22] On March 22, 1836, Senator Benton of Missouri reported out of the select committee a bill to admit Michigan to the Union. In the ensuing debate, Michigan saw its chances of retaining the Toledo Strip fade. The bill established the Harris line as the southern boundary of Michigan and established a line along the Menominee and Montreal rivers as its boundary with the territory of Wisconsin. Committee members gave to Michigan the western portion of the Upper Peninsula as a consolation prize for the loss of the Toledo Strip.

There was more. Insult was added to injury. Ohio was determined that Michigan should specifically accept the Harris line. An amendment was attached stating that Michigan would be admitted only after a majority of delegates elected by the people to a special convention should give their consent to the terms of the bill. In other words, Michigan would be given the green light for statehood if delegates to a convention of assent would accept the boundary compromise. It made no difference that Michigan was already a functioning state, that its constitution was republican in character, that its population exceeded the requirement of sixty thousand free inhabitants, or that its elected representatives were cooling their heels in Congress, waiting to be seated. And it made no difference that most of Washington's politicians probably agreed with John Quincy Adams's assessment of the matter, even if they did not vote that way.

This flawed bill passed the Senate on April 2, 1836, on a vote of 24–17, and was sent to the House. Adams again took up the cudgel for Michigan, in a lengthy speech during which he said, "Never in the course of my life have I known a controversy of which all the right was so clearly on one side, and all the power so overwhelmingly on the other; never a case where the temptation was so intense to take the strongest side, and the duty of taking the weakest so thankless."[23] Adams's speech failed to sway the House. The amended statehood bill passed that body, 143–50. On June 13, both the Michigan and Arkansas admission bills were approved by Congress. When President Jackson signed the Michigan statehood bill on June 15, 1836, it was, in Adams's clever turn of words, "in air perfumed with the 35 electoral votes of Ohio, Indiana and Illinois."[24] Adams's point was not lost. The act signed by Jackson was "an act to establish the northern boundary of Ohio, and to provide for the admission of the State of Michigan upon the conditions therein expressed."[25] That wording struck some as peculiar, given that Michigan was not a state in the eyes of the federal government and would not be for another seven months. In terms of real estate, Michigan yielded 468 square miles of rich farmland and swamp along its southern border for about nine thousand square miles of poor country in the Upper Peninsula.

One historian, Charles Grim, says, "The compromise offered to Michigan by the U.S. government was one of the shrewdest real estate deals of all time."[26] As historian of the Williams County Historical Society in Ohio, Grim suggests that the land deal was at Ohio's expense, even though Ohio was at the time considered the victorious party to the border dispute. The exchange of the Upper Peninsula for Toledo may not rank among such outstanding examples of getting something for nothing as the Louisiana Purchase and Seward's fire-sale purchase of Alaska, but for Michiganians today, the consensus is that Ohio got flimflammed in the deal. Another Ohio historian, W. V. Way, writes, "Congress gave Michigan the valuable mineral lands adjoining Lake Superior to make up the loss of the Territory given to Ohio; both parties thereby acquiring lands that neither had any legal right to, after having exhibited their prowess in a war without bloodshed."[27]

When the news of Congress's action reached Michigan, there were bitter attacks on the terms the bill contained. Signing off on Toledo in exchange for "a sterile region on the shores of Lake Superior" was deemed to be an act of sheerest folly. Many people believed Michigan had exchanged productive farmland and a window on Lake Erie for a wilderness of untamed Indians, as well as "selling out" those people who lived in the Toledo Strip. A former member of the legislature observed: "The Upper Peninsula isn't worth eighteen pence."[28]

Edward D. Ellis wrote to Senator Lyon, "I am willing to accede to Indiana, since I can see no way to help ourselves, but to yield to Ohio, it is what never will do, even though we should be reduced into a state of colonial vassalage for a century to come. The idea of assenting [to demands of Ohio as a condition for admission to Union] and then declaring our act a nullity would be unbecoming a Democratic community."[29] In a similar vein, delegates from several townships in Monroe County met on April 11 to address a bill in Congress that would "dismember" Michigan of a valuable portion of its territory as the price of admission into the Union. "Be it resolved," said the delegates, "that we rely on the Ordinance of 1787 and the Constitution of the U.S. for the preservation of the integrity of our territorial boundary." The *Detroit Free Press* called Michigan's newest acquisition "a region of perpetual snows," and the newspaper did not have winter sports enthusiasts in mind. It did not help that some residents of the remote region petitioned to be part of a new territory extending along the southern shore of Lake Superior, anticipating halfhearted petitions in the twentieth century for secession from Michigan to form a state of Superior.

Technically, Michigan did not get the Upper Peninsula in exchange for Toledo. The eastern portion of the Upper Peninsula had been considered to be part of Michigan even before the territory was established in 1805. Sault Ste. Marie, one of the oldest cities in the United States, had close economic ties with fur trading posts in the Lower Peninsula and at the Straits of Mackinac. The eastern one-third of the Upper Peninsula was Michigan before the Toledo War.

Senator Lyon said of the Upper Peninsula, "There we can raise our own Indians for all time to come and supply ourselves now and then with a little bear meat for a delicacy."[30] Someone else opined that the whitefish of Lake Superior might be a fair offset for "the lost bullfrog pastures of the Maumee." Eventually, as mentioned earlier, Lyon argued that Michigan got the better of the deal. He predicted that the Upper Peninsula would be worth forty million dollars in twenty years.

While the pressure from Michigan remained strong against the acceptance of anything that looked like a compromise, and although Norvell and Crary went with the flow of adverse public opinion, Lyon and Cass worked behind the scenes, with Schoolcraft encouraging them. This trio stood up against the blasts of negativity and hostile journalism. They secured for Michigan that region beyond the straits, predating by thirty years "Seward's Folly," the purchase of Alaska for a pittance, which proved to be of inestimable value despite the bleatings of the naysayers who cast Alaska as a region of perpetual snows.

Congress found it expedient to oppose statehood for Michigan on political grounds, of course, but also working against Michigan were fresh

memories of the Toledo War and of Michigan's role as alleged provoca-
teur of that dispute, given the Hotspur nature of Michigan's young governor. The arrest of Ohio officials and the violence that attended the
border war were remembered when it came time to discipline one of the
parties. It is always easier to administer the rod to a territory than to a
state. A political coalition of Whigs, congressmen (from Illinois, Indiana, and Ohio), and Southerners administered the coup de grâce.
Michigan's delegation to Congress could only listen in frustrated silence. A publication of the Michigan History Division would later report, "The southerly end of Lake Michigan did lie to the south of
Toledo, but in Washington in the 1830s political considerations could
bend surveyors' quadrants."[31]

Michigan was victimized by the double standard. When President
Jackson signed the statehood bills for Arkansas and Michigan, one state
was accepted unconditionally, while the other had conditions attached.
It was harsh medicine for Michigan to yield its rights to Ohio, but it was
bitter gall to be required to give its assent as a condition of statehood.
This is what is known in football as "piling on."

The same day Jackson signed the Michigan bill into law, with its
proviso for a convention of assent, Congress passed an act dividing federal surplus money. In these days of massive deficits, it is hard to believe
that there was once an excess of money in the federal treasury. Jackson's
last year in office would be marked by a division of federal largesse. But
there was a catch—no surplus dollars would be distributed to territories.
Michigan wanted its share of those excess federal funds before Jackson
left office and the deadline expired. Michigan politicians proved the rule
that money talks. Despite the onerous terms of the statehood bill, Governor Mason and other of the state's politicians moved to position the
state for the dollars it believed were rightfully its own. Economics—the
lure of lucre—drove the decision by Michigan to say yes to the unpalatable compromise brokered by Congress.

Michigan would receive about four hundred thousand dollars as its
share of surplus federal revenue. Other inducements were the prospect
of getting 5 percent of net proceeds from the sale of public lands within
Michigan's boundaries after it became a state. Additionally, there would
be patronage for "deserving" campaign contributors. Mason's Democratic Party, feeling victory beyond its reach, opted for acceptance of the
terms imposed by Congress. But opposition Whigs, confident of the
state's solid claim to Toledo, advocated holding out for justice, presum-

ably meaning an appeal to the Supreme Court. Both parties agreed that the Upper Peninsula was isolated, accessible only by water, and cut off from the capital of Detroit for six months of the year.

On July 11, Governor Mason called a special session of the legislature in Detroit to consider the compromise passed by Congress. In his message, he said that Congress had accepted Michigan's constitution and had agreed to admit the territory as a state, on condition that a convention of delegates elected for that purpose ratify the Harris line as the true boundary. Mason forcefully stated his belief that Congress had acted unjustly, but he agreed to abide by the decision of the people—a clear sign that he favored acceptance.

Two weeks later, the legislature approved an act authorizing the election of delegates to meet at a special convention in Ann Arbor on the second Monday in September to decide whether or not to accept statehood on Congress's terms. Ann Arbor, the site of the state's first public university, was a good compromise for the location of the convention. Detroit would not have been a good choice, because it was too closely associated with Mason's party in power. Instead, the convention would be held near the lands in dispute. That summer, Mason ordered yet another survey of the boundary. This survey confirmed the Fulton line and served to vindicate Mason's claim to the disputed territory.

As the September election neared, those favoring acceptance of the terms for statehood were mostly liberal Democrats, who argued that the state's southern boundary was now a dispute with the United States, not with Ohio. They stressed the potential value of the Upper Peninsula and said that Michigan needed to tap into the sale of public lands and the federal surplus. The Democrats felt that there was nothing to be gained by rejecting Congress.

Opposing Mason and standing on principle against any compromise, the Whigs favored rejection of the terms for statehood. They wanted to block Michigan from voting for Democrat Martin Van Buren in the upcoming national election, and they did not want elected Democrats Lyon, Norvell, and Crary seated. Besides, the Whigs said, not being in the Union means no federal taxes and no military service. As for the Upper Peninsula, the Whigs said it was too remote, with bad soil to boot. Newspapers of the day were fairly evenly divided. The *Ann Arbor Argus, Democratic Free Press,* and *Tecumseh Democrat* were in favor of statehood on the terms dictated by Congress; the *Detroit Advertiser, Pontiac Courier,* and *Monroe Sentinel* were against.

The election was September 12. On September 26, the delegates met in the Washtenaw County Courthouse in Ann Arbor, where a historical marker sits today. With only one question on the agenda, albeit a hotly contested one, the delegates could not indulge in the politicians' pastime of horse trading. This was a straight, vote-it-up-or-down matter. Still, there were points to be made. Delegates expressed resentment of the fact that Arkansas had been granted statehood unconditionally on the same day that Michigan had been offered admission only on terms that many found insulting and injurious to the state. To delegates, it appeared as though Ohio had succeeded in rubbing Michigan's nose in it. Emotions ran high because Ann Arbor was so near to the Toledo Strip, many of whose residents felt they had been betrayed.

From the *Journal of Proceedings* dated Tuesday, September 27, we read that Edward D. Ellis of Monroe presented a communication from Ira Smith and thirty others, "inhabitants of Toledo, in the disputed territory, claiming to be citizens of Michigan, and as such asking for protection."[32] Ellis, Robert Clark of Monroe, Wm. H. Welch of Kalamazoo, Seth Markham of Washtenaw, and S. A. L. Warner of Oakland signed their names on an address to the people of Michigan from the state convention at Ann Arbor. The flowery prose is a delight to read.

Shall our long and fondly cherished hopes be disappointed? Must Michigan participate in the national councils [if at all] mutilated, humbled and disgraced? Must she sell a portion of her brethren, like Joseph into Egypt, as the price of admission? No! Congress cannot bestow upon Ohio and part of our domain without our consent. . . .

Not content with her [Ohio's] own princely domains, she like the lordly Ahab of old, also covets the vineyards of poor Naboth— and we regret to say that Jezebels are not wanting who would willingly re-enact the tragical scenes of that sanguinary drama. When she [Ohio] found she could not gain her purpose by whining, she had recourse to blustering and bravado, talking of her million of freemen, and proceeded at once to nullify the Act of Congress of 1805, by erecting counties and townships within our territory, appointing officers and organizing courts of justice, etc. And in order to support this system of nullification, her chief magistrate ordered out a part of his "million" and boldly advanced within five or six miles of the true boundary line between Ohio and Michigan, and there made a glorious display of military prowess at a safe distance from the line claimed by the refractory inhabitants of Michigan.[33]

Forty-nine delegates representing twenty-seven counties debated for four days. On September 30, the vote was called, and the tally was 28–21 to reject Congress. Wayne and Lenawee counties voted for; Washtenaw, Livingston, Oakland, and Monroe counties voted no. The winners excoriated the expediency of linking the admission of Michigan to the "avarice" of Ohio. In a letter to John Quincy Adams, William Woodbridge, Michigan's leading Whig, said, "Our condition will be difficult, delicate and anomalous." As long as Michigan was not a state, it had no force to exert its will. But the Whigs held fast under a "moral obligation to insist upon our compact rights."

The vote was a blow to Mason and to the strong supporters of "statehood now." The vote left a bad feeling, like flat beer. Second-guessers had a field day. There clearly was not anything to be gained by thumbing one's nose at Congress, and it was just as obvious that Ohio was not going to be evicted from the Toledo Strip. Moreover, if Martin Van Buren was going to be the next president, Michigan could expect no help from that quarter. If Michigan were to claim its share of the federal surplus (four hundred thousand dollars was a lot of money in those days), it needed to be in the Union by early January 1837. In the aftermath of the vote at the First Convention of Assent, there was agitation to do something—anything—to get the would-be state onto a level playing field. Mason was urged to take some kind of official action. What followed was equal parts trickery, political doublespeak, and blatant illegality. It did not matter, because Congress eventually went along with the whole tainted piece of business.

Mason took the lead. He balked at calling another convention, and there was no time to bring the legislature back for a special session. He did not want to thwart the will of the people as it was expressed at the convention in Ann Arbor. But how was Mason to get around it? Successful, pragmatic politicians find the means to a desired end. Mason was driven by the goal of statehood, and he had been frustrated, time and again, by circumstances beyond his control. He had been beaten up in the Whig press prior to the convention, for being outsmarted politically by the wily Lucas of Ohio and for being too eager to accept the

proposal offered by Congress. So Mason, who circumvented Congress
in citing the "Tennessee precedent" for pushing statehood, figured he
could also circumvent the decision of the people at the convention of assent. In a remarkable display of doublespeak, he allowed as how the
people—in whom all sovereign power resides—had the right to over-
turn the decision of the convention if they found it "prejudicial to their
interests." Far be it from me, Mason seemed to be saying, to prevent
"spontaneous" gatherings of the people to demand another vote on the
question of statehood on Congress's terms. Right on cue, Michigan
Democrats initiated a movement to reconsider the decision of the convention. Mason did not quite come around to endorsing the venture,
but he did not fool anyone about where he came down on the subject.

On October 29,1836, the Democratic Party convention in Wayne
County urged meetings in all counties to persuade the people to call for
an election of delegates to a second convention of assent. Democrats in
Washtenaw, under the leadership of Ezekiel Pray, were not far behind in
support. A letter from Mason to Pray, reprinted in the *Michigan Argus*
on November 13, 1836, put it this way:

> It is asked if the proceedings of the late Ann Arbor convention are
> final upon the people of Michigan, and if there is no appeal from
> their decision. The answer is plain. The remedy is with the people
> themselves. They have an inherent and indefeasible right . . . to re-
> verse the acts of their agents if found prejudicial to their interests.
> If the people of Michigan are averse to the decisions of the late
> Ann Arbor convention, they possess the right and power to reverse
> it. No previous act of a convention precludes its acceptance by the
> people at a subsequent day.
>
> If the people are determined to make another effort for the ad-
> mission of the state previous to January, I would suggest that they
> take the measure into their own hands, and by delegates elected
> among themselves, they form a convention for the purposes con-
> templated by Congress. No one can question their right to do so.
> No one can impede their proceedings.[34]

Again as if on cue, Mason received a petition of about fifty-five signatures from the citizens of Bellevue in Calhoun County, requesting that
he call a convention to accept the conditions of the act of Congress. The
petition was dated November 7, 1836. A circular was sent to all counties, calling for an election of delegates on December 5 and 6. By No-

vember 7, a number of county meetings had been held. A "Committee of the People" was formed and called for delegates to meet in Ann Arbor on December 14. The candidates who ran on a platform favoring assent won by a large majority.

Mason then indicated that the people had spoken. This was only roughly so. The legislature did not authorize the second convention, and neither did Congress, acting on behalf of one of its territories. In addition, no other legal authority invoked the convention. This landmark event in Michigan history was the work of a Democratic central committee, requesting the people in the several townships to elect delegates. Delegates were chosen "direct from the people," in local caucuses. But the party caucus was not then recognized as a legal agency. George N. Fuller, in his lengthy treatise on Michigan history, said there was some doubt that this convention actually expressed the will of the majority of the people.

This time around, only eighteen counties participated in a highly questionable "election." Monroe County, for example, bitter over the loss of Toledo, sent no delegates. The people of that county condemned the vote to assent as a spineless capitulation. Other dissenters were equally vocal, claiming "sellout." Opposition Whigs, in boycotting the convention, said it was an administration scheme for forcing terms on the people.

As Yogi Berra might have said if he had been elected a delegate, this was déjà vu all over again. The Second Convention of Assent met in the same Ann Arbor courthouse. The charge was simple: agree to the act of June 15. That way, Michigan would share in the federal surplus, and a balance would be restored between free and slave states in the Senate. As at the first convention, angry comments were made of Arkansas's admission on June 15 without conditions—a free ticket that still rankled the Michiganians.

The seventy-eight delegates elected John R. Williams of Wayne president. It was cold in the courthouse that wintry December 14, and some jokester said, "Well, this sure is a frostbitten convention." The name stuck; the historical marker there today proclaims the courthouse as the site of the Frostbitten Convention—a major event in the life of the state.

On the third floor of the Toledo Public Library, there is an extremely rare copy of the *Journal of the Proceedings of the Convention held*

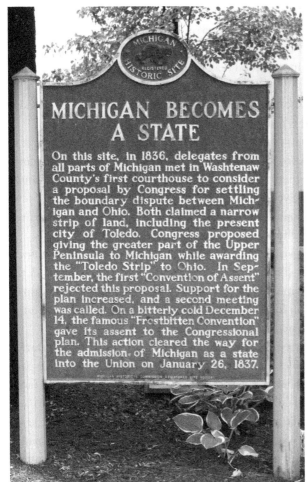

Historical marker in Ann Arbor at the site of the Frostbitten Convention, where Michigan delegates gave their assent to the terms of Congress ceding the Toledo Strip to Ohio. (Photograph by Jen Luton.)

MICHIGAN BECOMES A STATE

On this site, in 1836, delegates from all parts of Michigan met in Washtenaw County's first courthouse to consider a proposal by Congress for settling the boundary dispute between Michigan and Ohio. Both claimed a narrow strip of land, including the present city of Toledo. Congress proposed giving the greater part of the Upper Peninsula to Michigan while awarding the "Toledo Strip" to Ohio. In September, the first "Convention of Assent" rejected this proposal. Support for the plan increased, and a second meeting was called. On a bitterly cold December 14, the famous "Frostbitten Convention" gave its assent to the Congressional plan. This action cleared the way for the admission of Michigan as a state into the Union on January 26, 1837.

at Ann Arbor on the fourteenth day of December, A.D. 1836, for the purpose of giving the assent required by the Act of Congress of June 15th, 1836, previous to the admission of Michigan to the Union. The journal was published by order of the convention and printed by E. P. Gardner of Ann Arbor in 1836. The Toledoans paid a fancy price for this valued piece of Americana. To hold this rare document in one's hands is to be reminded of the passion and fury involved in the prosecution of the Toledo War and also of the fight for statehood. That little journal represents the final capitulation in the Michigan-Ohio war.

Without any Whigs to provide meaningful opposition, the result in Ann Arbor was predictable. Delegates swallowed hard and said yes to the conditions set by Congress, though stating to the end, "We do hereby most solemnly protest release of territory to Ohio." The consensus was that "it was better to be humiliated and to secure the civil and religious liberties inherent in statehood than to engage in an idle, unprofitable and hopeless contest for a boundary which is assuredly and forever lost to us."[35] Delegates also protested against the constitutional right of Congress to require this preliminary assent as a condition of admission.

The record shows that the chilled delegates voted to give assent to the congressional proposal on the first ballot. All but ten of the seventy-eight delegates signed the resolution. John R. Williams said in closing, "We bow to the power but question the right."[36] He and Hart L. Stewart of St. Joseph County were selected as special messengers to carry the resolution of assent to His Excellency, President Jackson.

Michigan had a right to be outraged. The requirement of assent was without precedent. Nothing like it appears in American history in the process of states joining the Union. Not only would Congress not pass enabling legislation for Michigan statehood, but now—at the behest of Ohio—it had attached special conditions.

Despite the irregularities that marked the life of the Frostbitten Convention, no official challenge was made to its legality. For his part, Mason strongly upheld the legal integrity of the convention. His biographer, the esteemed barrister Lawton Hemans, was moved to say, "However pleasantly this sort of thing might have appeared to the lay mind, the student of government and of legal form is hardly persuaded that in a government of laws and constitutions, their decrees and established forms can thus be lightly set aside."[37] Most scholars of the law would agree with him. One of them would say that in the ratification of the boundaries as laid down by Congress, the Second Convention of Assent had "no more authority than the crew of a Detroit schooner or a lumberman's camp in the valley of the Grand River." By any measure, then, the Second Convention of Assent was illegal, and the opposition Whigs were correct in saying so.

Michigan voted to submit for several reasons. Ohio had possession of the Toledo Strip, and nothing was to be gained by further stalling. Only Congress could right the wrongs, and it was now too late to undo the fraud whereby Michigan had lost territory. Once a state, Michigan could take the case to the Supreme Court and have the matter adjudicated there.

But Michigan's travail over statehood was not finished. On December 27, 1836, President Jackson received the resolution of assent and sent it on to Congress, with a message saying that Michigan had complied with the terms of the June 15 act of Congress. The only real objection now to Michigan's admission was the method used to call the Second Convention of Assent. Even after the convention seemingly paved the way for entry into the Union, Michigan found an unfriendly welcoming committee in Congress. The extralegality of the Frostbitten Convention delayed statehood even longer.

That a politics-riddled, easily influenced Congress suddenly became squeamish about legal technicalities in far-off Michigan may be attributable to Ohio's delegation, working overtime to accomplish its purpose. The boundary question arose yet again, and it was determined that it would be voted on separately, as would the question of Michigan's admission. On December 24, 1836, in the House of Representatives, Thomas L. Hamer of Ohio moved that the question of Michigan's admission be referred to the Judiciary Committee. Four days later, the House approved the motion, supported by Ohio and Indiana members. That same day, December 28, despite opposition from John Quincy Adams, still Michigan's most effective voice on the Capitol, the House voted to send the boundary question to the Judiciary Committee, chaired by Sam Beardsley of New York. Why? The majority of the committee was known to favor Ohio.

In the Senate, the boundary question was referred to the Judiciary Committee, and the admission question was referred to a select committee. The Senate debated the statehood bill for three days. In early January 1837, Senator Thomas Hart Benton of Missouri took up Michigan's case: "The people there had held a convention, by their own power, to accept a fundamental condition of their admission to the Union. They have accepted the condition; and the objection is that the convention was a lawless and revolutionary mob, and that law ought to be made to suppress and punish such assemblages in future." Benton continued, "At the last session of Congress, all this denunciation of lawless and revolutionary mobs had been lavished upon the conventions, both of Arkansas and Michigan because, being Territories, they had held conventions and framed without the authority of Congress. Our answer to these denunciations were the same that we give now, namely that they had a right to do so without our authority, and that all that we could require was, that they should send us their constitutions, that we might see if they were republican." Michigan, concluded Benton, had been debarred of its right for years: "She has a right to be admitted, and the admission of a state is a question of that dignity to be entitled, not only to a speedy decision, but to a preference over all other questions until it was decided."[38] On January 3, Senator James Buchanan of Pennsylvania, a future president of the United States, took a different tack.

> It was deemed of great importance at the last session to obtain the consent of Michigan to the settlement of the boundary between her and Ohio. To accomplish this purpose, we offered to Michigan a large territory on her northern boundary as a compensation for what she should yield to Ohio on the south, and we made her acceptance of this offer a condition precedent of her admission into the Union. We then believed, and I still believe, that this was the only mode of settling forever the disputed boundary between Ohio and Michigan, which has already involved us in so many difficulties, threatening bloodshed and civil war on that frontier.
>
> It became my duty at the last session to investigate this subject thoroughly, and I had many conferences upon it with the then chairman of the Judiciary Committee, Mr. Clayton. I am happy to state that, although we concurred in opinion that Michigan had no right to this territory under the compact of 1787, yet we also believed that the only mode of putting the question at rest forever was to obtain her own solemn recognition of the right of Ohio.[39]

The Senate, after focusing on the extralegality of the second convention, voted on January 5, 1837, to accept the Michigan statehood bill. The vote was 25–10 in favor. Whigs disgusted with the Democrats' rump convention cast the negative votes. Among the senators voting against the measure were the Old Nullifier himself, John C. Calhoun of South Carolina, and Henry Clay of Kentucky. The House passed the statehood bill on January 25 by a vote of 132–43; the no votes included eight from Ohio, and the bill was signed by President Jackson on the next day. Two future presidents—James K. Polk, who was then Speaker of the House, and Vice President Martin Van Buren—affixed their signatures to the statehood bill. Most astonishing of all, the two houses of Congress, by large majorities, then passed an act (approved on January 26, 1837) accepting the Second Convention of Assent as meeting the requirements of the act of admission. All the apparent untidiness over the legality of the Frostbitten Convention was swept under the rug, and Michigan was declared one of the states.

Congress did not exactly cover itself with glory in its handling of the Toledo Strip controversy, yet it maintained a kind of weird consistency. Because Michigan had no electoral votes and no voting representation in that body, Congress could—and did—choose to ignore its request for enabling legislation, siding with Ohio despite that state's flawed claim to the Toledo Strip. Similarly, when it came time to appease the territory of Michigan, Congress may have looked to Wisconsin because it had no vote and was waiting for admission. Taking a chunk of Wisconsin Territory to give to Michigan was an easy way out for cynical, expediency-minded politicians, and Congress showed no compunction in following that path.

After five years of waiting, during which time it fought a war with Ohio, drafted a constitution, and became a fully functioning state, Michigan entered the Union as the twenty-sixth state. Thus the number of the original thirteen states had doubled. Lucius Lyon and John Norvell were permitted to take their seats in the Senate, and Isaac E. Crary took his seat as Michigan's representative in the House. By early February, Michigan had received $95,383.83 in surplus federal revenue.

The date for statehood is commonly given as January 26, 1837, and January 26 is still celebrated as Statehood Day. But as mentioned earlier in this chapter, November 2, 1835, is the date stamped on Michigan's great seal. Resolving the details of the territorial swap (the exchange of the Toledo Strip for the western two-thirds of the Upper Peninsula) took years. Surveys and court suits to settle property matters and other issues lasted into the early years of the twentieth century. As late as 1973, the Michigan and Ohio boundary dispute still resonated when a dispute over which state owned the mineral rights to 206 square miles of Lake Erie bottomlands went all the way to the U.S. Supreme Court. Michigan lost in that arena, too. Today, the Toledo War reverberates in the annual titanic clash between the University of Michigan and Ohio State University on the gridiron.

Back on January 26, 1837, there was cause for spontaneous celebrations throughout Michigan. The Boy Governor had achieved his goal. On February 9, a special event was held in Detroit, and a public dinner was served at Woodworth's hotel. Toast followed toast. The most memorable one was offered to Ohio in a spirit of defiance: "Our neighboring sister, and her boasted million of freemen—Michigan neither forgets nor forgives!"[40]

CHAPTER FOURTEEN

BLOODLESS VICTORY AT TOLEDO LUCAS TRUMPS MASON

Have all the ammunition forwarded by boat. Do not forget the six-pounder. We have the balls here.

— GOVERNOR MASON TO COLONEL IKE ROWLAND

If you are women, go home; if you are men, do your duty as judges of the court; I will do mine.

— COLONEL MATTHIAS VAN FLEET OF THE OHIO MILITIA TO
JUDGES OF THE LUCAS COUNTY COURT OF COMMON PLEAS

For Michigan, the statehood celebration was still many months in the future when Ohio and the territory closed for final combat in the late summer of 1835. Stevens T. Mason, still Michigan's acting governor despite having been removed from office, ordered General Brown and his militia to Toledo to prevent the Lucas County Court of Common Pleas from convening there. Governor Robert Lucas sent Adjutant General Samuel C. Andrews to confer with the judges and county officials as to the most feasible means for holding the court. It was decided that the military, with a regiment under the command of Colonel Matthias Van Fleet, would escort the judges into Toledo to convene court on September 7, 1835.

Troops were converging on Toledo from three directions, including by steamship up the Maumee River. One dispatch from Mason to Colonel Ike Rowland read, "Have all the ammunition forwarded by to-

morrow's boat. Do not forget the six-pounder. We have the balls here."[1]
Mason's general orders to the army came from Mulholland's (a field
headquarters). Today, a historical marker there, one mile south of Erie
on South Dixie Highway in Monroe County, proclaims, "'War' with
Happy Ending." The marker reads:

> Michigan troops made their headquarters here during the blood-
> less Toledo "war" in 1835.
> Intense rivalry between the settlers of the two states fanned a
> controversy near flame. Original U.S. surveys had put in Monroe
> County the mouth of the Maumee River around which Toledo was
> taking form. When Ohio started the Miami Canal it obtained from
> Congress a new survey which showed these lands in Ohio.
> Months of disturbance ensued. Ohio partisans were seized on
> the contested frontier and tried in the Monroe County Court
> House. Militia of both states rushed to the border but never
> fought.
> The "war" ended with Michigan accepting the Upper Penin-
> sula in exchange for the Toledo Strip of Monroe County and with
> the admission of Michigan to statehood in 1837.

The object to be accomplished, Mason said, was "the protection of
the integrity of our Territorial limits, and the inviolability of our soil."
He added, "To effect this, it is believed is the determination of the citizens of Michigan."[2] General Brown would echo Mason's strong words:
"Our cause is just. We assemble to defend from invasion our constitutional privileges. The voice of law calls us to the field, and although
young in history, Michigan must be placed by us in the proud attitude of
seeking to do no wrong and never shrinking to defend the inviolability
of her soil."[3] There was never any doubt that the principals meant to
back up their words with action, and Ohio was no less determined to
push the margin.

The stage was set for a decisive confrontation. For all intents and
purposes, there would be a battle in Toledo over the issue of a court sitting there to establish the legitimacy of Ohio's claim. In its September 2
issue, the *Detroit Free Press* said, "Orders have been issued for volunteers
to resist the military encroachments of Ohio. We anticipate the most serious consequences from these reckless proceedings, and see no probability that they will be averted without the shedding of blood." The
writer of a September 3 letter from Detroit, taken from the *New York*

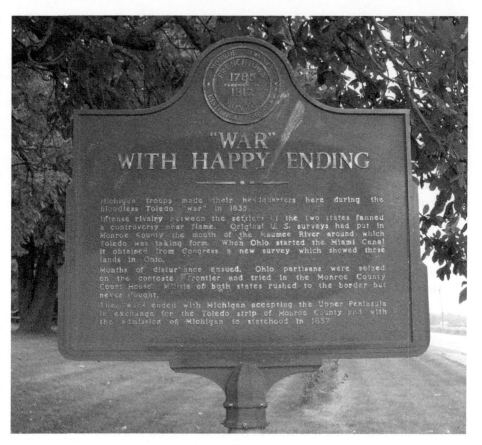

Historical marker south of Monroe, Michigan, marking the site where Michigan troops made their headquarters on their march to Toledo in September 1835. (Photograph by Jen Luton.)

Evening Star and reprinted in the *National Intelligencer,* said, "The Toledo War has again produced a great excitement, and things look more portentous than ever. I fear the worst. Nothing but the interference of the General Government, or a total backing out of one of the two belligerents can save the American name from eternal disgrace."[4]

The Michigan militia's march to Toledo lasted four days. Along the way, there was a nocturnal theft of a fine hive of honey, which resulted in the bees showing their displeasure and in some of the men overindulging. The senior officer must have had a sweet tooth, because even he got caught up in the beehive episode. One of his men reported that the commanding officer partook of the honey so freely that "at an early hour the next morning, I saw him bending over the fence in the rear of the house, with positive indications that he had taken more honey than he could carry."[5] A court-martial was convened in the morning, to which all commissioned officers were invited, but its members found no witnesses who claimed to know anything about the theft. The court-martial adjourned, subject to the call of the president, and nothing more came of the incident.

Accurate numbers are hard to come by, but Michigan's initial invading army probably amounted to 250 men. The Detroit militia arrived at Monroe on September 5. On the following day, the Michigan troops, augmented with volunteers from Monroe and Lenawee counties, pitched camp at Mulholland's, about eight miles from Toledo, expecting to meet Lucas's troops in open warfare. A scout reported that the Michiganians, in high spirits and led by Mason and Brown, marched into Toledo in numbers as high as twelve hundred, armed to a man with muskets and dragging artillery with them.

The truth is that a train of artillery did not exist, despite Mason's reference to a "six-pounder" (cannon) and boast "We have the balls here." He probably was hoping this piece of "intelligence" would fall into the hands of an enemy who would take fright. Brown stated that his main force stopped at Mulholland's on the night of September 6 and that he sent a subordinate forward to Toledo with an armed force of about one hundred men, to keep an eye on the judges, with orders to arrest them if they tried to hold court. The main force arrived at Toledo on the next day.

The third and final battle of the Toledo War took place on September 5–7. War fever was high on both sides. The Ohio commanders had their orders, and the Michigan militia was determined to follow up the territory's ongoing prosecutions of the Pains and Penalties Act with a victory in the field. The strange thing about it all was that during these giddy, tumultuous days of September, the territory was without official leadership. Nobody lost his life in the "Battle of Toledo," and there were no major injuries, unless you count loss of face.

Truth be known, this moment in history belongs to Ohio. Michigan was completely "out-Lucased" when Ohio's governor held "night court." Michigan was expecting its opponent to play by the rules, to come out in the open, to pit its manhood against the territory's mighty militia. Michigan did not foresee that Lucas, in his effort to establish indisputable jurisdiction over Toledo, would arrange for his court to be held in the dead of night, right under the noses of the Michigan fighting forces. No screenwriter for the Marx brothers or theater of the absurd could improve on what happened in the wee hours of September 7 in Toledo—which was either in the Michigan Territory or in Ohio, depending on your vantage point.

To hold court in defiance of the upstart Mason and his militia seemed to Governor Lucas to be a fine opportunity to show President Jackson that no one soiled the honor and dignity of Ohio with impunity, as well as to recover some prestige Lucas had lost that summer. After the Ohio threesome of Disney, Swayne, and Allen worked on getting President Jackson to sack Mason, Jackson advised Lucas to refrain from any jurisdiction over the territory, pending action of Congress. Lucas saw this as a blow to his ego; the eyes of the country were on him, and he needed to perform some act of jurisdiction to avoid the imputation of having backed down to cheeky Michigan. It was clear to him that an attempt to take forcible possession of the Toledo Strip would draw down the military force of the United States. Lucas wanted court to be held so that official records would show he had executed the laws of Ohio over the disputed territory.

Lucas rolled the dice and hit on the idea of holding court despite the show of force by Governor Mason and the recommendation of the president to abstain from further activity. He did not want to wait for Congress to act, and he probably felt that if he struck a sudden blow, it would be days before Washington learned of it. He called to his aid the adjutant general of the state of Ohio, and they devised a plan.

Lucas sent a colonel from the militia and a company-strength force as escort for the judges planning to open court in Toledo; this force would protect them in the discharge of their duty. The plan was to march from Maumee on the morning of September 7, but on the previous evening, a report was circulated by a scout that General Brown of Michigan was in Toledo with twelve hundred men, ready for any contingency. The report, as already mentioned, was of dubious truth, but it had an unsettling effect on the judges, who became faint of heart in the face of such opposition. They possibly even wondered why they had become jurists in the first place, as frontline service in a shooting war had no part in their job description. One judge bravely denied any "apprehension of a personal character" but admitted he would feel "acutely . . . the disgrace of the capture and abduction, by a Michigan mob, of a

branch of the Judiciary of the state when actually engaged in the performance of judicial functions."⁶ Judge Baxter Bowman was "in a state of
consternation." What should be done?

Backing down at this point was unacceptable to Lucas. To his chief
executive's assistance galloped the colonel of his command force,
Matthias Van Fleet. Excoriating the judges for their cowardice, he proposed to take the honor of the state into his own keeping. "If you are
women, go home; if you are men, do your duty as judges of the court; I
will do mine," Van Fleet told the cowed jurists.⁷

The presiding judge and his associates had assembled in Maumee,
about ten miles distant from Mason's troops, along with Van Fleet and
one hundred soldiers. State adjutant general Samuel C. Andrews, accompanied by Major General John Bell, took up quarters at a hotel in
Toledo, passing themselves off as private citizens who just happened to
be traveling through. If they used aliases, history does not record what
names they employed.

Van Fleet's fiery speech had the desired effect. Shaming the officials
into doing their duty, he then called for twenty brave men to sneak into
Toledo. Why did he employ only twenty when a hundred men were
available? Van Fleet knew that more could be accomplished with fewer
men, as they would be less likely to alert the enemy. Practicality dictated
the number, as he had only twenty horses available. He requested of his
men that such of them as were ready to risk a hazardous enterprise
should step forward four paces. When thirty or so did, he picked twenty,
with Captain Granville Jones of the Toledo Lucas Guards in charge of
the camp on the Maumee.

Van Fleet reminded the judges that September 7 would commence
immediately after midnight and that there was no hour specified in the
law when the court should be opened. Governor Lucas wanted the
court held, and furnishing the governor with the record was all that was
required. Accordingly, at one o'clock in the morning on September 7,
the officers of the court, accompanied by Van Fleet and twenty chosen
men, mounted and armed, started on horseback and followed the
Maumee River into Toledo. The colonel, three judges (Jonathan H.
Jerome, Baxter Bowman, and William Wilson), a bailiff, an acting sheriff, and the armed guards arrived shortly before 3:00 a.m. and utilized a
schoolhouse on Washington Street. They blacked out the windows, lit a
candle, and proceeded to hold a court session.

With Junius Flagg of Toledo acting as sheriff, the judges officially opened court. Dr. Horatio Conant of Maumee was appointed court clerk. Three commissioners—John Baldwin, Robert Gower, and Cyrus Holloway—were named for the new county of Lucas. After other necessary business was speedily transacted, the court adjourned. The session probably took all of ten minutes. But nothing was legal until the clerk prepared the official record. The proceedings were written on sheets of paper, which, when properly signed to certify the session, were given to Dr. Conant, who tucked them into his fashionable, tall, bell-shaped hat.

The men congratulated themselves on a job well done. No doubt tickled that they had put one over on the Michiganians, they found a nearby tavern kept by Munson H. Daniels and rousted him from a night's sleep. They encouraged him to open up the bar if he had an ounce of good Buckeye blood in him. There were drinks all around, but there was nothing of a too boisterous nature, because of the presumed proximity of the Michigan men.

One drink led to two, and just when they were filling their glasses a second time, the door burst open, and a local hollered at the top of his lungs that a strong force of Michigan men was near at hand, coming to arrest them. The jokester had the pleasure of watching confusion reign supreme; the court party dropped their glasses, spilling the libations they had intended as toasts to Lucas and his million of freemen. The justices of the newly formed, legally constituted Lucas County Court of Common Pleas threw dignity to the hindmost and took to their horses with all possible speed, cursing the foe who had crashed their victory party. The tavern keeper never collected for the second round.

The clerk's minutes were the court's proof of existence and certificate of legality. When they were safely stuffed into Dr. Conant's hat, the party hastily took the trail through the woods that led to Maumee, making an honest effort to stay as quiet as possible. The historian W. V. Way, in his *The Facts and Historical Events of the Toledo War of 1835*, wrote, "They went at such furious speed that if their charge had been made in the opposite direction towards the enemy, they would have pierced the most solid columns."[8]

At some point in the furious retreat, the party discovered that they had been given a false alarm. But far worse than the realization that they were fleeing a phantom force was the accident that befell Conant and his hat in transit. Holding the horse's reins with one hand and balancing his bell hat and its precious contents with the other, Conant came to

grief. The darkness concealed an overhanging tree limb. As his steed
passed under the tree branch, Conant's tall hat was knocked off his head
and lost somewhere along the trail. There was dismay all around. The
party had no choice but to backtrack through the woods, feeling their
way along until, mirabile dictu, the hat was retrieved with the minutes
of the midnight proceedings intact. Van Fleet permitted himself and his
party a two-gun salute. Ohio was saved from embarrassment, and the
party stumbled into Maumee at 6:00 a.m. They were clearly outside the
disputed territory but yet within Lucas County, where Michigan civil
officers or troops dared not pursue.

Its honor upheld, the state of Ohio was triumphant. It had won a
victory without shedding a drop of valiant Michigan blood, the men of
Michigan having been tricked by the justices' nineteenth-century version of night court. A record still exists today showing that on September 7, 1835, the state of Ohio exercised jurisdiction over the disputed
territory by holding a court of common pleas in due form of law. Not a
soul over whom the justices came to assert jurisdiction knew of their
comings, doings, or retreat.

Just as Michigan did not know that it was fighting the "Battle of
Toledo" without an official leader, the Michigan militia and General
Brown did not know that their march on Toledo was an exercise in fu-
tility. When Mason's forces arrived in Toledo in midmorning on September 7, there was not an Ohio soldier in sight. Mason and Brown
were chagrined to learn what had happened during the night. They had
plenty of men to prevent the holding of a court, as courts are normally
held. But they did not reckon with improvisational Ohio jurisprudence
and did not look for midnight tribunals held in blacked-out school-
houses under the glow of candles. They did not allow for Lucas's cunning or Van Fleet's challenging rhetoric.

Clearly, the failure to discover the judges or to anticipate Van Fleet's
move was no evidence of lack of vigilance on the part of the Michigan
authorities. General Brown had done his duty. It was not in his lifetime
of experience for justices to open court in the wee hours, conduct a bare
minimum of business, and then take to their heels like so many fleeing
felons.

When they learned they were too late, the enraged Michigan soldiers had excuse enough to extract some measure of pleasure for their
march from Monroe. They did what any soldiers would do under the

circumstances—they went on a rampage. Livestock, gardens, and orchards were the principal objects of revenge. Major Benjamin F. Stickney was singled out for particular judgment; the soldiers tore up his vegetable garden and stripped his orchard. A popular saying at Monroe started at Toledo and referred to the liberation of Stickney's garden by the men of Michigan. Offered in the form of a toast, it went, "Here's to Major Stickney's potatoes and onions—we drafted their tops and their bottoms volunteered." One story had a Michigan battalion raiding the major's wine cellar before disbanding and heading home.

In any event, the Michigan militia hung around Toledo, drinking, carousing, and plundering. No serious damage was done except for the butchery of some hogs and the death of two horses when soldiers fired into a barn. Finally, for good measure, the frustrated Michigan troops trashed the printing office of the *Toledo Gazette*. These were the dying gasps of the border war. The Michigan forces stayed three days before returning to Monroe, where they were reviewed by Mason. With Ohio troops disbanded, Mason ordered his own soldiers back to their farms and villages. And with that, the Toledo War passed from contested battle ground to the domain of the politicians.

The events of September, one observer wrote, were the ability of Buckeye brain to outwit Michigan brawn. Soon thereafter, at Toledo, a Michigan posse attempted to arrest the judges who had held the night court. During the ensuing melee, Deputy Sheriff Wood—the officer stabbed by Benjamin Stickney's son Two back in July—was shot in the arm, surely earning him the Purple Heart (if one were to be given) for the Toledo War.

With the petty depredations on his property, the colorful Major Stickney fades from the picture. We last hear from him in a letter of October 4, 1835, from Lower Sandusky, Ohio, where he writes to Governor Lucas concerning his self-exile due to trouble over the Michigan-Ohio boundary. He asks the governor for advice: "Your age and experience in the vicissitudes of life has afforded your excelancy amply opportunity to sympathize or at least bare with my impatience. Our situation appears bordering upon desparate. By your advice I have remained absent from my home and my business untill I am reduced nearly to this extremity of my means which were quite limited at the commencement of my exile."[9]

One of the last events relating to the Toledo War occurred on February 19, 1846, when the Ohio legislature appropriated three hundred

dollars in payment to Major Benjamin F. Stickney for the damage his
property sustained in Toledo and for the time he passed in prison in
Monroe. He died in 1852. He was eulogized in the *Toledo Blade* as "an extensive property holder, and a man generally esteemed by our citizens,
for uprightness and integrity of purpose, a clear philosophical mind, and
affable deportment. He had many eccentricities of character."

A song about the Toledo War, composed by a young veteran of the
war named Crawford, has survived the intervening years. It has about
seventeen verses. The principal ones follow.

> Come all ye Michiganians, and lend a hearing ear;
> Remember, for Toledo we once took up sword and spear,
> And now, to give that struggle o'er and trade away that land,
> I think it's not becoming of valiant-hearted men.
>
> In eighteen hundred thirty-five there was a dreadful strife
> Betwixt Ohio and this State; they talked of taking life.
> Ohio claimed Toledo, and so did Michigan;
> They both declared they'd have it, with its adjoining land.
>
> Old Lucas gave his order for all to hold a court;
> And Stevens Thomas [*sic*] Mason, he thought he'd have
>   some sport.
> He called upon the Wolverines, and asked them for to go,
> To meet the rebel Lucas, his court to overthrow.
>
> Our independent companies were ordered for the march;
> Our officers were ready, all stiffened up with starch;
> On nimble-footed coursers our officers did ride,
> With each a pair of pistols and sword hung by his side.
>
> When we got down to Toledo old Lucas was not there;
> He had heard that we were coming, and ran away with fear;
> To hear the wolves a howling scared the poor devil so,
> He said, before he'd fight them, he'd give up Toledo.
>
> Then let us drink a health to those honest, upright men.
> To all those true Republicans, the friends of Michigan;
> And when we have another war for the disputed land,
> May they be ready, cocked and primed to fight for Michigan.[10]

If Ohio was looking for heroes in the border fracas, it did not have to
look farther than Colonel Matthias Van Fleet, who was possessed of
more backbone than a million of Lucas's freemen. Historian W. V. Way

says, "It must be admitted that, according to the usual tactics in war, Ohio was justly entitled to the victory. It was no ordinary achievement. Colonel Van Fleet, with only twenty men, almost in the face of 1,200, sixty times his own number, by strategical movements, achieved a victory that another commander might have lost with the destruction of all his forces." Way goes on, "Whatever of honor or advantage the State of Ohio gained in this contest, she owes to Colonel Van Fleet, the General Jackson of Lucas County. General Jackson saved New Orleans and upheld the honor and glory of the American flag with the loss of only seven men in an engagement with more than twice his own number, while Colonel Van Fleet upheld the peace and dignity of the state of Ohio within the county of Lucas, against sixty times his own number without the loss of a single man or the shedding of one drop of blood."[11]

Way seems to elevate Van Fleet to the status of Pizarro, who defeated the mighty Inca with a handful of men. The figure of twelve hundred men is disputed; General Brown himself stated that his main force halted at Mulholland's. On the fiftieth anniversary of the war, a Michigan veteran recalled the march on Toledo from Detroit and Monroe in fond but less glorious terms: "Many of the soldiers were armed with broomsticks, but that did not matter. They were bound to strike terror to the Buckeyes. Our troops entered Toledo without opposition and stayed there three or four days, and were handsomely treated."[12]

With Ohio now riding high in the saddle, Governor Lucas believed that to carry the fight any further was to seriously run the danger of crossing President Jackson, while to wait was to win what his people wanted. His opponent had been dismissed from office, and the fight had been taken out of Michigan when the territory lost its leader. Mason felt it was better to keep the peace and to settle the question of boundary once Michigan was admitted as a state. In that, of course, he was mistaken, naively thinking statehood was imminent.

After the aborted endeavor of September 7, Mason and Michigan were preoccupied with setting up the new state. Oddly, even after Lucas's triumphant "night court," the war's end gave Michigan authority over the disputed tract—or so it thought—until Congress should act on the question of boundary. President Jackson concluded that the Toledo Strip lay within Michigan's jurisdiction, pending a final settlement by Congress. But it was becoming increasingly clear that Michigan would not win in Washington.

In actuality, the people in the disputed territory were left to regulate

matters in their own way. In November, Lucas's surveyors, so rudely in-
terrupted at Phillips Corners back in April, finished re-marking the
Harris line. A month later, Andrew Talcott completed his survey only a
hundred feet south of the old Fulton line. But now attention had shifted
to Congress, with old John Quincy Adams of Massachusetts taking up
the cudgel for the Michigan cause.

When the president removed Mason as Michigan's acting governor on
August 29, Jackson named Charles Shaler of Pennsylvania to the post of
secretary and acting governor of the territory. Shaler must have sensed
something untoward; he immediately declined the honor. On September 15, John Scott Horner of Virginia was named to the same position.
This unfortunate individual was a disaster from start to finish. Although
he was discredited, Mason was a genuine hero to his fellow Wolverines.
He was the Democratic Party's nominee for governor and would, in a
few short weeks, be elected to the state's highest position. Mason had
been the victim of some low-blow politicking in Washington, but he
had taken his lumps in manly fashion. Now his people were prepared to
reward the Boy Governor for his pluck in telling old Lucas where to get
off.

Horner was treated with indifference at first and then scorn. From
the moment of his appointment, trouble dogged him. On his way to Detroit on September 19, his boat ran aground at the mouth of the Detroit
River after he had taken passage from Cleveland. Barely had he arrived
than the people of Michigan, on October 5, ratified their new state constitution and elected Mason governor.

So just who actually was governor? Was it Mason, freely elected by
the people of a state not yet officially recognized, or Horner, the president's man, who held title to the job? The Whig press in Michigan continued to maintain that Michigan was not a state until admitted to the
Union. The Whigs said Horner, not Mason, was the only legal governor. The Democratic press considered Michigan to be a state and held
that Horner had no claim to the job. On October 19, in a letter from
Detroit, Horner wrote of his troubles.

> My condition was this; at Monroe, the seat of strife, amidst a wild
> and dangerous population, without any aid, a friend, servant or bed
> to sleep in, in the midst of a mob excited by the enemies of the ad-
> ministration, and bad men, I could not enlist a friend, or an officer

of the Territory. Under the most disadvantageous and embarrassing circumstances which anarchy could present, the wishes and instructions of Government have been constitutionally fulfilled and complied with.

On Saturday at noon, Judge Swayne and myself left Tecumseh for Detroit, and on our arrival that evening at Ypsilanti, were mobbed, the house somewhat injured; no bones, however, were broken, and not a word was said by me on the subject.

My labors, both mental and bodily, have been very arduous, almost insupportable. It was not until this morning that I could procure a clerk or private secretary, such was the state of the public mind, from some cause or other. I mention mobs and details only to exhibit the true state of things; personally, I care nothing for them. Doctrines are afloat here monstrous and dangerous. There never was a government in Christendom with such officers, civil and military, and filled with such doctrines as Michigan. One of the judges at Monroe expressed publicly his desire to become a martyr to the cause. I have used my utmost exertions in executing the duties of my office at the sacrifice of my own health. P.S. There are no funds here within my control, and, to discharge my duties, I have exhausted my own pecuniary resources.[13]

Horner proceeded to pardon Ohio partisans who had been prosecuted under the Pains and Penalties Act. This only confirmed among Michiganians that he was a tool of Washington. George S. May, in his fine updating of Willis F. Dunbar's *Michigan: A History of the Wolverine State*, writes: "He released from jail those Ohioans who had been apprehended trespassing on what Michigan regarded as its territory, giving rise to the suspicion that Horner was in league with Governor Lucas of Ohio. These suspicions were well founded, for Horner kept Lucas informed on developments in Michigan, broadly hinting that affairs would be managed in such a way as to redound to the benefit of Ohio."[14]

When the people of Ypsilanti heard that Horner had freed the Ohioans, they gathered beneath his hotel window (in the incident described by Horner in the letter previously quoted) and pelted him with stones, unsavory eggs, and blobs of horse dung. Luckily, says Horner, "They did no damage to my person." Later, the Monroe County prosecutor refused to cooperate with Horner when he tried to carry out the president's instructions to dismiss the suits against Ohio officials.

To be sure, Horner was dealing with a frontier people, raw in their politics and deportment. But his pardoning of all the Ohio men previously arrested or sought, with the exception of Two Stickney, was seen as unacceptable by the local populace. Demonstrations against him in Monroe and Ypsilanti were typical of the low regard in which he was held. Horner's physiognomy did not help his cause. He apparently was obese and sour-faced and possessed a raspy voice. It was not long before he was dubbed "little Jack Horner." He stuck it out until March, when he accepted appointment as secretary of the newly formed Wisconsin Territory. He was much safer there.

The war was over, but there followed a lively dispute over the source of the weapons Michigan employed and who may have authorized their use. A controversy erupted involving Governor Lucas, Secretary of War Cass, and (to a lesser extent) Stevens T. Mason. At the Battle of Phillips Corners, a veteran named Benjamin Baxter recalled being furnished with "U.S. arms and ammunition," an allegation his commanding officer denied; he said muskets for his men were supplied by the territory of Michigan. In their report to Lucas of what happened at Phillips Corners, Ohio survey commissioners Jonathan Taylor, Uri Seely, and John Patterson said, "An armed force of about fifty or sixty men hove in sight within musket shot of us, all mounted upon horses, well armed with muskets."[15]

Recall that in February 1835, acting governor Mason had authorized General Joseph Brown, head of the militia, to take "any necessary measures" to prevent Ohio officials from acting in the disputed area. Later, Mason would write to Brown saying, "I shall assume responsibility of sending you such arms, etc. as may be necessary for your successful operations, without waiting for an order from the Secretary of War."[16] The confident Mason also told Secretary of State John Forsyth, "A collision is inevitable."[17] As secretary of war, Cass, the longtime Michigan territorial governor, had tried to maintain a hands-off attitude in the border dispute. But he had never balked at promoting the interests of Michigan, and his views on the rightful owner of the Toledo Strip coincided with those of his protégé Mason.

Sebried Dodge, who was employed as a surveyor marking the Harris line, wrote from Maumee on April 10 to say that Michigan had "300 men under arms and 1,500 stands of arms taken from the U.S. arsenal at White Pigeon." This was two weeks before Phillips Corners. But were these fifteen hundred stands of arms "taken," or was there legitimate authorization for their use? Since Michigan was only a territory and therefore a "possession" of the central government, was its militia in fact armed by the federals? Or were federal arms not used at all by Michigan in the Toledo War? There are plenty of reports that when Michigan militiamen marched off to do battle with the Ohioans, the former were armed only with broomsticks and homemade weapons.

Governor Robert Lucas was not one to let loose ends go untied. Since Congress had not yet acted on the border dispute, for all Lucas knew, Michigan still held title to the Toledo Strip. True, there was now a record proving he had held court, and his commissioners had resumed re-marking the Harris line, unmolested. But it still rankled Lucas that the secretary of war, a Michiganian first and foremost, had arranged for his state a convenient access to federal arms and ammunition in the shooting war with Ohio. Or so Lucas believed.

In a letter to the secretary of state at Washington dated November 10, 1835, Lucas formally accused Cass of helping to supply arms to Michigan. Lucas stated that he was informed by General Haskall, a member of the Michigan legislature, that Governor Mason procured the key to the U.S. arsenal at Detroit and, in that way, came into possession of government arms for use by his forces. Lucas expressed the belief that such use of the arms was made by "private special permission of the Secretary of War."[18] He further wrote that in private letters (seen by Lucas) to friends in Ohio, Cass stated that while not appearing publicly in the controversy, he was doing all he could privately do in support of the Michigan claim. At one point early in 1835, Cass wrote, "I am doing all I can in my private capacity as a mediator between the parties, and I have written to Michigan advising a course of forbearance so much more moderate than any which seems to have occurred to them."[19] On another occasion, Cass advised Mason to stick to his guns, figuratively speaking, because he had right on his side.

L. G. Stuart says that when Mason was arming for the Toledo fracas, he made a demand on Colonel Henry Whiting, who was in command of the government store in Detroit, for "1,000 stand of arms and 75,000 ball cartridge." The arms were given out, Stuart writes, without waiting to hear from the War Department at Washington. A veteran of the Toledo campaign, Edward Peck, says that on nearing Toledo, "it was found that the men had loaded their rifles with powder and ball without any authority, and entirely without the knowledge of the officers."[20] Mason's demand on Colonel Whiting gave Governor Lucas occasion to accuse Cass of taking advantage of his official position to lend aid and encouragement to Michigan. The subsequent letters Cass wrote denying any responsibility for what had been done, declaring that Colonel Whiting had acted without orders and that what he had done had not been approved by the department, are preserved among the documents of Congress and Ohio.

Colonel Whiting wrote to George Bomford, colonel of ordnance, to say, "A requisition on the War Department by the Acting Governor of Michigan for arms and ammunition had already been received and this requisition was duly submitted to the President of the U.S. who promptly directed the Secretary of War to advise the governor of Michigan that the requisition could not be approved."[21] Bomford was also in receipt of a letter from C. A. Harris, acting secretary of war, to Secretary of State John Forsyth, in which he says, "I refer you to the enclosed report of the colonel of ordnance, from which it will be perceived that the arms and munitions of war, alluded to by Governor Lucas, as being lately in the possession of ex-Secretary Mason of Michigan, were NOT taken from the U.S. store at Detroit."[22]

Back on March 5, Mason had urged Cass to send two companies of U.S. regulars from Fort Gratiot to occupy the border area. Mason informed Forsyth that he would meet Lucas's force by a force of like character if the latter tried to establish jurisdiction over the Toledo Strip. The governor also placed the Michigan militia on alert, with General Brown in command. When too few men responded to a call for volunteers, Mason resorted to a draft to muster five hundred men, whom he planned to place under Brown's command. To arm these men, Mason requested one thousand muskets and seventy-five thousand cartridges from Colonel Whiting, acting quartermaster at the U.S. arsenal in Detroit. In *Michigan's Early Military Forces*, LeRoy Barnett and Roger Rosentreter pick up the story: "Feeling that the urgency of the situation required him to honor the request before notifying his superiors in Washington D.C., Colonel Whiting gave Mason the armaments. Whiting did, however, refuse to give Mason the cannon he requested. After being notified of Whiting's action, a distraught Cass ordered him to retrieve the weapons immediately."[23] A report dated April 30, 1835, says that the stores requested by Mason "are reported as having been returned by the acting governor of Michigan, with the exception of 1,446 musket cartridges."

Cass lost no time in responding to the charges made by Lucas. In a letter to Forsyth from the War Department dated November 19, 1835, Cass alluded to a letter he received from Governor Lucas on October 6. In it, Lucas remarked, "The late military invasion of the northern boundary of Ohio, by ex-secretary Mason, with a force armed and equipped in fact, if not in the whole, with arms and munitions of war, taken from the United States store at Detroit, we think can be viewed in no other light than as being in contempt of the authorities of the United States."[24]

Cass denied "in the most solemn manner" that he ever advised the adoption of any course that would or could lead to the use of arms. He maintained, "The error of his expectation is shown by the simple statement that I do deny, in my own name, and in the most unequivocal terms, that any arms belonging to the U.S., taken from the stores at Detroit or from any other place, were in the possession of the authorities or militia of the Territory of Michigan at the period alluded to by Governor Lucas in his letter of October 6, so far as the records of this Department show, or my personal knowledge or information extends. I am perfectly satisfied that Gov. Lucas has been misinformed on the subject." The secretary was careful to throw in some qualifiers here, such as "so far as the records show" and "or my personal knowledge or information extends." He says Lucas was in error when he suggested that "the arms and munitions of war or a part of them at least that were in possession of ex-secretary Mason and his invading army on the 7th of September last were drawn from the same source and that these things were done with the knowledge at least, if not with the special permission of the Secretary of War."[25] In further reply, now to Mason, Cass said he would be happy to see an inquiry by Congress into the matter, "which will remove any doubt upon the subject." Now that the war was over, he argued,

> Circumstances render it proper that I should state my views. My opinion then was that Michigan was entitled to the possession of the district in dispute, until that possession was changed by the rightful authority. I thought the Territory should continue to exercise its jurisdiction by the use of the ordinary civil power until this was formally obstructed, and that then all proceedings should stop, and that the circumstances should be officially reported to the President for his consideration and review.
>
> I now state most unequivocally that there is no letter of mine in existence which contradicts in the slightest degree this representa-

tion, and that no person ever heard me advise a different course. It is well known in Michigan that the proceedings by which a considerable armed force was embodied did not accord with my opinion, and that my views were opposed to it. Governor Lucas states that I am considered in Ohio as the "master spirit" that has directed this controversy. . . . Never was the course of any man more mistaken.

I venture to predict that the investigation I have directed the Ordnance department to make into the facts will result in showing that there has been an entire misapprehension, and that no stores of any description were thus issued or taken, and that the issues of March 21st were the only ones made. It is common knowledge arms are distributed annually to states and territories in proportion to their militia, and it is possible the arms belonging to Michigan may have been used.[26]

There was no congressional inquiry into the matter of who issued what orders or from what source or sources the arms were issued. Cass's word and his integrity were sufficient to carry the day. There is no evidence of Mason procuring the key to the U.S. arsenal in Detroit in pursuit of maintaining the integrity and laws of Michigan. Mason had made a requisition on the War Department for arms and ammunition, but his requisition was not approved. He asked for the use of U.S. arms, and some were issued to him from federal arsenals in the Michigan Territory, but not by authority of the secretary of war.

CHAPTER FIFTEEN

WAR'S END

*The stiffness of the Michigan back gave us the Upper Peninsula—
worth a dozen Toledo Strips.*

—J. WILKIE MOORE, VETERAN OF THE TOLEDO WAR

*Both parties acquired lands (Ohio the Toledo Strip, Michigan the
Upper Peninsula) that neither had any legal right to.*

—W. V. WAY, OHIO HISTORIAN

When General Joseph Brown marched his men into Toledo only to discover that Ohio's Lucas County Court of Common Pleas had already met, put the proceedings into an official record, and fled, nothing could have deflated the Michiganians more. As if the embarrassment of September 7 were not enough, Governor Mason learned on September 10 that he had been sacked. The Toledo War ended with the sound of muffled hoofbeats along the Maumee River as the "court of stealth" made its way to safety. But although the shooting was over, the Toledo Strip War echoes in history to the present day; indeed, as shall be seen, the boundary dispute was far from over when the war ended in 1835.

Casualties of the war included several livestock; the farm animals foraged by the Michigan troops en route to Toledo; and, of course, Deputy Sheriff Wood, who survived his stab wound. The property of Major Benjamin F. Stickney suffered, as did the newspaper office in Toledo, but real harm to person and property was averted during the hostilities of 1835. The soldiers, as has been noted, were a pretty scruffy bunch. But whatever they lacked in training, they made up in zeal. The Toledo affair gave rise to many myths and stories. Added to the recollections of the veterans themselves, they give color and a human dimension to a dispute that rattled cages in Detroit, Columbus, and Washington, D.C.

One story that made the rounds was that a pious justice of the peace, under Ohio commission, fled to a sugar camp in the woods and lived there for days nourished in daily food by robin redbreasts. The be-

lief in this "miracle" sustained many a Buckeye partisan that summer of
1835. On another occasion, a Michigan officer attempted to arrest a
man in the night. The man only had a moment's warning and ran for his
life. He reached the Maumee River, threw himself on a log, and used his
hands and feet to paddle to safety on the opposite shore. This alleged act
of heroism in flight likewise received wide currency in the Ohio camp.

In Toledo on September 5 or thereabouts, a Michigan force poured
a broadside into the pine siding of a barn that intelligence had told them
might contain a cache of arms of the enemy. Upon entering the barn, all
the Wolverines found was a fine horse, dying from the fusillade of bul-
lets he had received. The Michiganians had come for blood, and they
had shed it. It was rumored that in Toledo, an Ohio flag had been torn
from its staff and cruelly dishonored. The Michigan version of the story,
as reported in the *Monroe Sentinel*, had patriotic citizens tearing the dis-
graceful badge of treason from its perch, dragging it through the streets,
and burning it in Monroe, "with suitable demonstrations of contempt."
The Ohio version had General Brown taking the flag down and tying it
to the tails of several horses in his troops, where, it may be assumed, it
was defecated on with truly equine equanimity.

A small volume might be written relating the incidents of this
bloodless struggle and the story of the privations endured by the soldiers—privations that were relieved by raids on chicken coops, melon
patches, and potato fields. The acts of bravado and bluster, the narrow
escapes, and the ludicrous incidents all make for entertaining reading.
There are letters from the period addressed to "Postmaster,
Tremainsville, State of Uncertainty" and to the equally ambivalent
"Tremainsville, Lucas or Monroe County, Ohio or Michigan."
Tremainsville was located in the Toledo Strip.

Throughout the summer of 1835, people in the Toledo area were
arrested and hauled away to jail. There were reports of fistfights, as-
saults, murders, and atrocities. A correspondent from Defiance, Ohio,
reported "citizens being carried off and women abused." Wolverines
and Buckeyes were equally guilty of exaggeration. Ohio newspapers described in detail the mob tactics employed by the champions of Michigan, but similar charges could be made on the other side with equal
truth. An overexcited patriot from Ypsilanti, A. S. Millington, reported
knowledge of a band of a hundred Chippewa and Potawatomie Indians
engaged to assassinate Governor Lucas and his aides. An anonymous
"Buckeye" in Philadelphia wrote to Governor Lucas, "Michigan has

inflicted a stain on the citizens of Ohio which must be washed out with their blood, and that without delay."[1]

The Michigan Pioneer and Historical Collections is a rich treasure trove of veterans' personal recollections of how they fought. In the mid-1880s, J. Wilkie Moore, then a wiry and active old man of seventy-one living on Cass Avenue in Detroit, was interviewed. "Yes, I was a soldier in the Toledo War," Moore said. He continued,

> It was so long ago, however, that the whole affair seems to me now just like a dream. It was a time of great excitement in Michigan, and when we won our "glorious victory" the Territory was wild with enthusiasm. The whole Toledo war may seem very funny to look back at, but most of us went down expecting to risk our lives. Everyone expected bloodshed. Some of us were armed with guns, but the great majority carried long broom handles.
>
> We had a vast amount of fun on the march to the front. The farming people *en route* generally welcomed us enthusiastically because we were fighting for Michigan. They did a great deal for our creature comforts, giving us mush and milk and cooking us regular meals. We returned these favors by stealing pigs and chickens—of course we called it foraging. When we entered the town [Toledo] we were finely entertained there. We occupied the city four days and then, matters being temporarily adjusted, we returned to Detroit. The Toledo War was of great importance. The stiffness of the Michigan back gave us the Upper Peninsula—worth a dozen Toledo Strips.[2]

In contrast to Moore, for whom the war seemed "like a dream," J. P. Cole, another veteran of the war, remembered plenty: "I ought to know something about the old Toledo war. I fought, bled and died in that war; laid out thirteen nights on the cold, cold ground, and the State of Michigan has never given me a pension. All I ever got . . . was $7.35, and I fear it is all I ever will get. Let me give you a reminiscence. When we had passed the disputed line, and were on the ten-mile territory, we one day saw a well and went to get some water, and a woman came out of the house to which the well belonged, and began to scold us because we were fighting against Ohio. We asked her what difference it made to her. She said it made a good deal of difference, she wouldn't live in Michigan for anything in the world; it was a miserable

country full of the fever and ague. She would a great deal rather live in
Ohio. The territory on which she lived was pretty near the line of the
disputed territory!"[3]

Other veterans of the war recounted vivid memories. Edward W. Peck of Pontiac recalled, "We proceeded to the seat of war at Toledo, and by a forced march on a sultry day in September, we reached the River Raisin. The troops marched on to Monroe on the Sabbath. On nearing Toledo, it was found that the men had loaded their rifles with powder and ball without any authority and entirely without the knowledge of the officers. Approaching the landing, no resistance being offered, we landed and remained two or three days."[4] Rev. R. C. Crawford of the Michigan Conference of the Methodist Episcopal Church had sharp memories of the march to Toledo in early September.

> Being myself of a military mind and fond of excitement, I cheerfully obeyed my country's call and started out with a humble knapsack on my back. . . . Our march lasted the best part of four days, traveling most of the time at good speed, and occasionally sitting down to a lunch of fresh chicken and a bunch of well filled honeycomb, brought in by some foraging party. . . .
>
> But what grieved us most of all was the fact that after marching all the way to the banks of the Maumee, we found Governor Lucas had stayed away with all his forces, and left us to do our fighting with the only man we could find, who was ready for the fight, and he preferred sending out his pigs and chickens to the slaughter rather than to come out himself. We spent two nights and one whole day in drill, under the leadership of General Brown, showing the Buckeyes what Michigan troops could do in the matter of fight, if they could find a foe worthy of their steel.[5]

In the poem "My Seventy-eight Years," J. H. Tappan of Toledo recalls, "I came to Toledo in the fall of 1835, a few days prior to the Toledo War, and saw the Michigan soldiers with flags in the air, marching down Monroe Street to take Toledo. Perhaps I am the only one now living [in 1905] in Toledo who was present upon the occasion. Toledo was then but a very small village and there was not a railroad in the State of Ohio. Toledo then being a very sickly place, the settlers died off very fast. Funeral cars and funeral directors were unknown. These were the conditions of Toledo in 1835."[6]

After the war, the Michigan legislature appropriated $13,658.76 to pay the expenses incurred in the unsuccessful effort to retain the Toledo Strip. The war was over, and statehood was an accomplished act, but bad feelings about the land exchange remained. Charles C. Trowbridge, Mason's Whig opponent for governor in 1837, made an already bitter contest even more so by portraying Mason as selling out for Michigan's role in the Toledo War. Trowbridge was a hero because he fought in the war. The national financial panic of 1837 further clouded the picture and ruined Mason's political career.

As for the boundary issue itself, the matter was as restless as Hamlet's ghost. In 1844, the Army Corps of Engineers placed the state line in Lake Erie at a forty-five-degree angle from the north cape of Maumee Bay. For whatever reason, no question was raised by Michigan. Two years later, the Clayton bill (after Senator John M. Clayton of Delaware, chair of the Judiciary Committee) finally established Ohio's boundary claims and defined the boundaries of Ohio, Michigan, and Indiana. In 1889, because of innumerable problems that had arisen over the uncertainty of their exact location, the Michigan legislature asked for a new survey of the Michigan-Ohio and Michigan-Indiana lines. Washington refused to comply, saying that the boundary lines in question were disposed of long ago.

In 1915, Ohio and Michigan jointly sponsored a survey because of mutual difficulties involving taxation of landowners whose property was adjacent to the state line. It basically was a resurvey of the Harris line. The governors of the two states met at the boundary and shook hands in the spirit of letting bygones be bygones. But with Michigan and Ohio, on the question of boundary, bygones do not stay bygones. On April 20, 1915, an act of the Michigan legislature, signed by Governor Woodbridge N. Ferris, provided for the sum of $3,600 "for a relocation, establishment and imperishable monumenting" of the boundary between Michigan and Ohio.[7] On November 30, a report from the engineer at Toledo said, "The eastern terminus of the line, originally the most northerly cape of Maumee Bay, has been washed away for many years and did not furnish a definite starting point."[8]

There matters stood until 1922, when Ohio made a survey to determine the location of the Michigan-Ohio boundary in Lake Erie. Using the act of June 1836 as its basis, Ohio extended the interstate land boundary due east to the international line between Canada and the United States. This gave Michigan control over the northwest end of

Lake Erie and over the Lost Peninsula, 240 acres of land that can be reached only by water or through Ohio.

Nothing else happened on the issue for ten years, but apparently the boundary arrangement proved unsatisfactory to Ohio. In 1932, it redrew the line northeast at a forty-five-degree angle from Maumee Bay to the international border. By awarding a triangular two hundred square miles of former Michigan land to Ohio, the new survey laid the basis for the controversy of the 1940s, when Lake Erie bottomlands were discovered to be potentially rich in oil and gas.

At first, Michigan supported Ohio's possession of the lake area, but in 1947, Michigan made a formal claim to be the area's rightful owner. Then, in 1952, the U.S. Geological Survey Erie Quadrangle, published with the collaboration of the Michigan highway commissioner, indicated the Lake Erie boundary at a forty-five-degree angle from the north cape of Maumee Bay. In 1965, Republican governors James Rhodes of Ohio and George Romney of Michigan met where the line cuts across the Lost Peninsula, to celebrate the fiftieth anniversary of the 1915 get-together of governors at the line. A tablet erected at the site in 1965 reads:

> 50th Anniversary of Michigan-Ohio Boundary Survey
> On 19 September, 1965, officials of the states of Michigan and Ohio, and leaders of both states in civic, engineering and historical organizations, met here to celebrate the 50th anniversary of the 1915 survey and monumenting of the boundary line between these two great states of the union
> "Good Fences Make Good Neighbors"

The Rhodes-Romney photo op would seem to suggest that all was peace and love, but with Ohio and Michigan, that is never the case, and despite the optimism expressed on the site's monument, good fences do not necessarily make good neighbors. Amity lasted a year. In 1966, Michigan filed suit against Ohio for the Erie Triangle. In 1967, the U.S. Supreme Court awarded the disputed Lake Erie area to Ohio; in regard to the Lake Erie boundary, the Supreme Court accepted "northeast" to mean halfway between due north and east. In the 1970s, the dispute over the Toledo Strip erupted again. Both Ohio and Michigan laid joint claim to two hundred square miles of Lake Erie bottomlands reputed to be rich in minerals. The federal courts decided in Ohio's favor.

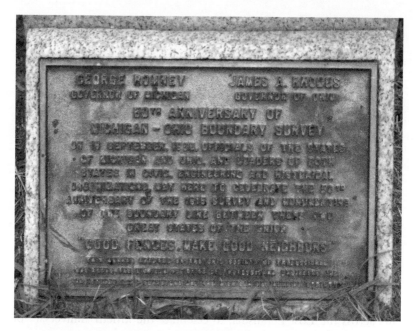

Tablet on the boundary marker in Michigan's Lost Peninsula, claiming that "good fences make good neighbors." It has not always worked out that way for Michigan and Ohio. (Photograph by Jen Luton.)

The matter was not entirely cleared up yet. In 1971, basing his ruling under the 1967 U.S. Supreme Court decision on Michigan's claim, Special Master Albert B. Maris, a retired federal appeals court judge, gave his decision for settling the dispute in favor of Ohio. Finality came in 1973, as reported by the *Monroe Evening News* on February 22 from Washington: "The Supreme Court today awarded a potentially rich stretch of Lake Erie bottom to Ohio, ending a 136-year dispute with Michigan. A 200-square mile area of the lake is potentially rich in minerals, oil and gas. Special master Albert B. Maris, retired federal appeals court judge, ruled. Michigan argued that the border should not take a northward swing over the lake but that it should extend straight out to the Canadian line. Maris recommended that the line be set to extend on a north 45 degrees east course from a point in Maumee Bay where Maris judged the north cape of the bay to have been located in 1836, when Ohio's northern boundary was set. The Supreme Court followed Maris's recommendation."

The high court's decision against Michigan underscores a supreme irony. The Boy Governor, Stevens T. Mason, all along had wanted the Toledo Strip controversy to go to the federal Supreme Court. Michigan's claims and Attorney General Butler's opinion would likely have confirmed Michigan's ownership of the Toledo Strip. As a result, Toledo now would have a Michigan zip code. But after waiting for 137 years to get to the Supreme Court, Michigan came up dry.

Also in the 1970s, a group of Toledoans cheekily campaigned to extract eleven billion dollars in "war reparations" from Michigan. Reporting in the *Monroe Evening News* on November 24, 1990, writer Elisa Tomaszewski said, "The money was supposed to compensate for the taxes Michigan received from Ohio residents before the border was settled, 'wear and tear' on Ohio troops, and destruction of a Toledo cabbage patch." Of course, no one took the campaign seriously. Or maybe people took it as "seriously" as the Upper Peninsula's infrequent campaigns to secede and establish a separate state of Superior.

Today, three historical markers help to explain the Toledo War. Two are in Michigan; one is in Ohio. The " 'War' with Happy Ending" marker is sited in Erie, south of Monroe; the "Frostbitten Convention" marker is in Ann Arbor; and the "Battle of Phillips Corners" plaque is just inside Ohio, fourteen miles south of Adrian, Michigan.

In 2003, the year Ohio celebrated its bicentennial, a provocative postscript to the Toledo War was provided by Dave Hobson, U.S. congressman from Ohio's Seventh District. On February 27 of that year, in his weekly column, Hobson reported the startling discovery that due to an oversight, a bill admitting Ohio to the Union was never formally approved in 1803 when Ohio became a state. That, of course, would make Ohio "illegal" when the Toledo War was being fought in 1835.

Ohio officially became legal at the first session of the Eighty-third Congress of the United States, "begun and held at the City of Washington on Saturday, the third day of January, one thousand nine hundred and fifty three." On April 27 and May 5, 1953, the Subcommittee on Territories and Insular Possessions held hearings on House Joint Resolution 121, a resolution for admitting the state of Ohio. The record shows that the resolution was approved on August 7, 1953. The approval document bears the signatures of Speaker of the House Joseph W. Martin Jr., Vice President Richard M. Nixon, and President Dwight D. Eisenhower. Ohio's bicentennial celebration in 2003 was in actuality only the fiftieth anniversary of statehood. The ghosts of Stevens T. Mason, General Joseph Brown, and Lewis Cass must have chortled at Ohio being referred to as a territory. On the other side, the shades of Lucas and Stickney must have groaned in travail. How could Ohio be an oversight? How could its "million of freemen" be illegal aliens? Just who did Michigan go to war with in 1835?

Only after Michigan was severely taken to task for the extralegality of the Second Convention of Assent did Congress do an about-face and vote to overlook the illegality. Michigan was admitted to the Union on the false statement by Congress that Michigan was satisfied with the terms of the act of Congress of June 15, 1836 (which, of course, it was not). Michigan never actually gave the assent required by the act of Congress, because the Second Convention of Assent was illegal and contrived. Purely and simply, there was no statutory authority for the vehicle Michigan rode into the Union. As Ohio historian W. V. Way said in his history of the Toledo War, "both parties acquired lands (Ohio the Toledo Strip, Michigan the Upper Peninsula) that neither had any legal right to."[9]

Illegalities, oversights, phantom states, purchased electoral votes, the lure of lucre, political expediency, movable boundaries—somehow the Toledo War provided them all. Both states gained territory without burying a single veteran hors de combat, and both states still can claim they never lost a war. If there was one real loser in all this, it was Wisconsin, which lost the lands extending to the eastern border of Michigan. But Wisconsin was not a state yet and had no say in Congress. And that is all familiar territory, is it not?

EPILOGUE

Michigan has been called "a misfit of two diverse peninsulas within the boundaries of a single state." That may be a bit harsh. As we have seen, the state's birth was extraordinarily complicated and drawn out. It is not the norm for a state to have to shoot its way into the Union as Michigan did with the Toledo War. The Toledo conflict was no normal war, but in any contest such as was waged in 1835 by Michigan and Ohio, it is only natural to look for winners and losers.

Stevens T. Mason, the Boy Governor, was often depicted as a youthful hothead, while his Ohio opponent, Governor Robert Lucas, came off as the seasoned political veteran. Lucas was, of course, three decades older than Mason. Holding a court of common pleas in the morning hours of September 7 was a stroke of genius on Lucas's part and shows a political cynicism that is the mark of an experienced politician.

Mason had exceptional ability for a young man in his twenties. When the committee judging his fitness for office was holding its deliberations, he took the trouble to tell them, "Yes, gentlemen, I am young, but it will be the most natural thing in the world for me to take advice of those older than myself, and I trust that if you leave matters in my hands, the affairs of this territory will be conducted to your liking."[1] Mason was not trying to get himself confirmed at any cost. Reminding his elders that they were young once themselves, he asked where they would be if someone older had not taken them under wing. This was a telling point. President Jackson perceived in the young man administrative qualities that warranted elevating him, at age twenty, to the post of secretary of the Michigan Territory.

In the battle of principle, Michigan more than upheld its honor in standing on its rights. Organized government in the Toledo Strip was under the banner of the Michigan Territory. The Pains and Penalties Act, which so galled Ohio, was upheld as valid law by the nation's top legal officer. In the exchange of the Toledo Strip for the western Upper Peninsula, Michigan was enriched territorially and economically. The mining of copper and iron ore benefited Michigan immensely. Lumbering soon followed. Now, tourism floats the region's economy. The picture is smudged, however, by the Upper Peninsula's continuing economic depression and occasional desperate attempts to create a separate state of Superior. Still, most Michiganians congratulate themselves for hoodwinking Ohio.

Mason biographer Lawton T. Hemans suggests that Michigan's border war with Ohio had the beneficial effect of advertising the state's prospects and possibilities. The Erie Canal may have been the vehicle for a westward migration, but the incentive was an interest throughout the East in Michigan's resources and people. The Toledo War kept Michigan in the headlines, "so that it seemed," writes Hemans, "as though there was hardly a hamlet of New England or New York that was not sending its delegation of pioneers."[2]

When Governor Mason's remains were exhumed and reinterred at Detroit in 1905, one of the speakers at the ceremony was Clarence M. Burton, president of the Michigan Pioneer and Historical Society. In accepting the northern peninsula, Mason, said Burton, "builded better than he knew, for it was the laying of the foundation of the immense lake traffic that we now have." Mason had sponsored the idea of building the Soo Canal. With rare foresight, his first message to the legislature asked for an appropriation for the construction of a ship canal around the falls of the St. Marys River. The locks at Sault Ste. Marie, as every Michigan schoolkid knows, handle more tonnage than the Panama and Suez canals combined. The majestic ore carriers that ply the waters of the Great Lakes and the scenic lighthouses that guide them are images that are distinctly Michigan.

Mason "builded better than he knew" in at least one other major area, that of education. His father's library provided young Mason with most of his instruction. The experience, says Hemans, "left him with a profound reverence for universal free education." Hemans continues, "His boyhood had been passed in a state where free schools and universal education were unknown, and yet one of the greatest services of the young man to the State of his adoption was to be in the cause of free schools. There is scarce a message to the Legislature in which Mason does not urge the need of universal education."[3]

The state constitution of 1835, drafted while Mason was prosecuting the Toledo War, was endorsed by the people of Michigan, who hailed its educational provisions as a milestone in American government. College training was to be a part of every child's birthright. There

would be universal education for men and women. Rather than allow
money from land grants to be drained off by township boards, a certain
amount would automatically be set aside for schools. There would be a
state superintendent of public instruction. A board of regents, free of
political influence from politicians in the state capital, would be in
charge of the state university in Ann Arbor. These provisions incorporated in the state's first charter were radical and far-reaching indeed.
Michigan's present constitution, enacted in 1963, provides the state's
Big Three institutions of higher education with a broad grant of constitutional autonomy.

Stevens T. Mason served two terms as Michigan's governor, from
November 1835 to January 1840. After the Toledo War, his stature
among the people of Michigan eroded badly. No sooner did Michigan
become a state than it was caught up in the national financial panic of
1837. Mason's financial inexperience made matters worse, and the
Whigs reminded him of his deficiencies. While still in office, on November 1, 1838, he married Julia Phelps of New York, a society girl.

His mother's death in 1839, his own discredited administration, and
his failure to support lavish state construction projects with sound currency ruined Mason's second term of office. An attendee at a dinner that
friends gave him in 1841 in Detroit described a downcast Mason: "He
was so choked he could not utter a word and finally giving way to his
feelings he cried like a child which . . . proved so infectious that there
were kerchiefs drawn out and heads held down without number."[4] Broken in heart and spirit, he moved to New York with Julia and practiced
law—not successfully as it turned out, because he had become thoroughly disillusioned with himself and with life. Mason fell victim to
pneumonia and died on January 5, 1843, only thirty-one years old. He
was buried in Marble Cemetery in New York.

Lawton T. Hemans spearheaded an effort to bring the body of
Stevens Thomson Mason home to Michigan, to Detroit, to the state to
which he had given so much and that was so indebted to him. In 1905,
in a ceremony that attracted thousands, including his ninety-year-old
sister, Emily, Mason's remains were lowered directly below the spot
where his office had been in the state's first capitol. Clarence Burton
said, "His ashes repose on the spot where the greatest achievement of
his life took place—the site of the first capitol of a mighty state." The
site is tiny, debris-blown Capitol Park in downtown Detroit. If one goes

to the foot of Griswold, one will find a statue of Stevens T. Mason, dwarfed by the towers of the Motor City. His body lies beneath the statue, in the soil of a grateful state.

Robert Lucas was a staunch Jacksonian Democrat when he ran a losing race for governor of Ohio in 1830. Running again in 1832, he triumphed, and he was inaugurated on December 7. At the time of the Toledo War, Lucas was a comparatively creaky fifty-four. Prior to the 1836 state nominating convention, Lucas said he would not be a candidate for reelection, preferring to run for the state senate in 1837, an election he promptly lost. Memories must have been short in Ohio.

The book hardly closes on Lucas at this point, however. When Congressman Thomas Hamer of Ohio suggested Lucas for the post of governor of the Iowa Territory, President Martin Van Buren readily complied. After two years of "retirement," Lucas became territorial governor of Iowa from 1838 to 1841, becoming involved in, of all things, another boundary dispute. This time, Lucas was the territorial governor dealing with a neighboring state governor. The controversy was over the territory's southern border. The true identification and location of "the rapids of the river Des Moines" were the basis of contention. When Lucas learned that Missouri officials assessed property and collected taxes in territory claimed by Iowa, he issued a proclamation stating that the "Act to prevent the exercise of a foreign jurisdiction within the limits of the territory" was in full force and effect in the territory of Iowa.

If this sounds repetitive, it is because Lucas apparently learned well from his experiences with the Pains and Penalties Act. As it turned out, Lucas copycatted Stevens T. Mason and won. The Supreme Court made the final decision and substantiated the claims of Lucas and the people of Iowa. In 1840, the Whigs won the elections, and Lucas was removed as territorial governor the next year. In 1852, Lucas threw over the Democratic Party and supported the Whig nominee for the presidency, General Winfield Scott. Lucas died in 1853. As in Ohio, a county in Iowa is named after him.

Lewis Cass, statesman, died full of years and honors. He anticipated the Toledo War in 1817, when he penned a note to the surveyor general of Ohio saying that "a disputed jurisdiction is one of the greatest evils which can happen to a country." In 1830, Cass warned Stevens T.

Mason about the disputed southern boundary with Ohio. A longtime territorial governor, Cass designed the original state seal. Of Cass, John D. Pierce, father of the Michigan school system, said, "To him more than to any other man is the state indebted for its subsequent rapid development."[5] Cass served his country as secretary of war under President Jackson and as secretary of state under President James Buchanan. He ran for president in 1848 but lost to General Zachary Taylor. Cass served as a U.S. senator from Michigan from 1844 to 1857; before that, he was a University of Michigan regent. He died on June 17, 1866, and is honored today in the National Statuary Hall in the U.S. Capitol.

Lucius Lyon served his state as a most useful citizen to the end of his days. He was Michigan's first U.S. senator. It was largely through his efforts that the Upper Peninsula was made a part of Michigan. At first opposed to any cession of the Toledo Strip to Ohio, Lyon read the political tea leaves and switched his position to one of getting as much land in compensation for the loss of Toledo as Michigan could get. In that, he played politics like an organ. Lyon decided not to seek reelection when his term was up, and he refused the nomination for governor. He served one term in 1843 as representative from the Second Congressional District and was one of the first regents of the University of Michigan. He accepted the appointment of surveyor general for Ohio, Indiana, and Michigan in 1845 and served in that post until 1850. On his death in 1851, the *Detroit Free Press* called Lyon "a well known, much beloved and most intelligent citizen" who "has left behind him an example worthy of all praise and imitation."

President Andrew Jackson, the "hero of New Orleans," served two terms as president. He put down the nullification doctrine advanced by South Carolina over the issue of tariffs. A champion of the spoils system, he won the support of the masses by vetoing a bill to recharter the Bank of the United States, portrayed by Jackson as an instrument of special privilege and profitable mainly to foreigners. Old Hickory retired to his home in Nashville in 1837, but he remained a force in politics. He worked for the annexation of Texas. His health deteriorated badly until he died on June 8, 1845.

President John Quincy Adams was not exactly a has-been at the time of the Toledo War. He served only one term as president but got himself elected as a Republican to the U.S. House of Representatives. Adams's presidency, from 1825 to 1829, was the second to go one term, the first being that of his father, John. His bid for reelection defeated by Andrew Jackson, John Quincy Adams returned to public life in a lesser capacity. He gave several speeches in support of Michigan during the time of the Toledo War. The most famous, the "Never in the course of my life" oration, was rendered in vain. By that time, Adams had turned Whig. A long life in the service of Massachusetts and his country ended in the U.S. Capitol, where Adams died on February 23, 1848.

Michigan is a state of many peninsulas, of which the most famous are the Upper Peninsula, the Garden Peninsula, the Leelanau Peninsula, the Keweenaw Peninsula, and Old Mission Peninsula. A native of Michigan instinctively points to parts of his or her hand to identify a place in the Lower Peninsula, which is shaped roughly like a mitten. But even most Michiganians cannot locate the Lost Peninsula.

In the *Toledo Blade Sunday Magazine* of February 18, 1968, writer Pat Eckhart said that "the Lost Peninsula was given to Michigan in 1836 in the treaty that ended the Toledo War." Actually, it was not a treaty so much as a brokered deal. In 1922, Ohio made a survey to determine the location of the Michigan and Ohio boundary in Lake Erie. Using the act of June 15, 1836, as its basis, Ohio extended the interstate land boundary due east to the international line between Canada and the United States. This gave Michigan control over the northwest end of Lake Erie and over the Lost Peninsula.

So just what is the Lost Peninsula, and where exactly is it? It is 240 acres of Michigan land that can be reached only by water or through Ohio. The Lost Peninsula can be found in Maumee Bay, squeezed between the Ottawa River and the bay. Michigan owns the tip that extends as a spur of land north of Toledo. The spit of land was named through the whimsy of a newspaperman, who noted in 1946 that Michigan had its Upper and Lower Peninsulas and now its Lost Peninsula. At one time, the Wyandot Indians lived there. To get to the Lost Peninsula from Michigan without a boat, one can take Summit Street in Toledo to 131st Street and drive from there to Edgewater Drive and then north to the Ottawa Shores subdivision. Ottawa Shores is the name of the private association of Lost Peninsula residents.

On November 24, 1915, Michigan governor Woodbridge Ferris

and Ohio Governor Frank B. Willis met at the end of Point Place Road, now known as Edgewater Drive, in the Lost Peninsula. Standing before the American flag, the governors declared that the "War of the States" had finally ended and dedicated a monument that pinpoints the Ohio-Michigan boundary line. A survey marking the state line was finished in 1915 after taking three months; the last land marker to be erected, post 70, was the one the governors dedicated on the Lost Peninsula. At the same boundary marker is a plaque showing that Governors James Rhodes of Ohio and George Romney of Michigan met on the site in September 1965 to celebrate the fiftieth anniversary of the boundary survey.

What is it like to live on the Lost Peninsula? "It's like being on vacation every day of your life," proclaims a sign on a porch there. More to the point, what is it like to be a part of Ohio but to pay taxes to and receive services from Michigan? I spent most of a day on the Lost Peninsula and quizzed several residents about life there.

There are about fifty modest homes on the 240 acres. Speed laws are enforced through the simple expedient of asking motorists to slow down and by posting speed limits. The residents' private association sees to road repairs. Michigan allocates no money for Lost Peninsula road improvements. Residents get no snow removal or garbage pickup, although if they were annexed to Toledo, they would receive city water and waste removal. Lost Peninsula residents' children are served by Mason Consolidated Schools in Monroe County and bused to mainland Michigan. Taxes are collected through Erie Township in Monroe County. The Lost Peninsula post office and mail service are through Erie Township, under the zip code 48133. Electricity comes from Consumers Energy of Michigan, whose lines run underneath the Ottawa River. Telephone service is through Erie Township; fortunately for Lost Peninsula residents, it is not a long-distance call to Toledo. Water comes from wells, and peninsula residents have septic fields. Erie Township provides police protection; the Moran Point (Michigan) volunteers provide fire protection. Most of the residents subscribe to the *Toledo Blade* newspaper.

Rick Knapp, resident of the Lost Peninsula since 1988, told me of life there, "It's magical when you enter the gates. There's no crime and we know our neighbors." *Magical* is also the word fifty-six-year-old Mick Johnson uses. A resident for twenty-seven years, Johnson is a retired pipe fitter who lives alone but was once married. He is a boat owner who sometimes complains about the "high water" from the Ottawa River.

"When I first moved here," Johnson told me, "we had a Toledo mailing address. I paid $23,000 for the house, but it's worth $230,000 or $300,000 on the water [Ottawa River]. It's a diverse bunch of people here, a great place for kids. The really neat thing about the Lost Peninsula—you can't dig anywhere without finding Indian pottery shards. Indians chose to live here—that tells you something!" From his window, Johnson has a great view across what he calls the "polluted" Ottawa River. He points to a bald eagle's nest across the river. He said, "I'd just as soon have Toledo take us back. We'd get water and sewer from Toledo. We'd have road service and garbage pickup." When asked if he has any feelings on the rivalry between Michigan and Ohio State, he says, "I'm a Buckeye but not hard core." It is pretty clear he likes life on the Lost Peninsula. "Once you move here, you'll die here," he said.

Over at the Lost Peninsula Marina, which the boundary line runs right through, owner Ray Roche says he serves about six hundred vessels. "Boat ownership is about 50/50 Michigan and Ohio residents." Roche lives in Ohio. He complains, "Michigan doesn't pay attention to us. They won't dredge us."

Ohio, it seems, is never quite content about the status of its northern boundary. Ohio House Bill 780, which died in 1958, empowered the governor to enter into negotiations for the acquisition of the Lost Peninsula and take it into Ohio. Some Ohioans would like to make the Lost Peninsula a Toledo recreational area. But in 1965, speaking to Toledo's efforts to acquire the Lost Peninsula Marina property for recreational purposes, Michigan attorney general Frank Kelley said to a gathering of Michigan and Ohio officials, "This threatens the sovereignty of Michigan. As far as Michigan is concerned, it will never cede an inch of Lost Peninsula lands to Ohio." That same year, state representative Raymond Kehres of Monroe proposed that the Michigan Waterway Commission purchase the land and the bayside marina for development as a Michigan state park. His proposal met with little enthusiasm.

Twenty years after Kelley's claim that Michigan would "never cede an inch" of the Lost Peninsula, Roy Hamlin, managing editor of the *Monroe Evening News*, reported a modest proposal by the Toledo City Council. In an effort to revive a long-standing border dispute, the council suggested that Michigan cede the Lost Peninsula to Toledo, which borders it on the south, if Ohio State won the annual pigskin war with Michigan. The council said that if Michigan won, Toledo would "forever waive claim to the land." Michigan governor James Blanchard, a Michigan State University graduate, turned down the wager, as Ohio was giving up nothing.

TIME LINE FOR THE TOLEDO WAR AND MICHIGAN STATEHOOD

1755: Mitchell's map places the southern end of Lake Michigan too far north of its true site.

July 13, 1787: The Northwest Ordinance provides for not less than three or more than five states, including Michigan and Ohio.

1803: Ohio becomes a state, with its northern border angled to include Maumee Bay.

January 11, 1805: Michigan becomes a territory, with its southern border at the line described by the Northwest Ordinance.

1812: Congress orders a survey of the Northwest Ordinance line, but the War of 1812 intervenes.

1816: Indiana becomes a state, with its northern border placed ten miles into the Michigan Territory.

1817: The Harris survey marks the boundary desired by Ohio.

1818: The Fulton survey line puts the mouth of the Maumee River in the Michigan Territory.

October 1832: Michigan citizens vote to petition Congress for admission as a state.

December 1833: Lucius Lyon presents the first formal petition of Michigan for admission as a state. From this date, the admission of Michigan and the boundary controversy became inseparable.

1834: The line of the Talcott survey, authorized by Congress in 1832, is found to be nearly identical with the Fulton line. In September, Governor Stevens T. Mason calls for a census.

February 12, 1835: Michigan passes the Pains and Penalties Act.

February 24, 1835: Ohio names three commissioners to re-mark its boundary.

April 1, 1835: Michigan holds elections for township officials in the disputed Toledo Strip area.

April 4, 1835: Michigan residents vote to elect delegates to a constitutional convention.

April 6, 1835: Ohio holds elections in the disputed Toledo Strip area.

April 26, 1835: The Battle of Phillips Corners opens the Toledo War.

May 11, 1835: Michigan begins its constitutional convention.

June 1835: The Ohio legislature creates Lucas County, with its seat
   at Toledo.

July 15, 1835: Two Stickney stabs Deputy Sheriff Wood, in the only
   real bloodshed of the Toledo War.

August 29, 1835: President Jackson removes Mason from office, with
   Mason officially notified on September 10.

September 7, 1835: Ohio's Lucas County Court of Common Pleas
   meets after midnight in Toledo.

September 19, 1835: John Horner arrives in Detroit to assume
   Mason's job.

October 5, 1835: Michigan ratifies its first constitution, 6,299–1,359,
   and elects Mason as its governor.

November 1, 1835: Michigan state government begins.

June 15, 1836: Jackson—seeking the electoral votes of Ohio, Indiana,
   and Illinois—signs enabling legislation for Michigan statehood,
   contingent on Michigan giving up the Toledo Strip.

September 25, 1836: The First Convention of Assent in Ann Arbor
   rejects Congress's terms.

December 14, 1836: The Second Convention of Assent (the Frostbitten Convention) approves Congress's terms for statehood.

January 26, 1837: Michigan officially becomes a state.

1843: Governor Mason dies in New York City at age thirty-one.

NOTES

CHAPTER ONE

1. Stevens T. Mason Papers, Burton Historical Collection, Detroit Public Library, Detroit, MI.
2. George N. Fuller, *Michigan Centennial History* (Chicago: Lewis Publishing, 1939), 1:230.
3. Robert Lucas Papers, Ohio Historical Society Archives/Library, Columbus.
4. Quoted in Jim Path, *The Toledo War and the Battle of Phillips Corners* (Adrian, MI: Lenawee County Historical Museum, 2001), 12.
5. LeRoy Barnett and Roger Rosentreter, *Michigan's Early Military Forces* (Detroit: Wayne State University Press, 2003), 239.
6. Quoted in Clara Waldron, *One Hundred Years, a Country Town: The Village of Tecumseh, Michigan, 1824–1924* (Tecumseh: T. A. Riordan, 1968).
7. Michigan Pioneer and Historical Collections, vol. 12, 1887, 411. Michigan Pioneer and Historical Collections is a series of volumes created from materials that were presented at meetings of the Michigan Pioneer and Historical Society. These volumes are available at a number of libraries throughout the state. The series is particularly useful to studies of early Michigan.
8. Ibid., 413.
9. Ibid.
10. Ibid.
11. Ibid.
12. Quoted in Waldron, *One Hundred Years.*

Other useful source material for this chapter includes Sister Mary Karl George, *The Rise and Fall of Toledo, Michigan: The Toledo War!* (Lansing: Michigan Historical Commission, 1971); *Cleveland Herald*, March 28, 1835; *Cleveland Whig*, April 22, 1835; Charles E. Slocum, *History of the Maumee River Basin* (Indianapolis and Toledo: Bowen and Slocum, 1905); F. M. Holloway, "A Report from Hillsdale County," in Michigan Pioneer and Historical Collections, vol. 1, 1874–76; *Monroe Courier and Ad-Venture*, November 16, 1971.

CHAPTER TWO

1. John Dann, "The Northwest Ordinance," in *Liberty's Legacy: Our Celebration of the Northwest Ordinance and the United States Constitution* (Columbus: Ohio Historical Society, 1987), 16.
2. Quoted in Willis F. Dunbar, *Michigan: A History of the Wolverine State* (Grand Rapids: Eerdmans, 1965), 61.
3. Carl Wittke, "The Ohio-Michigan Boundary Dispute Re-examined," *Ohio State Archaeological and Historical Quarterly* (October 1936).

4. Quotations by James Monroe are from George N. Fuller, *Michigan Centennial History*, vol. 1 (Chicago: Lewis Publishing, 1939), 223.

5. Dann, "Northwest Ordinance," 16–17.

6. Pauline Maier, "The Philadelphia Convention and the Development of American Government," *Liberty's Legacy*, 63.

7. George Willard, "The Making of Michigan," in Michigan Pioneer and Historical Collections, vol. 17, 1890, 299.

8. Nathan Dane to Rufus King, July 16, 1787, New York, signed autograph letter, 3 pages, State Historical Society of Wisconsin, in *Liberty's Legacy*, 34.

9. Thomas H. Smith, *An Ohio Reader, 1750 to the Civil War* (Grand Rapids: Eerdmans, 1975), 33.

10. Peter S. Onuf, "The Importance of the Northwest Ordinance," in *Liberty's Legacy*, 11.

11. Smith, *Ohio Reader*, 33.

Other useful source material for this chapter includes Sister Mary Karl George, *The Rise and Fall of Toledo, Michigan: The Toledo War!* (Lansing: Michigan Historical Commission, 1971); *Cleveland Herald*, March 28, 1835; *Cleveland Whig*, April 22, 1835; Clara Waldron, *One Hundred Years, a Country Town: The Village of Tecumseh, Michigan, 1824–1924* (Tecumseh: T. A. Riordan, 1968); Charles E. Slocum, *History of the Maumee River Basin* (Indianapolis and Toledo: Bowen and Slocum, 1905); F. M. Holloway, "A Report from Hillsdale County," in Michigan Pioneer and Historical Collections, vol. 1, 1874–76; *Liberty's Legacy: Our Celebration of the Northwest Ordinance and the United States Constitution* (Columbus: Ohio Historical Society, 1987); Willis Dunbar, *Michigan through the Centuries*, vol. 1 (New York: Lewis Historical Publishing, 1955); Carl Wittke, "The Ohio-Michigan Boundary Dispute Re-examined," *Ohio State Archaeological and Historical Quarterly* (October 1936): 10–21; Dr. Martin J. Hershock, "Michigan's Path from Territory to Statehood" (lecture, Ann Arbor District Library, January 12, 2005); David S. Pollack, editorial guest viewpoint, *Ann Arbor News*, July 21, 1992; Russell B. Nye, *Michigan* (Toronto: Longmans Canada Limited, 1966), especially 104–7.

CHAPTER THREE

1. Quoted from Frank E. Robson, "The Michigan and Ohio Boundary Line," in Michigan Pioneer and Historical Collections, vol. 11, 1887, 218–19.

2. Letter published by the Michigan constitutional convention in 1835 in its *Appeal to the People of the United States*, as quoted by Annah May Soule in *The Southern and Western Boundaries of Michigan* (Ann Arbor, MI, 1896), reprinted in Michigan Pioneer and Historical Collections, vol. 27, 1896, 350. *The Southern and Western Boundaries of Michigan* is also reprinted in Michigan Political Science Association publications, vol. 2, 29–81. The Michigan Political Science Association publications are a series of volumes created from papers and lectures that were delivered at MPSA gatherings throughout the state.

3. John H. Doyle, "A Story of Early Toledo," *Commerce Club News* (1919), 24ff.

Other useful source material for this chapter includes Sister Mary Karl George, *The Rise and Fall of Toledo, Michigan: The Toledo War!* (Lansing: Michigan Historical Society Commission, 1971); Alec R. Gilpin, *The Territory of Michigan, 1805–1837* (East Lansing: Michigan State University Press, 1970); *Historical Sketch of Lucas County* (Columbus, OH: Works Progress Administration, 1937), in Inventory of the County Archives of Ohio, Lucas County Public Library, Toledo.

CHAPTER FOUR

1. Quoted in Lewis Cass Papers, William L. Clements Library, Ann Arbor, MI.

2. A. C. McLaughlin, "The Influence of Governor Cass on the Development of the Northwest," American Historical Association Papers, vol. 3, p. 347, and quoted in George N. Fuller, *Economic and Social Beginnings of Michigan* (Lansing: Wynkoop Hallenbeck Crawford, 1916), 52.

3. J. Morse, *Traveller's Guide* (New Haven, CT: New Haven Press, 1826), 169, reprinted in Fuller, *Economic and Social Beginnings of Michigan,* 52.

4. Annah May Soule, *The Southern and Western Boundaries of Michigan* (Ann Arbor, 1896), reprinted in Michigan Pioneer and Historical Collections, vol. 27, 1896, 343. *The Southern and Western Boundaries of Michigan* is also reprinted in Michigan Political Science Association publications, vol. 2, 29–81.

5. Cass Papers. See also Frank E. Robson, "The Michigan and Ohio Boundary Line," in Michigan Pioneer and Historical Collections, vol. 11, 1887, 221.

6. Quoted in Cass Papers.

7. Ibid.

8. Quoted in Fuller, *Economic and Social Beginnings of Michigan,* 53–54.

9. Quoted in Willis F. Dunbar, *Michigan: A History of the Wolverine State* (Grand Rapids: Eerdmans, 1965), 193. Dunbar cites this as an "Emigrant's Song," first published in a Detroit newspaper in 1831.

10. "A Michigan Emigrant Song," from *Detroit Post and Tribune,* Feb. 13, 1881, as found in Michigan Pioneer and Historical Collections, vol. 3, 1879–80, 265.

11. Kent Sagendorph, *Michigan: The Story of the University* (New York: E. P. Dutton, 1948), 44.

Other useful source material for this chapter includes Kent Sagendorph, *Michigan: The Story of the University* (New York: E. P. Dutton, 1948); Elizabeth M. Farrand, *History of the University of Michigan* (Ann Arbor: Register Publishing House, 1885); Wilfred B. Shaw, *A Short History of the University of Michigan* (Ann Arbor: George H. Wahr, 1937); Annah May Soule, "The Controversy over the Michigan-Ohio Boundary," in *The Southern and Western Boundaries of Michigan* (Ann Arbor, 1896), reprinted in Michigan Pioneer and Historical Collections, vol. 27, 1896; Howard Peckham, *The Making of the University of Michigan, 1817–1992* (Ann Arbor: University of Michigan Bentley Historical Library, 1967); John H. Doyle, "A Story of Early Toledo" *Commerce Club News* (1919), 24ff.; Ethel Rowan Fasquelle, *When Michigan Was Young* (Grand Rapids, MI:

Eerdmans, 1950); Richard A. Santer, *Michigan: Heart of the Great Lakes* (Dubuque, IA: Kendall/Hunt Publications, 1977); Charles Richard Tuttle, *General History of the State of Michigan*, vol. 2 (Detroit: Detroit Free Press, 1873); George Willard, "The Making of Michigan," in Michigan Pioneer and Historical Collections, vol. 17, 1890.

CHAPTER FIVE

1. September 20, 1834, Papers of the Monroe County Historical Commission, Monroe, MI.

2. Lawton T. Hemans, *The Life and Times of Stevens T. Mason* (Lansing: Michigan Historical Commission, 1930), 115.

3. Ibid., 114.

4. Quoted in Kit Lane, *Lucius Lyon: An Eminently Useful Citizen* (Douglas, MI: Pavilion, 1991), 67.

5. Ibid., 66.

6. Stevens T. Mason Papers, Burton Historical Collection, Detroit Public Library, Detroit.

7. George N. Fuller, *Michigan Centennial History*, vol. 1 (Chicago: Lewis Publishing, 1939), 230.

8. Stevens T. Mason Papers, Bentley Historical Library, Ann Arbor, MI.

9. Letter from John Thomson Mason, September 6, 1834, Mason Papers, Burton Historical Collection.

10. Fuller, *Michigan Centennial History*, 253.

11. Kent Sagendorph, *Michigan: The Story of the University* (New York: E. P. Dutton, 1948), 51.

12. Annah May Soule, *The Southern and Western Boundaries of Michigan* (Ann Arbor, 1896), reprinted in Michigan Pioneer and Historical Collections, vol. 27, 1896, 358. *The Southern and Western Boundaries of Michigan* is also reprinted in Michigan Political Science Association publications, vol. 2, 29–81.

13. Quoted in Hemans, *Life and Times of Stevens T. Mason*, 144.

Other useful source material for this chapter includes F. Clever Bald, *Michigan in Four Centuries* (New York: Harper and Row, 1954), especially 188–202; C. Warren Vanderhill, *Settling the Great Lakes Frontier: Immigration to Michigan, 1837–1924* (Lansing: Michigan Historical Commission, 1970); Lucius Lyon Papers, William L. Clements Library, Ann Arbor, MI; George S. May, *Pictorial History of Michigan: The Early Years* (Grand Rapids: Eerdmans, 1967); Willis F. Dunbar and George S. May, *Michigan: A History of the Wolverine State* (Grand Rapids: Eerdmans, 1970); Dr. Martin J. Hershock, "Michigan's Path from Territory to Statehood" (lecture, Ann Arbor District Library, MI, January 12, 2005); Kent Sagendorph, *Stevens Thomson Mason, Misunderstood Patriot* (New York: E. P. Dutton, 1947); John Kern, *A Short History of Michigan* (Lansing: Michigan History Division, Michigan Department of State, 1977); John T. Blois, *Gazetteer of Michigan* (Detroit: Rood; New York: Robinson, Pratt, 1838); Clarence Edwin Carter, *The Territorial Papers of the United States*, vol. 12, *The Territory of Michigan, 1829–1837* (Washington, DC: United States Government Printing Office, 1945).

1. Robert Lucas Papers, Ohio Historical Society Archives/Library, Columbus.
2. Ibid.
3. Ibid.
4. Lawton T. Hemans, *The Life and Times of Stevens T. Mason* (Lansing: Michigan Historical Commission, 1930), 139.
5. Letter of February 20, 1835, Stevens T. Mason Papers, Bentley Historical Library, Ann Arbor, MI.
6. Ibid.
7. Ibid.
8. Ibid.
9. Quoted in Frank E. Robson, "The Michigan and Ohio Boundary Line," in Michigan Pioneer and Historical Collections, vol. 2, 1887, 223.
10. Lucas Papers.
11. Letter of February 28, 1835, Mason Papers, Bentley Historical Library.
12. Francis Weisenburger, *History of the State of Ohio*, vol. 3 (Columbus: Ohio State Archaeological and Historical Society, 1941), 297–307.
13. Letter of March 6, 1835, Mason Papers, Bentley Historical Library.
14. Mason Papers, Bentley Historical Library; also in Stevens T. Mason Papers, Michigan State Archives, Lansing.
15. Lucas Papers.
16. Ibid
17. Ibid.
18. Mason Papers, Bentley Historical Library.
19. Ibid.
20. Letter of March 20, 1835, Stevens T. Mason Papers, Burton Historical Collection, Detroit Public Library, Detroit.
21. Letter of March 21, 1835, Mason Papers, Bentley Historical Library.
22. Quoted in letter to Secretary of State John Forsyth, April 2, 1835, Mason Papers, Burton Historical Collection. See also Claude S. Larzelere, "The Boundaries of Michigan," in Michigan Pioneer and Historical Collections, vol. 30, 1905, 22; George N. Fuller, *Michigan Centennial History* (Chicago: Lewis Publishing, 1939), 1:233.
23. Sister Mary Karl George, *The Rise and Fall of Toledo, Michigan: The Toledo War!* (Lansing: Michigan Historical Commission, 1971), chap. 3.
24. Letter to Mason, May 1, 1835, marked "confidential," Mason Papers, Burten Historical Collection.
25. Quoted in Fuller, *Michigan Centennial History*, 1:232–33.
26. Letter of March 23 to Forsyth, Mason Papers, Bentley Historical Library; Letter of March 23 to Jackson, Mason Papers, Burton Historical Collection.
27. Quoted in Hemans, *Life and Times of Stevens T. Mason*, 141.
28. Mason Papers, Bentley Historical Library.

Other useful source material for this chapter includes Alec R. Gilpin, *The Territory of Michigan, 1805–1837* (East Lansing: Michigan State University Press, 1970); *Annals of Cleveland*, vols. 18–19, part 1 (Cleveland, OH: Works Progress

Administration, 1938), in State Archives of Ohio, Columbus; *National Intelligencer*, March 26, 1835.

CHAPTER SEVEN

1. Quoted in David S. Pollack, "The Frostbitten Convention," *Ann Arbor Observer*, January 1997.

2. Robert Lucas Papers, Ohio Historical Society Archives/Library, Columbus.

3. Quotations from Carl Wittke, "The Ohio-Michigan Boundary Dispute Re-examined," *Ohio State Archaeological and Historical Quarterly* (October 1936): 11, 12.

4. Quoted in *Cleveland Whig*, April 8, 1835.

5. Letter of April 2, 1835, Stevens T. Mason Papers, Burton Historical Collection, Detroit Public Library, Detroit.

6. Letter of March 20, 1835, Lucas Papers.

7. Stevens T. Mason Papers, Bentley Historical Library, Ann Arbor, MI, and Michigan State Archives, Lansing.

8. Lawton T. Hemans, "Michigan's Debt to Stevens T. Mason," in Michigan Pioneer and Historical Collections, vol. 35, 1905–6, 246.

9. Michigan Pioneer and Historical Collections, vol. 35, 1905–6, June 7–8, 1905, 38. Quotation is from the re-interment ceremonies in Detroit held on June 4, 1905.

10. Carl Wittke, "The Ohio-Michigan Boundary Dispute Re-examined," *Ohio State Archaeological and Historical Quarterly* (October 1936): 13.

11. Letter of April 2, 1835, Stevens T. Mason Papers, William L. Clements Library, Ann Arbor, MI.

12. Thomas H. Smith, *An Ohio Reader: 1750 to the Civil War* (Grand Rapids: Eerdmans, 1975), 69.

13. Letter of April 5, 1935, Mason Papers, Burton Historical Collection.

14. Quoted in William D. Hoyt Jr., "Benjamin C. Howard and the 'Toledo War': Some Letters of a Federal Commissioner," *Ohio State Archaeological and Historical Quarterly* 60 (July 1951): 303, 304.

15. John C. Parish, *Robert Lucas* (Iowa City: State Historical Society of Iowa, 1907).

16. Quoted in Hoyt, "Benjamin C. Howard and the 'Toledo War,'" 306.

17. Richard Rush and Benjamin C. Howard to Mason, April 10, 1835, Mason Papers, William L. Clements Library.

18. Message to the second session of the Thirty-third General Assembly, June 8, 1835, 3, Lucas Papers.

19. Letter of April 9, 1835, Mason Papers, Burton Historical Collection.

20. Annah May Soule, *The Southern and Western Boundaries of Michigan* (Ann Arbor, 1896), reprinted in Michigan Pioneer and Historical Collections, vol. 27, 1896, 361. *The Southern and Western Boundaries of Michigan* is also reprinted in Michigan Political Science Association publications, vol. 2, 29–81.

21. Mason Papers, William L. Clements Library.

22. Quoted in Randolph C. Downes, ed., "How Andrew Jackson Settled the Ohio-Michigan Boundary Dispute of 1835," *Northwest Ohio Quarterly*, Autumn 1951, 186.

23. See LeRoy Barnett and Roger Rosentreter, *Michigan's Early Military Forces* (Detroit: Wayne State University Press, 2003), 238; Goodsell's quote comes from Lucas Papers.

24. Lucas Papers.

25. Quotations from, respectively, Hoyt, "Benjamin C. Howard and the 'Toledo War,'" 304; Barnett and Rosentreter, *Michigan's Early Military Forces*, 238.

26. R. Carlyle Buley, *The Old Northwest*, vol. 2 (Indianapolis: Indiana Historical Society, 1950), 190–203.

27. Barnett and Rosentreter, *Michigan's Early Military Forces*, 239.

28. Letter of April 10, 1835, Mason Papers, Burton Historical Collection.

29. Smith, *An Ohio Reader*, 69.

30. Quoted in Frank E. Robson, "The Michigan and Ohio Boundary Line," in Michigan Pioneer and Historical Collections, vol. 2, 1887, 223–24; also quoted in Claude Larzelere, "The Boundaries of Michigan," in Michigan Pioneer and Historical Collections, vol. 30, 1905, 21.

31. Rush and Howard to Mason, April 14, 1835, Mason Papers, Burton Historical Collection.

32. Mason to Rush and Howard, April 18, 1835, Mason Papers, Burton Historical Collection.

33. Mason Papers, Burton Historical Collection.

34. Letter of April 18, 1835, Lewis Cass Papers, William L. Clements Library, Ann Arbor, MI.

35. Smithsonian-Schoolcraft Papers, in Michigan Pioneer and Historical Collections, vol. 37, 1908, 341–42.

36. Mason to Lewis Cass, April 25, 1835, Mason Papers, Burton Historical Collection.

Other useful source material for this chapter includes Alec R. Gilpin, *The Territory of Michigan, 1805–1837* (East Lansing: Michigan State University Press, 1970); Charles E. Slocum, *History of the Maumee River Basin* (Indianapolis and Toledo: Bowen and Slocum, 1905); Talcott E. Wing, *History of Monroe County, Michigan* (New York: Munsell, 1890); W. V. Way, *The Facts and Historical Events of the Toledo War of 1835* (Toledo, OH: Daily Commercial Steam Book and Job Printing, 1869); Sister Mary Karl George, *The Rise and Fall of Toledo, Michigan: The Toledo War!* (Lansing: Michigan Historical Commission, 1971); *Indiana Journal* (Indianapolis), May 1, 1835; "The First Blow Struck!" *Detroit Free Press*, May 9, 1835; *National Intelligencer*, May 12 and 16 and June 27, 1835.

CHAPTER EIGHT

1. Jim Path, *The Toledo War and the Battle of Phillips Corners* (Adrian, MI: Lenawee County Historical Museum, 2001), 11, 12.

2. As quoted in the *Cleveland Whig* and reprinted in *National Intelligencer*, May 9, 1835.

3. Charles R. Tuttle, *General History of the State of Michigan*, vol. 2 (Detroit: Detroit Free Press Co., 1873), 464.

4. Letter of May 3, 1835, Stevens T. Mason Papers, William L. Clements Library, Ann Arbor, MI, and Michigan State Archives, Lansing.

5. *Columbus Hemisphere*, as reprinted in *National Intelligencer*, May 12, 1835.

6. *Cleveland Whig*, May 13, 1835, as reprinted in *Annals of Cleveland*, vols. 18–19, part 1 (Cleveland, OH: Works Progress Administration, 1938), in State Archives of Ohio, Columbus.

7. Quoted in William B. Saxbe Jr., "Battle of the Transits: The Toledo War," *Timeline* (Ohio Historical Society, Columbus), October–November 1987, 8.

8. Mason Papers, William L. Clements Library, and Michigan State Archives, Lansing.

9. Robert Lucas Papers, Ohio Historical Society Archives/Library, Columbus.

10. Mason Papers, William L. Clements Library, and Michigan State Archives, Lansing.

11. Mason Papers, Burton Historical Collection.

12. The May 7 resolution and the Hamer letter to Lucas quoted in Francis Weisenburger, *History of the State of Ohio*, vol. 3 (Columbus: Ohio State Archaeological and Historical Society, 1941), 307; see 297–307.

13. Letter of May 10, 1835, Lewis Cass Papers, William L. Clements Library, Ann Arbor, MI.

14. Weisenburger, *History of the State of Ohio*, 307.

15. Letter of May 10, 1835, Cass Papers, William L. Clements Library.

16. Quoted in Weisenburger, *History of the State of Ohio*.

17. Quoted in Tana Mosier Porter, *Benjamin Franklin Stickney, 1775–1852* (Toledo: Toledo Sesquicentennial Commission, 1987), 3.

18. Ibid., 2.

19. Sister Mary Karl George, *The Rise and Fall of Toledo, Michigan: The Toledo War!* (Lansing: Michigan Historical Commission, 1971), chap. 4.

20. *Toledo Gazette*, dateline Maumee, April 13, 1835.

21. Lucas Papers.

22. Lucas Papers.

23. Quoted in Frank E. Robson, "The Michigan and Ohio Boundary Line," in Michigan Pioneer and Historical Collections, vol. 2, 1887, 224.

24. Lucas Papers. The message was recorded by J. B. Gardiner.

25. Charles R. Tuttle, *General History of the State of Michigan*, vol. 2 (Detroit: Detroit Free Press Co., 1873), 463.

26. Letter of June 26, 1835, Lucas Papers.

27. Both quotations in Saxbe, "Battle of the Transits."

Other useful source material for this chapter includes *Detroit Journal and Courier*, May 6, 1835; Charles E. Slocum, *History of the Maumee River Basin* (Indianapolis and Toledo: Bowen and Slocum, 1905); Richard L. Hawk, "Ohio's 'War' With Michigan," *Columbus Dispatch*, January 20, 1963; George S. May, *Michigan: An Illustrated History of the Great Lakes State* (Northridge, CA: Windsor Publications, 1987); Bruce Catton, *Michigan: A Bicentennial History* (New York: W. W. Norton, 1976); Thomas H. Smith, ed., *An Ohio Reader, 1750 to the Civil War* (Grand Rapids, MI: Eerdmans, 1975) ; E. D. Antes, *The Toledo War* (Hamilton, OH: privately printed, 1959); Karl F. Zeisler, "When Michigan 'Fought' Ohio," *Detroit Saturday Night*, October 15, 1927; *National Intelligencer*, May 16, 1835; *Detroit Journal*, June 19 and 27, 1835.

1. Quotations in *Annals of Cleveland, 1818–1835*, vols. 18–19, part 1 (Cleveland, OH: Works Progress Administration, 1938), in State Archives of Ohio, Columbus.

2. Letter of July 11, 1835, Stevens T. Mason Papers, Bentley Historical Library, Ann Arbor, MI.

3. Report of July 16, 1835, from the district attorney's office, Monroe, MI, to Stevens T. Mason, "Report on the Toledo War," box 197, Michigan State Archives, Lansing.

4. Talcott Wing, *History of Monroe County, Michigan* (New York: Munsell and Co., 1890), 190.

5. "Report on the Toledo War."

6. Ibid.

7. Ibid.

8. Letter of July 16, 1835, *Annals of Cleveland*, vols. 18–19, part 1.

9. Letter of July 17, 1835, Mason Papers, Bentley Historical Library.

10. Quoted in LeRoy Barnett and Roger Rosentreter, *Michigan's Early Military Forces* (Detroit: Wayne State University Press, 2003), 241.

11. Sister Mary Karl George, *The Rise and Fall of Toledo, Michigan: The Toledo War!* (Lansing: Michigan Historical Commission, 1971), chap. 4.

12. *Toledo Gazette*, July 20, 1835; see also Richard L. Hawk, "Ohio's 'War' With Michigan," *Columbus Dispatch*, January 20, 1963, 18.

13. Reprinted in *Annals of Cleveland*, vols. 18–19, part 1.

14. Letter of July 20, 1835, "Report on the Toledo War."

15. Stevens T. Mason Papers, Bentley Historical Library, Ann Arbor, MI.

16. Letter of July 17, 1835, Mason to Forsyth, Mason Papers, Bentley Historical Library.

17. *Cleveland Whig*, August 26, 1835, reprinted in *Annals of Cleveland*, vols. 18–19, part 1. See also *Cleveland Whig*, August 26, 1835.

Other useful source material for this chapter includes *Cleveland Whig*, July 22 and 29, 1835; Michigan Pioneer and Historical Collections, vol. 6, 1883; Rowland H. Rerick, *State Centennial History of Ohio* (Madison, WI: Northwestern Historical Association,1902); Emilius O. Randall and Daniel J. Ryan, *History of Ohio*, vol. 3 (New York: Century History, 1912), 438–46; Francis Weisenburger, *History of the State of Ohio*, vol. 3 (Columbus: Ohio State Archaeological and Historical Society, 1941).

CHAPTER TEN

1. Letter of June 8, 1835, from Bethel, Ohio, Lucas County Public Library, Toledo, OH.

2. L. G. Stuart, "Verdict for Michigan: How the Upper Peninsula Became a Part of Michigan," in Michigan Pioneer and Historical Collections, vol. 27, 1986, 390–99.

3. Senator John M. Clayton, *Report to the Senate Committee on the Judiciary, March 1, 1836* (Washington, DC: Blair and Rives, 1836).

4. Ibid.

5. Ibid.

6. Lucas County Public Library, Toledo, OH.

7. December 21, 1835, *Speech of Senator Thomas Ewing* (Washington, DC: Gales and Seaton, 1835), in Lucas County Public Library, Toledo, OH.

8. Ibid.

9. Ibid.

CHAPTER ELEVEN

1. Speech of June 4, 1834, as quoted by L. G. Stuart in "Verdict for Michigan: How the Upper Peninsula Became a Part of Michigan," in Michigan Pioneer and Historical Collections, vol. 27, 1896, 399.

2. Ibid.

3. Lucius Lyon Papers, William L. Clements Library, Ann Arbor, MI.

4. Ibid.

5. *Appeal, by the Convention of Michigan, to the People of the United States; With Other Documents, in relation to the Boundary Question, between Michigan and Ohio* (Detroit: Sheldon McKnight, 1835). See also "The History and Times of the Hon. John Norvell," paper presented at the annual meeting of the Michigan State Pioneer Society, February 4, 1880, printed in Michigan Pioneer and Historical Collections, 140–47.

6. Stevens T. Mason Papers, William L. Clements Library, Ann Arbor, MI.

7. Message to the Legislative Council, November 19, 1834, Stevens T. Mason Papers, Bentley Historical Library, Ann Arbor, MI.

Other useful source material for this chapter includes Charles Grim, *The Ohio and Michigan War and Tales of the Border* (n.p., 1962); W. V. Way, *The Facts and Historical Events of the Toledo War of 1835* (Toledo, OH: Daily Commercial Steam Book, 1869).

CHAPTER TWELVE

1. Stevens T. Mason Papers, Burton Historical Collection, Detroit Public Library, Detroit.

2. Stevens T. Mason Papers, Bentley Historical Library, Ann Arbor, MI, and Michigan State Archives, Lansing.

3. Mason Papers, Bentley Historical Library.

4. Letter of March 11, 1832, Mason Papers, Burton Historical Collection.

5. Mason Papers, Burton Historical Collection.

6. Letter from General Brown at Tecumseh, Box 152, Michigan State Archives, Lansing.

7. Mason Papers, Bentley Historical Library.

8. Ibid.

9. Executive order of August 25, 1835, "Report on the Toledo War," box 197, Michigan State Archives, Lansing.

10. Letter of August 29, 1835, *Annals of Cleveland, 1818–1935*, vols. 18–19,

part 1 (Cleveland: Works Progress Administration, 1938), in State Archives of Ohio, Columbus.

11. Michigan Pioneer and Historical Collections, vol. 35, 1905–06.

Other useful source material for this chapter includes Patricia J. Baker, "Stevens Thomson Mason," *Michigan History* (Michigan Historical Center, Lansing), 1st ser., 5 (2001): 1–4; George Weeks, *Stewards of the State* (Ann Arbor: *Detroit News* and Historical Society of Michigan, 1987); undated article from the *Monroe Sentinel*, Lucas County Public Library, Toledo, OH; Robert Lucas Papers, Ohio Historical Society Archives/Library, Columbus; Carl Wittke, "The Ohio-Michigan Boundary Dispute Re-examined," *Ohio State Archaeological and History Quarterly* (October 1936): 15.

CHAPTER THIRTEEN

1. Debate in the House of Representatives, printed in *National Intelligencer*, March 24, 1835.

2. Quoted in Kit Lane, *Lucius Lyon: An Eminently Useful Citizen* (Douglas, MI: Pavilion, 1991), 77–78.

3. Letter of November 15, 1835, "Letters of Lucius Lyon," in Michigan Pioneer and Historical Collections, vol. 27, 1896, 462.

4. Alec R. Gilpin, *The Territory of Michigan, 1805–1837* (East Lansing: Michigan State University Press, 1970).

5. Letter of December 6, 1835, "Letters of Lucius Lyon," 464.

6. Letter of December 29, 1835, box 5, Lucius Lyon Papers, William L. Clements Library, Ann Arbor, MI.

7. Quoted in Lane, *Lucius Lyon*, 74.

8. "Letters of Lucius Lyon," 470.

9. Letter of January 19, 1836, box 5, Lyon Papers.

10. Letter of February 21, 1836, "Letters of Lucius Lyon," 479.

11. Message to the legislature, February 1, 1836, Stevens T. Mason Papers, Bentley Historical Library, Ann Arbor, MI.

12. "Letters of Lucius Lyon," 475.

13. Ibid., 479.

14. L. G. Stuart, "Verdict for Michigan: How the Upper Peninsula Became a Part of Michigan," in Michigan Pioneer and Historical Collections, vol. 27, 1896, 402.

15. "Letters of Lucius Lyon," 475.

16. Ibid., 485.

17. Ibid., 488.

18. Message to the legislature, February 1, 1836, Mason Papers, Bentley Historical Library.

19. Ibid.

20. Ibid.

21. House of Representatives, *Remonstrance of the Citizens of the Township of Whiteford, Monroe County, Michigan, on the Disputed Tract, against the Bill Reported in the H.R. Giving That Tract to the State of Ohio, April 1, 1836*, 24th Cong., 1st sess., 1835–36, in *Journal of Proceedings*, Lucas County Public Library, Toledo, OH.

22. Letter of March 23, 1836, "Letters of Lucius Lyon," 489.

23. Quoted in Frank E. Robson, "The Michigan and Ohio Boundary Line," in Michigan Pioneer and Historical Collections, vol. 2, 1887, 227.

24. William B. Saxbe Jr., "Battle of the Transits: The Toledo War," *Timeline* (Oct.–Nov. 1987): 10; see also Lawton T. Hemans, *The Life and Times of Stevens T. Mason* (Lansing: Michigan Historical Commission, 1930), 144.

25. Edward W. Peck, "Disputed Questions in the Early History of Michigan," Michigan Pioneer and Historical Collections, vol. 11, 1887, 157.

26. Charles Grim, *The Ohio and Michigan War and Tales of the Border* (n.p., 1962).

27. W. V. Way, *The Facts and Historical Events of the Toledo War of 1835* (Toledo, OH: Daily Commercial Steam Book, 1896), 48.

28. Peck, "Disputed Questions," 158.

29. Letter of April 8, 1836, box 6, Lyon Papers.

30. Dr. A. Philes, Galena, Ill., Letter of February 18, 1836, box 5, Lyon Papers.

31. Patricia J. Baker, "Stevens Thomson Mason," *Michigan History* (Michigan Historical Center, Lansing), 1st ser., 5 (2001): 2.

32. *Journal of Proceedings*, found in box 200, entry of Sept. 27, 1836, Michigan State Archives, Lansing.

33. Address of October 15, 1836, box 200, Records of the Executive Office, 1810–1910, Michigan State Archives, Lansing.

34. *Michigan Argus*, November 13, 1836, Bentley Historical Library, Ann Arbor, MI.

35. Quotations from, respectively, box 200, Records of the Executive Office, 1810–1910, Michigan State Archives, Lansing; *Journal of the Proceedings of the Convention at Ann Arbor, December 14, 1836* (Ann Arbor, MI: E. P. Gardner, 1836).

36. Box 200, Records of the Executive Office, 1810–1910, Michigan State Archives, Lansing.

37. Kent Sagendorph, *Stevens Thomas Mason, Misunderstood Patriot* (New York: E. P. Dutton, 1947), 244.

38. Mason Papers, Bentley Historical Library.

39. Ibid.

40. Gilpin, *Territory of Michigan*.

Other useful source material for this chapter includes F. Clever Bald, *Michigan in Four Centuries* (New York: Harper and Row, 1954), esp. 188–202; Dr. Martin J. Hershock, "Michigan's Path from Territory to Statehood" (lecture, Ann Arbor District Library, MI, January 12, 2005); David S. Pollack, "The Frostbitten Convention," *Ann Arbor Observer*, January 1997; Willis F. Dunbar and George S. May, *Michigan: A History of the Wolverine State* (Grand Rapids: Eerdmans, 1970); Claude S. Larzelere, "The Boundaries of Michigan," in Michigan Pioneer and Historical Collections, vol. 30, 1905; Sister Mary Karl George, *The Rise and Fall of Toledo, Michigan: The Toledo War!* (Lansing: Michigan Historical Commission, 1971), chap. 8; Senate, *Report of the Committee on the Judiciary, to Whom Were Referred a Bill to Settle and Establish the Northern Boundary Line of the State of Ohio*, 24th Cong., 1st sess., 1835–36; House of Representatives, *Report of the Committee on the Judiciary, to Whom Were Referred a Bill to Settle the Northern*

Boundary Line of the State of Ohio and the Admission of Michigan into the Union, 24th Cong., 1st sess., 1835–36; *National Intelligencer,* March 24 and 26, April 11, and May 2, 1835; U.S.

207
———
Notes to
Pages
157–69

Department of State, *Message from the President of the United States, with Reports from the Secretaries of State and War, Relative to the Boundary Line between Ohio and the Territory of Michigan, January 12, 1836* (Washington, DC: Gales and Seaton, 1836), in Ohio Historical Society Archives/Library, Columbus; Lucius Lyon, *Letter to the Honorable Lewis Williams, Chairman of the Committee on Territories, respecting the Boundary Line between Ohio and Michigan; also, the Report of said Committee on the Subject of Admitting Michigan into the Union* (Washington, DC: Gales and Seaton, 1834), in Ohio Historical Society Archives/Library, Columbus; U.S. War Department, *Boundary—Ohio and Michigan* (Washington, DC: Blair and Rives, 1835); Talcott Wing, *History of Monroe County, Michigan* (New York: Munsell and Co., 1890), esp. 198; George N. Fuller, *Michigan Centennial History,* vol. 1 (Chicago: Lewis Publishing, 1939), esp. 236.

CHAPTER FOURTEEN

1. Quoted in Kent Sagendorph, *Stevens Thomson Mason, Misunderstood Patriot* (New York: E. P. Dutton, 1947), 200.

2. Quoted in W. V. Way, *The Facts and Historical Events of the Toledo War of 1835* (Toledo, OH: Daily Commercial Steam Book, 1869), 49.

3. Quoted in ibid., 49–50.

4. *National Intelligencer,* September 16, 1835.

5. Edward W. Peck, "Disputed Questions in the Early History of Michigan," in Michigan Pioneer and Historical Collection, vol. 11, 1887, 155.

6. Quoted in William B. Saxbe Jr., "Battle of the Transits: The Toledo War," *Timeline* (Ohio Historical Society, Columbus), October–November 1987, 9.

7. Quoted in Way, *Facts and Historical Events of the Toledo War,* 42.

8. Ibid., 44.

9. Letter of October 4, 1835, *Annals of Cleveland, 1818–1935,* vols. 18–19, part 1 (Cleveland: Works Progress Administration, 1938), in State Archives of Ohio, Columbus.

10. *Lansing Republican,* September 5, 1873, reprinted in Michigan Pioneer and Historical Collections, vol. 7, 1884, 60–61.

11. Way, *Facts and Historical Events of the Toledo War,* 46–47.

12. *Monroe Commercial,* September 11, 1885.

13. Letter to Secretary of State Forsyth, Lucas County Public Library, Toledo, OH; also found in Michigan Pioneer and Historical Collections, vol. 30, 1905, 328–31.

14. Willis F. Dunbar and George S. May, *Michigan: A History of the Wolverine State* (Grand Rapids: Eerdmans, 1970), 249.

15. Letter of May 1, 1835, Robert Lucas Papers, Ohio Historical Society Archives/Library, Columbus; also found in Michigan Pioneer and Historical Collections, vol. 12, 1887, 413.

16. Quoted in Frank E. Robson, "The Michigan and Ohio Boundary Line," in Michigan Pioneer and Historical Collections, vol. 2, 1887, 223.

17. Letter of March 15, 1835, Lucas County Public Library, Toledo, OH.

18. Quoted in Talcott E. Wing, *History of Monroe County, Michigan* (New York: Munsell, 1890), 195; see also letter of November 10, 1835, Lucas Papers.

19. Quoted in L. G. Stuart, "Verdict for Michigan: How the Upper Peninsula Became a Part of Michigan," in Michigan Pioneer and Historical Collections, vol. 27, 1896, 402.

20. Peck, "Disputed Questions in the Early History of Michigan," 156.

21. Undated letter *Annals of Cleveland,* vols. 18–19, part 1.

22. Letter of October 23, 1835, Toledo Lucas County Public Library, Toledo, Ohio.

23. LeRoy Barnett and Roger Rosentreter, *Michigan's Early Military Forces* (Detroit: Wayne State University Press, 2003), 237.

24. Letter of November 19, 1835, box 20, Lewis Cass Papers, William L. Clements Library, Ann Arbor, MI.

25. Ibid.

26. Letter of November 19, 1835, Stevens T. Mason Papers, Burton Historical Collection, Detroit Public Library, Detroit.

Other useful source material for this chapter includes Sister Mary Karl George, *The Rise and Fall of Toledo, Michigan: The Toledo War!* (Lansing: Michigan Historical Commission, 1971), esp. chap. 7; Charles E. Slocum, *History of the Maumee River Basin* (Indianapolis and Toledo: Bowen and Slocum, 1905); *Detroit Free Press,* September 2, 1835; Alec R. Gilpin, *The Territory of Michigan, 1805–1837* (East Lansing: Michigan State University Press, 1970); E. D. Antes, *The Toledo War* (Hamilton, OH: privately printed, 1959); Carl Wittke, "The Ohio-Michigan Boundary Dispute Re-examined," *Ohio State Archaeological and Historical Quarterly* (October 1936); Tana Mosier Porter, "Benjamin Franklin Stickney, 1775–1852," in *A Sesquicentennial History* (Toledo Sesquicentennial Commission, 1987); Jim Schutze, "The Rip-Roaring Michigan-Ohio War: We Won—They Got Toledo," *Detroit Free Press,* May 9, 1971; Richard L. Hawk, "Ohio's 'War' With Michigan," *Columbus Dispatch,* January 20, 1963.

CHAPTER FIFTEEN

1. Letter of May 1, 1835, and letter of May 24, 1835, *Annals of Cleveland, 1818–1935,* vols. 18–19, part 1 (Cleveland: Works Progress Administration, 1938), in State Archives of Ohio, Columbus.

2. "How They Fought," in Michigan Pioneer and Historical Collections, vol. 7, 1884, 69–71.

3. "How They Fought," in Michigan Pioneer and Historical Collections, vol. 13, 1888, 23.

4. Edward W. Peck, "Disputed Questions in the Early History of Michigan," in Michigan Pioneer and Historical Collections, vol. 11, 1887, 155–56.

5. R. C. Crawford, "Reminiscences of Pioneer Life in Michigan," in Michigan Pioneer and Historical Collections, vol. 7, 1884, 45–46.

6. Boxed material of Toledo War, Monroe County Historical Commission, Monroe, MI.

7. *The Ohio-Michigan Boundary,* vol. 1, *Ohio Cooperative Topographic Survey* (Mansfield: Press of Ohio State Reformatory, 1916), 3.

8. Arthur Meier Schlesinger, *Basis of the Ohio-Michigan Boundary Dispute*, part 3 (1916), 113–15.

9. W. V. Way, *The Facts and Historical Significance of the Toledo War of 1835* (Toledo, OH: Daily Commercial Steam Book, 1869), 48.

EPILOGUE

1. Letter mailed to U.S. Senate in 1831, Stevens T. Mason Papers, Bentley Historical Library, Ann Arbor, MI, and Michigan State Archives, Lansing.

2. Quoted in George Weeks, *Stewards of the State* (Ann Arbor: Detroit News and Historical Society of Michigan, 1987), 15.

3. Lawton T. Hemans, "Michigan's Debt to Stevens T. Mason," in Michigan Pioneer and Historical Collections, vol. 35, 1905–6, 246.

4. November 5, 1841, Stevens T. Mason Papers, William L. Clements Library, Ann Arbor, MI.

5. Quoted in Kent Sagendorph, *Michigan, the Story of the University* (New York: E. P. Dutton, 1948), 45.

Other useful source material for this chapter includes Sister Mary Karl George, *The Rise and Fall of Toledo, Michigan: The Toledo War!* (Lansing: Michigan Historical Commission, 1971); Dr. Martin J. Hershock, "Michigan's Path from Territory to Statehood" (lecture, Ann Arbor District Library, MI, January 12, 2005); Arthur Meier Schlesinger, *Basis of the Ohio-Michigan Boundary Dispute*, part 3 (1916), 113–15; R. Carlyle Buley, *The Old Northwest*, vol. 2 (Indianapolis: Indiana Historical Society, 1950), 190–203; C. S. Van Tassel, *Maumee Valley, Toledo, and the Sandusky Region*, vol. 1 (Chicago: S. J. Clarke Publishing, 1929), 750–77; F. Clever Bald, *Michigan in Four Centuries* (New York: Harper and Row, 1954), 188–202; Annah May Soule, "The Controversy over the Michigan-Ohio Boundary," in *The Southern and Western Boundaries of Michigan* (Ann Arbor, 1896), reprinted in Michigan Pioneer and Historical Collections, vol. 27, 1896 (*The Southern and Western Boundaries of Michigan* is also reprinted in Michigan Political Science Association publications, vol. 2, 29–81); C. E. Sherman, *The Ohio-Michigan Boundary*, vol. 1, *Ohio Cooperative Topographic Survey* (Mansfield: Press of Ohio State Reformatory, 1916); Thomas C. Kingsley and Kenneth H. Priestley, "Territorial Postal History of the Toledo Strip," *American Philatelist* 89, no. 9 (September 1975); Kent Sagendorph, *Stevens Thomson Mason, Misunderstood Patriot* (New York: E. P. Dutton, 1947); LeRoy Barnett and Roger Rosentreter, *Michigan's Early Military Forces* (Detroit: Wayne State University Press, 2003); Representative Dave Hobson, Seventh Congressional District of Ohio, column of February 27, 2003; Henry Howe, *Historical Collections of Ohio*, vol. 2 (Cincinnati: Krehbiel, 1888), 148–50; Fred Folger, "The Man Who Saved Toledo for Ohio," *Toledo Blade Sunday Magazine*, September 15, 1985; *Monroe Commercial*, March 14, 1872; papers of Lewis Cass relating to arms and ammunition dispute, Lewis Cass Papers, William L. Clements Library, Ann Arbor, MI; personal recollections of veterans of the Toledo War from "How They Fought," in Michigan Pioneer and Historical Collections, vol. 7, 1884, and vol. 13, 1888; "Reminiscences of Pioneer Life in Michigan," in Michigan Pioneer and Historical Collections, vol. 13, 1888.

INDEX

Text design by Mary H. Sexton
Typesetting by Delmastype, Ann Arbor, Michigan

Text Font: Janson Text
Designed by the Hungarian Nicholas Kis in about 1690, the model for
Janson Text was mistakenly attributed to the Dutch printer Anton Janson.
Kis' original matrices were found in Germany and acquired by the Stempel
foundry in 1919. Its strong design and clear stroke contrast combine to
create text that is both elegant and easy to read.
 —courtesy www.adobe.com

Display font:
FFQuadraat, designed by Fred Smeijers, launched by
FontShop International in 1992.
 —courtesy www.fontfont.com

Printed and bound by CPI Group (UK) Ltd, Croydon, CR0 4YY

13/04/2025

14656533-0002